CITY OF DREAMS

Latino Immigration to Chicago

Wilfredo Cruz

University Press of America,® Inc.
Lanham · Boulder · New York · Toronto · Plymouth, UK

Copyright © 2007 by
University Press of America,® Inc.
4501 Forbes Boulevard
Suite 200
Lanham, Maryland 20706
UPA Acquisitions Department (301) 459-3366

Estover Road
Plymouth PL6 7PY
United Kingdom

Library of Congress Control Number: 2007926937
ISBN-13: 978-0-7618-3820-3 (paperback : alk. paper)
ISBN-10: 0-7618-3820-1 (paperback : alk. paper)

⊖™ The paper used in this publication meets the minimum
requirements of American National Standard for Information
Sciences—Permanence of Paper for Printed Library Materials,
ANSI Z39.48—1984

For my wife, Irma,
and our children, Wilfredo Jr.,
Alexandra Irma, and Daniel Cesar.

And also for my parents
Aida Rodríguez and Juan Cruz

Cover photos top to bottom:

Guatemalan children and adults participate in the September 1998, annual Central American Parade in downtown Chicago. (Courtesy *La Raza*.)

Mexican children do their holy communion in 1935 at Our Lady of Guadalupe Church in South Chicago. (Courtesy Southeast Historical Society.)

Former first ward alderman Jesse Granato, Ann Alvarez (middle), president of Casa Central, and Pastora San Juan Cafferty, professor, University of Chicago, participate in a 1997 ribbon cutting for Casa Central's new, $4 million Community Services Center. (Courtesy Ann Alvarez.)

Gilberto and Martha Hernandez came from Puerto Rico to Chicago in 1952. They met in Chicago and married in 1954. Gilberto worked in the steel mills, and later drove his own taxi. Martha worked in factories. They had two sons and five daughters. (Courtesy Martha Hernandez.)

Contents

List of Maps

Map

Acknowledgments

I wish to thank Columbia College Chicago for granting me a semester sabbatical, and release time from teaching. The time was most valuable in helping me to research and write a major portion of the book.

I extend a deeply felt thank you to Eduardo Camacho and various anonymous reviewers. Their suggestions on improving the chapters, and the organization of the book, were invaluable.

I appreciate the semester of research assistance provided by John Colon. Colon graduated from Columbia College Chicago.

I appreciate the work of Kathryn Koch in transcribing many of the English interviews, and to Yessenia Vindell for transcribing many of the Spanish-language interviews.

Special gratitude is extended to all the individuals who allowed me to interview them for the book. They warmly welcomed me into their offices, businesses, and homes. They generously offered their time, often spending hours at a time with me. They willingly shared their personal stories even when I asked probing, personal questions about themselves and their families. They did not have to divulge personal information to a stranger, and yet they trusted me with the information. I am grateful for that trust. This book would not be possible without their cooperation and participation.

Thank you to Alexandra Cruz and Oscar Valdez for your assistance with editing.

A very special thank you to my wife Irma. I appreciate the assistance and motivation you provided me during the years I worked on this book.

Introduction

Since its incorporation as a city in 1837, Chicago has always been a magnet attracting immigrants and newcomers. Even when Chicago was little more than a trading post, the influence of immigrants was shaping the city's history. Successive waves of immigrants historically flocked to the city by the lake. At the turn of the 19th century, hundreds of thousands of Irish, Italians, Germans, Poles, Jews, and other European ethnic groups, crossed oceans to come to Chicago. They came searching for economic opportunities, jobs, and a better life for themselves and their children. These European groups worked hard in the city's heavy industries. They worked in the steel mills, packinghouses, stockyards, and factories. They carved out their own distinct ethnic neighborhoods throughout the city. They made good money and after a few generations they climbed the ladder of success into middle-class America. Many eventually left the city and moved to the suburbs.

Like European groups, African Americans also flocked to Chicago. During the mid-1900s, in the "Great Migration," five million African Americans migrated from the rural South to Northern cities like Chicago. Like previous waves of immigrants, African Americans came to Chicago searching for good-paying, steady jobs, and a better overall quality of life. They came searching for freedom, racial equality, and a chance to integrate and enter the American mainstream. They too toiled in many of the city's heavy industries. Previous immigrant groups had a big impact on Chicago's development. They helped establish many of the city's cultural, educational, economic, and political institutions. Numerous scholarly articles and books have been written richly detailing the experiences of these diverse immigrant groups in Chicago. Even today, new books are being written telling the histories, struggles, and contributions that various European groups and African Americans have made to the growth of the city.

Yet surprisingly, there exist few books chronicling the story of Latino immigration to Chicago. It is a story that has not been adequately recorded. Even though Latinos have had a presence in Chicago since the early 1900s, very little has been written about their experiences. Some journalistic reports and a few academic books have been published on specific Latino groups in Chicago, or on particular events in the Latino community. However, a social history of major Latino groups in Chicago is missing. Since many major Eastern and Southwestern United States cities have concentrations of one major Latino group, much of the written literature on Latinos usually focuses on the specific experiences of one Latino group. There are studies on Mexicans in the Southwest, Puerto Ricans in New York, Cubans in Miami, Florida, and Central and South Americans in Houston and Los Angeles.

However, Chicago is uniquely different. It is one of a handful of major American cities with large populations of different Latino groups. In addition, Latino immigrants continue to settle in the city. Nationally, Latinos are now the fastest growing population group in America. From 1990 to 2000, their numbers increased 58 percent in the United States. They are now over 35.3 million Latinos in America, and they have surpassed Africans Americans as the nation's largest minority group. Like previous immigrants, Latinos are an important part of Chicago's history. Latinos are now the fastest growing ethnic group in the city. In 1990, Latinos were 19.2 percent of Chicago's 2,783,726 residents. However, the 2000 U.S. Census showed explosive growth in the city's Latino population. For the first time since the 1950 census, Chicago's population increased 4 percent to 2,896,016. The city's population growth was mainly due to a large influx of Latino residents. The number of Latinos in Chicago increased by nearly 210,000 from 1990 to 2000. During the same period whites in the city decreased by 150,000 and blacks declined by 20,000. According to the 2000 U.S. Census, there were over 753, 644 Latinos in Chicago or 26 percent of the city's population.[1] Additionally, from 2000 to 2004, the number of Latinos in Illinois' suburbs increased by a third to 862,000.

It is projected that in the coming decades African Americans and whites in Chicago will continue to decline, while Latinos will continue to grow. Since Latinos are younger than African Americans or whites, Latino growth will come about mainly through births, combined with continued immigration. By 2010, Latinos could be 33 percent of Chicago's residents. Due to their growing numbers, Latinos undoubtedly are key players in the city's future. They are helping to shape the character of the city, including its politics, its neighborhood, and its economy. This book is an attempt to tell the social history of Latinos in Chicago. I try to tell their story through their own voices. Over a two and a half year period, I interviewed one hundred individuals in Chicago. The vast majority of the interviews were with Latinos. A handful of interviews were with non-Latinos who are familiar with Latino communities. The interviews were conducted in person, and usually lasted from one to two hours. The interviews were tape-recorded and then transcribed. Several interviews were done by telephone. The majority of interviews were conducted in English. About one fourth were conducted in Spanish.

This book does not explore one central, overarching theoretical argument. Instead, through these oral interviews, along with other data, I try to capture and highlight the voices of Latinos. I want to show how Latinos view themselves. I attempt to probe various related major themes and questions. For instance, why do Latinos come to Chicago? Why do people leave their country of birth and familiar surroundings to venture to a new, strange place thousands of miles away? The decision to uproot a family and move to a new country is not an easy one. It is a bold, pioneering decision. What are the dreams and aspirations of Latinos?

Like previous immigrants, Latinos perceive Chicago as a good place to plant deep family roots. Therefore, Latino immigrants come with high expectations and aspirations. Some say they come pursuing a small piece of the American dream. But how do they define the American dream? And, after living and working for many years in Chicago, have they fulfilled their aspirations and dreams? The book also examines how Latino groups adjust and adapt in Chicago. Many Latinos who come to Chicago are often poor, uneducated and do not speak English. How did the early Latino immigrants, and those coming later, go about surviving and making it? What jobs did they hold, and continue to hold? How do their neighbors receive them? How do they get along with white groups, African Americans and other Latinos?

Moreover, after many years in Chicago, how do Latinos view their religion, assimilation, culture, and ethnic identity? What cultural traditions and values do they see as important? Some Latinos live and work in Chicago for many years and still only speak Spanish. Some Latinos and their children speak only English and seem to have completely assimilated into American culture. They see no need to hold on to an ethnic identity. Yet many others are bilingual and speak both English and Spanish. To many Latinos, maintaining a strong sense of their Latino culture is important in how they perceive themselves. Other themes explored are the experiences of Latinos in building their communities. How are they interacting with major institutions like the church, school, police and government? What are some problems, obstacles, and struggles still facing Latinos? And how are they dealing with these obstacles?

I personally selected the persons interviewed for the book. Over the years I have written various journalistic and academic articles on issues affecting the Latino community. In writing these articles, I established contact with many key persons in the Latino community. I tried to select individuals who through their jobs were actively involved with Latinos, and knowledgeable about various aspects of the Latino community. Also, pastors and priests in Protestant and Catholic churches in Latino neighborhoods put me in contact with some of the individuals interviewed. Some interviewees were referred to me by social service agencies in Latino neighborhoods. In selecting the interviews, I tried to be as inclusive as possible. I interviewed Latinos from many walks of life. I wanted interesting stories, but I also wanted people with different viewpoints and perspectives. There were interviews with different generations of Latinos, interviews with men and women, with elders, middle-aged persons and with youth. Some individuals come from poor, working-class, middle-class, and upper-middle-class backgrounds. They are from varied occupations like laborers, factory workers, teachers, businesspeople, writers, priests, politicians, reporters, professors, community activists, and persons on public aid.

Several persons, especially those struggling economically, refused to be interviewed. They did not want intimate and often painful aspects of their lives to become public. That was understandable. Yet, all the others willingly shared their life stories with me, often revealing very personal details of their lives. I believe their stories give the book a personal, human touch. One hundred interviews cannot possibly represent the full range of emotions and experiences of well over half a million Latinos in Chicago. I had to make difficult decisions about which persons to interview, and what specific themes to highlight. No doubt, I have missed the personal testimonies of many important individuals who should be included. Surely, there are important issues that are not covered in the book. I take full responsibility for the omissions. Hopefully, the voices in this book present a snapshot of how Latinos see themselves.

I use the voices of interviewees as much as possible throughout the book. However, to give their voices context and richness, some sociological analysis, history, and narration are included. Besides interviews, I referred to past and current books, reports, newspaper articles, U.S. Census data, government reports, and unpublished dissertations. As the stories in this book demonstrate, the immigration experiences of Latino groups are different. Some Latino groups in Chicago are making great strides. They are progressing and moving up into the American economic mainstream. Yet, others are making slower progress. Still, others are struggling to put food on the table. Some Latinos came to the city when good-paying, industrial jobs were plentiful. Others came much later, when opportunities in heavy industries dried up. Some Latinos who immigrated to the city were educated, middle-class, and professional. Others were poor, uneducated, undocumented, and did not speak English. They took low-paying, menial jobs. Some Latino groups have lived in Chicago for several generations. Others arrived yesterday.

The Latino community of Chicago is a rich ethnic tapestry, not a monolithic group. Latinos do not speak in a single, united voice. Over 20 Spanish-speaking groups fall under the umbrella term of "Latino." There are no two groups completely alike. There are obvious racial, socioeconomic, educational, and political differences among the groups. To assume that Latino groups should be united in a single, permanent coalition is unrealistic. As differences and diverse viewpoints exist among African Americans and whites, there are differences among Latino groups. Sometimes, Latino groups are divided and clash over cultural, educational and political issues. They hold damaging stereotypes about other Latino groups. At times, Latinos work together in temporary coalitions on specific issues. Occasionally different Latino groups come together in community activism to promote the civil rights of the larger Latino community.

In the Midwest, "Latino" became a common term in the 1970s, emerging from the interaction of different groups. While most Latino groups identify themselves first by their own nationality group, they also invoke the term "Latino" as a show of force to the outside world. In temporary coalitions, diverse Latino groups do express a Latino consciousness. Latinos oftentimes use the word "Latino" as a political, unifying ethnic term.[2] In Chicago, many Latinos prefer the term "Latino" over terms like "Hispanic," "Spanish-speaking," or "Latin Americans." Also, in Chicago, there is a high rate of intermarriage among different Latino groups. This intermarriage is helping to break down stereotypes, and create better understanding among the groups. This book does not try to cover most Latino groups in Chicago. Instead, it focuses on the struggles and stories of the major Latino groups in the city. Traditionally, Mexicans and Puerto Ricans have been the two largest Latino groups in the Midwest. Of

Chicago's Latino population, Mexicans are about 70.4 percent and Puerto Ricans comprise 15 percent. Together the two groups are about 85 percent of Latinos in Chicago. Therefore, much of the book focuses on these two larger groups.

Mexicans are the largest Latino group in the city, and their numbers continue to swell. They were the first Latino group to set roots in Chicago, and secure a foothold in the city's industries during the early 1900's. Chapters one and two examine the experiences of Mexicans since they first arrived in Chicago, up to the present time. How do different generations of Mexicans view the struggles of their parents? How do they see their own challenges? Chapter three and four explore Puerto Rican migration to the city. Puerto Ricans are the second largest group in the city. Puerto Ricans came to the city in the 1950s and 1960s looking for steady work. Unlike most other Latino groups, Puerto Ricans came as American citizens. Yet they faced many of the same hardships most Latino immigrant groups encounter when coming to a new city. While they are still facing certain problems like high rates of poverty, others are college educated and middle-class. Many Puerto Ricans are optimistic that things in Chicago will only get better.

Chapter five looks at Guatemalans, and to a lesser extent, at Salvadorans. In the 1970s, 1980s, thousands of Latinos from throughout Central and South America came to Chicago. Many continue coming to Chicago. Guatemalans are now the third largest Latino group in the city, and their numbers steadily grow. But very little is known about Guatemalans or Salvadorans. They are the most recent Latino arrivals to the city. Little is written about these two groups. They are called "invisible communities" because their presence is not well established in the city. Both communities have a large percentage of undocumented workers. Still, some immigrants from both countries are adapting well in the city. Others appear to be having a harder time making it.

Chapter six looks at Cubans. Between 1959 and 1973, thousands of middle-class Cubans, fleeing Fidel Castro's revolution, came as political refugees. Others came in later waves. Their presence in the city continues to decline as they move to the suburbs or relocate to Miami, Florida. Yet economically, they are doing better than most Latino groups in the city. Generous financial aid from the U.S. government helped many in their transition to Chicago. Cubans in the city are influential in business, media, social services, and institutions of higher learning. The experiences of some political refugees from the three major waves of Cuban immigration are explored. The Epilogue briefly highlights some of the challenges facing the newest Latinos arrivals to Chicago. It also attempts to summarize the major themes covered in the book. What do the interviewees say about their experiences in Chicago? Have their dreams and aspirations been fulfilled? What concerns do they still face? And how do they see the future?

This book is by no means a definitive history of Latinos in Chicago. Much more can be written about each Latino group. At the dawn of the 21st century, Latino immigrants continue coming to the city. They are bringing new problems, challenges, and contributions. Like other immigrants, they are coming with their hopes and dreams packed tightly in their suitcases. They are adding to the continuing story and history of Latinos in this city. Surely, the Latino community of Chicago will look different in the coming decades.

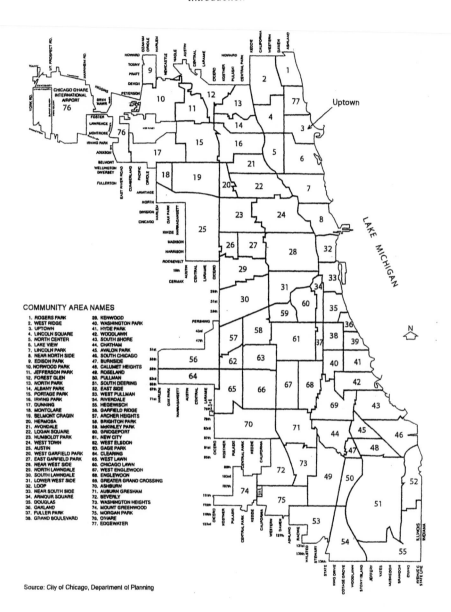

Map 1. Chicago Community Area Map.

Source: City of Chicago, Department of Planning

Chapter One: Mexicans

The Old Hull-House Neighborhood

Frank Duran, 87, and his wife Jovita, 85, clearly recall why their parents immigrated from Mexico to Chicago. Their parents, like waves of previous immigrants, came seeking better economic opportunities. They came with high hopes and dreams of a better life for themselves and their children. The Duran's parents came to the city by way of seeking railroad work. "My father came to Texas in 1911 from Guanajuato, Mexico," says Frank. "My three brothers and sisters were born in different U.S. cities because my dad was working on the railroads. My father followed railroad work that took him to different United States cities. My father worked for the Santa Fe and Topeka railroads. He heard there were good jobs in Chicago. We came to Chicago in 1929, when I was 10 years old. My dad worked for the Santa Fe railroad for a dollar a day. He was a laborer. In Chicago, we lived in the Hull-House neighborhood at 14th and Peoria. This area was mostly Jewish, Italian, Greek and Mexican."[1]

"My parents came to Texas in 1921," adds Jovita. "My father was a lumber jack in Oaxaca, Mexico. "He came to Texas in 1921. He worked as a lumberjack in Texas. He heard there were many Hispanics in Chicago, so my parents decided to come and make a living here. We came to Chicago's Hull-House area in 1927. My father also worked on the railroads." The Durans grew up on Chicago's Near West Side in a neighborhood known as the Hull-House area. The area's poverty led to the establishment of Hull-House, the famous settlement house founded in 1889 by renowned social reformers Jane Addams and Ellen Gates Starr.

Mexicans have historically flocked to Chicago in hopes of finding good-paying jobs. In 1910, there were only about 1,000 Mexicans in the Chicago metropolitan area. But by 1980 the U.S. Census counted 368,981 Mexicans in Chicago and its suburbs.[2] The number of Mexican residents in Chicago grew about 50 percent from 1990 to 2000 to more than 530,000. Mexicans were the largest Latino group in Chicago representing about 70.4 percent of Latinos in the city. Chicago passed San Antonio and Houston to become the United States city with the second largest Mexican population after Los Angeles. The Mexican population throughout Illinois continued to swell. For instance, in Illinois, the Latino population grew from 904,446 to 1.53 million over the last decade, with Mexicans making up 75 percent of the total. Illinois is now home to 1.14 million Mexicans.[3]

Certain push and pull factors brought Mexicans to the city. The first Mexican immigrants to Chicago came as contracted workers. The onset of World

War I, created severe labor shortages in the United States. Yet large Midwestern industries needed a plentiful supply of cheap and unskilled labor. These industries looked to African Americans from Southern states, and Mexicans from Southwestern states, to fulfill the need. During the 19th century, Chicago was the nation's railroad hub. As early as 1916, Chicago area railroad companies recruited 206 Mexican railroad track workers from the Texas-Mexican border.[4] Companies like Santa Fe, Topeka, and Burlington sent enganchadores, or labor recruiters, to Texas to recruit Mexican laborers. The number of Mexicans working for Chicago railroad companies rose from 206 in 1916 to over 5,255 in 1926. Mexicans were 40 percent of the total railroad maintenance crews of Chicago.[5]

Most early Mexican railroad workers were solos, or single, young men. They lived in boxcars owned by railroad companies on the outskirts of the city. The single men and families shared boxcars that were crude, cold, and lacked water or indoor plumbing. "My father was about 16-years-old when he immigrated to the United States. He was from Jalisco, Mexico. He fought in the Mexican Revolution with Pancho Villa. He started working on the railroads laying down railroad tracks," says Dennis Prieto, 63, commander of Chicago's tenth police district. "He started working in Kansas and moved west through Colorado, Nebraska and finally coming to Chicago. He came to Chicago looking for work around 1918. He left railroad work and worked for the steel mills. We lived in the Hull-House area."[6]

Chicago area railroad companies confined Mexicans to the hard laborer jobs, constructing new railroad lines or maintaining existing ones. Mexican laborers performed physically strenuous work, often in below-freezing weather. Some employers and the local public held prejudiced attitudes against Mexicans, and considered them as foreign, cheap labor. White railroad workers were usually placed in the higher-paying, skilled jobs as engineers, motormen, and conductors. Some companies even paid white workers higher wages than Mexicans for similar work. Mexicans usually received the lowest wages, thirty-five to thirty-nine cents an hour.[7] Sugar beet companies also recruited Mexicans to the Midwest. By 1927, over 20,000 betabeleros or Mexican sugar beet workers, labored for four large sugar beet companies in Michigan, Ohio, Indiana, Iowa, and Minnesota. Entire families worked together in the fields over 12 hours a day on their hands and knees, planting and harvesting endless rows of sugar beets. Railroad workers and betabeleros eventually left railroad work and farm work, and came to large cities like Chicago hoping to find better paying jobs in factories and industries.[8] Political revolutions in Mexico during the early 1900s pushed Mexicans toward Chicago. They came escaping revolutions, social upheavals, and poverty. Some were educated members of Mexico's middle-class. Most, however, were poor and uneducated.

Labor and Racial Tension

Mexicans arrived in Chicago at a time when the city was undergoing strikes, labor unrest, and racial conflict. Competition for jobs and housing between white ethnic groups and African Americans migrating from the South, created intense racial tension in Chicago. In 1919, large steel mill companies in Chicago and the Calumet Region faced a nationwide strike, as returning war veterans demanded unions. Management responded by recruiting hundreds of Mexicans as strikebreakers.[9] The few Mexicans who already worked in the steel mills supported the strike and walked out with their fellow Polish, Serbian, and Slovak workers. However, the hundreds of recruited Mexican workers took their place. When the union drive failed, and the strike was over, many of the recruited Mexican workers were fired.[10]

The city's racial tension came to a head during the summer of 1919. That year the city experienced a deadly race riot between whites and blacks. The riot began when whites threw rocks at five black boys who were swimming in a beach that whites had claimed as their own. One black boy was hit on the head with a rock and drowned. Groups of blacks and whites attacked each other in the streets. When the smoke cleared, 23 blacks and 15 whites had been killed. Another 537 people were injured.[11] Company management continued to pit racial and ethnic groups against each other. In 1921, thousands of Chicago stockyard workers went out on strike demanding higher wages. Companies like Armor and Swift recruited African Americans and Mexicans as strikebreakers. The few Mexicans who worked in the stockyards supported the strike. Yet many recruited Mexican workers crossed the picket line.[12]

Employers were pleased that Mexicans worked hard and long hours for low wages. By 1928, Mexicans were 11 percent of the workers in fifteen of Chicago area's meatpacking, steel, and other plants. However, employers used Mexicans as cheap, temporary workers. For Mexicans, layoffs were common in the railroads, stockyards, and steel mills. Some white ethnics resented Mexican workers, and viewed them as illegal foreigners who were anti-union, undercut wages, and took jobs from Americans. Some white ethnic workers and employers saw Mexicans as racially inferior Indian peons, who were docile, indolent, and backward.[13] Some white employers preferred to hire light-skinned Mexicans. Some Mexicans passed themselves off as European or Spaniard.[14]

"My father was very light-skinned. He could have been mistaken for either Italian or Greek," says Dennis Prieto. "My father insisted that his children learn English. He did not want us speaking Spanish. We lived mostly with Italians and Greeks. Later I found out why he didn't want us to speak Spanish or live among Mexicans. It was because my father was illegal and he was afraid of being deported. My father learned very little English. My father finally retired in 1968 and he had to collect his pension from the Santa Fe railroad. We had to get my father a resident alien card so he could collect his pension. He got the pension."

Early Mexican immigrants regularly returned back and forth between Chicago and Mexico. They motivated relatives and friends to try their luck in Chicago. While the jobs in Chicago were dirty, hard, and often dangerous, they were better than migrant fieldwork which was backbreaking work, low-paying, and seasonal. Early immigrants complained about Chicago's freezing winter weather and lack of Mexican culture. Some came planning only a temporary sojourn. They dreamed of making a small fortune, and then returning and buying a small business or home in Mexico. Hoping to return to their homeland, they remained Mexican rather than American in culture or legal nationality.[15]

As the Mexican community grew in Chicago, marriages took place and new families developed. Mexicans settled in neighborhoods close to industries that recruited them. The railroad workers and betabeleros settled in the crowded colonial of Hull-House around Taylor and Halsted. This was one of the early Mexican communities in the city. The area was attractive to Mexican immigrants because of its low rents, employment agencies, and light industries. By the end of the 1920s, over 2,500 Mexicans lived in the area.[16]

Hard Depression Years

The Great Depression years were economically difficult for Americans, but they were especially hard for Mexicans. Their attempt to build communities was dealt a serious setback. Besides poverty, Mexicans faced discrimination. Native-born whites accused Mexicans of being illegal aliens, and taking American jobs. They were accused of being a drain on private and public relief rolls. Employers laid off many workers, and Mexicans were the first to go. Chicago employers refused to hire Mexicans for even menial jobs. Private and public relief agencies, and employers, often required that applicants be citizens. Most Mexicans were not naturalized citizens.[17]

A national program of voluntary and forced repatriation set in. Employers and local government offered to pay train fare costs if Mexicans returned to Mexico. Some Mexicans in major cities took up the offer to leave. Others were forcibly deported. Nationally, almost 500,000 Mexicans—about one-third of Mexicans in the United States—many American citizens, were deported to Mexico between 1927 and 1937.[18] Unemployment combined with voluntary forced repatriation reduced Chicago's Mexican population from 20,000 in 1930, to 14,000 in 1933 and to 12,500 in 1934.[19] Frank Duran recalls the racial tension during the 1930s. "I didn't experience any discrimination because I'm not that dark. People thought I was Italian or Greek. But my three brothers were more dark-skinned than I was. They had a rough time. People would call them bad names. They were always fighting the whites. But Chicago was not as bad as Kansas. I recall as a boy that in Topeka, Kansas restaurants and theaters had signs saying, 'Blacks and Mexicans Not Allowed'."

During the 1930s, theaters in Gary and East Chicago, Indiana, forced Mexican steelworkers and their families to sit in the balconies or back rows. Some hotels and restaurants refused to admit Mexicans. Mexicans fought back and boycotted theaters, hotels, and restaurants that practiced discrimination. Mexicans in Indiana often preferred to come to Chicago's Mexican neighborhoods for entertainment.[20] Some Mexicans who stayed in Chicago during the depression years struggled to make ends meet. "During the Great Depression my family moved to Gary, Indiana, where my father tried to find work in the steel mills," recalls Dennis Prieto. "He wanted to work in the steel mills because that was where the good money and jobs were. But he only worked in the steel mills for a short while. There was a lot of unemployment and jobs were scarce. He came back to Chicago looking for employment. Around the 1940s, my father had a small stand in the Maxwell Street area. He used to sell used clothes, shoes, and musical instruments. He would go to all the Jewish merchants and buy from them at a discount. Then he would sell them to people at retail. I used to go with my father to Maxwell Street on Sundays. Later, he started working for the railroads again. He retired from the Santa Fe railroad company. He was a hardworking man. He died when he was 93-years-old."

Frank Duran's father luckily found steady work during the depression. "In Chicago my father left the railroads. Although it was the depression, he found work at the Curtis Candy Company making thirty-five cents an hour. My three brothers also found work there. I was the youngest in the family. Despite the low wages, we always had a roof over our heads, clothing, and food. I don't recall any poverty." But Jovita Duran recalls poverty. "Life was not easy during the Great Depression. My father always wanted to go back to Mexico. He didn't like Chicago. He got hit by a truck here in Chicago. He passed away when I was 10. My mother stayed in Chicago and supported us. My mother worked as much as she could. She never knew any English.... My mother was out cleaning homes and selling clothes. She went down to Maxwell Street to get a whole barrel of clothes. She used to knock on doors and sell used clothes."

Hull-House, the famous settlement house, reached out to help Mexicans. "There was no work during the depression, and many people were hurting," recalls Jovita. "But Jane Addams here at Hull-House helped many immigrants. They helped us. It was like being on relief. You waited in line. They gave us clothes shoes and food. We had to get everything we could from Hull-House" Mexican children spend countless hours at Hull-House enjoying arts and crafts, pottery, and music lessons. Hull-House sponsored social dances, a day care, a music school, and English and citizenship classes for immigrant children and adults. Hull-House activities helped Mexican boys avoid trouble. Yet, like previous white immigrants, some poor Mexican youth joined street gangs. They hung out on corners and engaged in minor delinquent acts. Irish and Polish police and judges often saw Mexican youth as troublemakers. Arrests and convictions for minor offenses were much higher for Mexican males compared to white ethnics.[21]

With World War II, economic opportunities again surfaced in Chicago. Mexicans began immigrating back to the city. Eager to show their American patriotism, many Mexican young men enlisted for military service. "I joined the U.S. Army infantry," says Frank Duran. "I saw combat in Europe. I was wounded and earned the Purple Heart. After the war when I returned home, I drove a taxi for four years. I then opened my own bar in the Hull-House neighborhood. Mexicans came to the bar to drink, dance, and have a good time. I had the bar for fifteen years. The bar business was good. Then one day I had a fight in there. Somebody got cut up, and they canceled my insurance. That forced me to close. I then worked for the City of Chicago as a pipe yard foreman for twelve years until I retired."

World War II created a labor shortage as men went off to war. American companies needed a supply of cheap labor. Again, they looked to Mexicans. The governments of the United States and Mexico agreed to let temporary, contracted workers from Mexico—braceros or helping arms—come to America to work. Most braceros worked mainly as farm workers and on railroads in the Southwest and Midwest. Originally a wartime measure, the bracero program lasted from 1942 to 1964. Over four and a half million braceros came to the United States.[22] Between 1943 and 1945, railroads in the Chicago area imported 15,000 braceros. Some braceros settled in the Hull-House area. Braceros and other Mexicans were poor, and could not afford quality medical care. Thus, their health often suffered.   Unpaved streets and alleys, poor housing, and crowded living conditions made the health situation worse. Mexicans often lived in dingy basement apartments, with little fresh air or sun. Families complained of rat-infestation. Periodic tuberculosis epidemics hit the Hull-House area.[23] "My mother died of tuberculosis in 1954," says Frank Duran. "There was an epidemic around that time and they didn't have a cure. They used to put them in a sanitarium, and segregate them from other patients. Rest and fresh air was all they would give tuberculosis patients. She was 62 when she died.... My father was killed in an auto accident. An auto hit him at the corner of Taylor and Ashland."

Recognizing that Mexicans needed good health care, Dr. Jorge Prieto established a medical office in the Hull-House area in 1954. Dr. Prieto was a family doctor, and one of the first Mexican physicians in Chicago. Word quickly spread that Dr. Prieto was a compassionate doctor. He treated patients despite their ability to pay. Dr. Prieto passed away in 2001, at the age of 83. "I came to Chicago in 1950 to serve the medical needs of braceros," said Dr. Prieto. "With help from Roman Catholic priests, I set up a private practice in an old wooden convent near Maxwell Street. There, I spent twenty years providing medical care to poor Mexican families. There were thousands of poor Mexicans in Chicago without immigration papers. It's a doctor's obligation to serve people regardless of whether they can pay. I used to charge three dollars per appointment. First, I saw many alcohol related illnesses. Second was diabetes. Third were diet diseases, gall bladder and digestive system problems. There were also many Latinos with injured backs from working in the fields and stockyards."[24]

Dr. Prieto made house calls and treated sick children. "The children were sick a lot in the winter because they lived in apartments with insufficient heat," said Dr. Prieto. "Many apartments had small heaters that didn't provide good heat. I visited homes where I saw ice and snow inside the windows because the apartments were so cold." Mexican women especially sought out his services. "Many women came asking me for birth control. They had large families and didn't want to have more children. In those days, it was a moral sin to use birth control. I am Roman Catholic. Then I realized they didn't have enough to eat.

To poor to feed children

They were too poor to keep having kids. If they were poor, why should I tell them to keep having children. I started giving them birth control. I figured with all the problems and poverty they faced, they should have a doctor on their side." Because of his lifelong dedication to the poor, a medical center serving the Mexican communities of Pilsen and Little Village, was named in Dr. Prieto's honor in the early 1990s. Dr. Prieto published two books about his life.[25]

St. Francis of Assisi, once an Italian Roman Catholic Church at 813 W. Roosevelt Road became a center of social and religious activity for Mexicans. It was here where they baptized their children, received communion, married, and sought burial rites. Many small Mexican mom-and-pop businesses emerged and catered to Mexican patrons. There were restaurants, grocery stores, shoemakers, bakeries, meat markets, print shops, tailors shops, and music stores. Mexican-owned pool halls catered to single men. "Before my father passed away, I understand he was one of the first Mexicans to open up a bakery in the area," says Jovita. "He opened a bakery on Morgan Street. He had the bakery for a few years. Then he went to work for the steel mills in South Chicago." While many Mexican women were homemakers, others worked outside the home helping their families. Jovita worked most of her life on the assembly lines of factories. She recalls the good times growing up in the Hull-House area. "Many young men organized baseball leagues. We enjoyed going to the public parks to see the young men play baseball. Later, my girlfriends and I organized a woman's baseball team. We played baseball with other young women from the neighborhood. We also organized a woman's bowling league."

The Hull-House neighborhood met a sudden death in the early 1960's. Chicago's Mayor Richard J. Daley pushed to build a massive public university, the University of Illinois at Chicago, smack in the heart of the neighborhood. Longtime Mexican, Greek and Italian residents had to sell their homes and stores to the city of Chicago. Their homes and stores were bulldozed, and the university was built. In 1999, the University of Illinois won city approval to expand even farther south. The university expanded into the Maxwell Street area and Pilsen. The University's $525 million, 10-year south campus project called for construction of on-campus housing, residential units, academic building and retail space.[26] Most Mexicans from the old Hull-House neighborhood moved south to the Lower West Side neighborhood known as Pilsen.

The Years at South Chicago

Up through 1944, most Mexicans in Chicago worked mainly for the railroads, stockyards, and steel mills. But steel mill jobs paid the best. A worker did not need an education to land a good-paying, steel mill job. All he needed was a strong back, strong arms, and a willingness to work hard. Generations of white ethnics like the Irish, Germans, and Poles worked in the mills. Mexicans proved themselves as reliable workers. By 1926, Chicago steel mills employed over 6,000 Mexicans, or 14 percent of the total workforce. In 1926, Inland Steel employed 2,526 Mexican, or 35 percent of the company's force work.[27] South Chicago, Gary, and East Chicago, Indiana, was home to large steel mills like Wisconsin Steel Works, United States Steel South Works, Inland Steel, and Bethlehem Steel Works. In their heyday, these steel mills in the Chicago-Calumet area employed hundreds of thousands of men. Mexican communities developed in Gary and East Chicago, Indiana. In Chicago, a large Mexican community emerged in South Chicago, referred to by local residents as Millgate. Another large Mexican community emerged in the neighboring area of South Deering, referred to as Irondale.

Dolores Garcia Reyes, 73, vividly recalls her years growing up in South Chicago. She came from a family of steel workers. Her husband, brother-in-law and sister worked many years in the steel mills. "I'm from a family of five sisters and a brother. My mother was 16, and my dad was 18 when they married. Both came from Mexico. My father immigrated to the South Deering neighborhood around 1922. Like other immigrants, he came hoping to establish himself. Two years later, he sent for my mother and their first child. Most Mexican families came to South Chicago to work in the steel mills. My father's brother worked in the mills. But my father never worked in the mills. My father opened a barbershop on East 90th Street. I was born in that building."[28]

Mexicans were not docile steel workers. Instead, during the 1930s, Mexicans, along with their white ethnic co-workers, actively participated in efforts to unionize steel workers. Workers demanded decent wages, steady hours, and improved working conditions. Mexican workers participated in strikes. For instance, the Steel Workers Organizing Committee signed a contract with U.S. Steel in 1937. But Republic Steel and other smaller mills refused. Workers called a strike against those companies. On Memorial Day 1937, hundreds of strikers marched toward Republic Steel in South Chicago. Mexicans made up about 15 percent of the strikers. Chicago police employed by Republic Steel fired at the strikers, killing 10 and injuring one-hundred and twenty-five people. Of those injured, 11 were Mexican. This Memorial Day massacre ended the strike. However, in 1941, the United Steelworkers gained recognition. In subsequent years, Mexican workers increasingly joined steel mill unions in Chicago and Indiana.[29]

Mexican steel workers took pride in their work. Their employment as industrial workers in the Midwestern United States was a source of status, winning them respect from co-workers, family, and bosses.[30] Some Mexican steel workers, like Dolores' husband, worked themselves up into skilled and supervisory positions. "I started working at Island Steel in East Chicago, Indiana. I had a skilled job as a fitter in a machine shop," says Dolores' husband, Emilio, 72. "I worked there for about 10 years. From there I did ironwork out of Local 395 in Hammond, Indiana. Then I went to Burnside Steel, a large foundry on East 92nd Street. Burnside had about 300 employees mostly black and white, with a few Mexicans. I worked there about 11 years. I worked myself up to a foreman. Burnside went bankrupt in 1979. I got my pension from there."

During World War II the steel mills faced a shortage of workers. The mills hired women to fill the void. Dolores' sister Katie, and other Mexican women worked in the mills. These women saw their work as patriotic duty to the war effort. They performed the same sweaty, hard work as men. Though women were paid less than men, few ever complained. When the war ended, women were encouraged to quit work, and give returning veterans their jobs back. Most women became homemakers. But some women refused to assume traditional female roles. "My sister Katie, was 20 years old when she started working in the steel mills during World War II. She didn't give up her job after the war. My sister Katie never married. She loved the steel mills. She worked there for many years and liked making money. She was an oiler. She carried cans of oil and oiled the freight cars and trains. At work she wore heavy shoes, a hard hat, high overalls, and carried a metal lunch bucket.... We made Katie retire from the mills at age 62. Katie died at 69."

Ironically, the same steel unions Mexicans workers supported in the mid-1930s, became the focus of complaints from Mexicans by the 1950s. For decades many white steel workers were promoted into better-paying, skilled jobs like electricians, mechanics, and welders. Yet over 80 percent of Mexicans in most steel mills worked mainly as laborers in lower-paying, more dangerous jobs. Mexicans believed the United Steel Workers of America union supported the discriminatory practices. The Civil Rights movement of the 1960s, followed by a series of lawsuits against the steel companies and the United Steel Workers of America, slowly opened skilled employment opportunities for Mexicans.[31]

Steel mill jobs allowed residents of the blue-collar community of South Chicago to enjoy a middle-class lifestyle. Mexican steel mill workers averaged over $12,500 a year by the late 1960s, and skilled workers earned as much as $25,000. The elite of the Mexican community lived in South Chicago.[32] First, second, and third generations of Mexicans lived side by side. Families purchased small bungalows, frame two-flats, and cottages. The homes, with their small backyards, were well maintained. Friendships developed among different ethnic groups in the steel mills. But after work, workers usually went their own ways. The Poles, Serbians, Croatians, Germans, Italians, and Mexicans lived in their own areas. Ethnic groups often maintained animosities against each other.[33]

Dolores recalls a painful incident in South Chicago. "I got married in 1957 and we were looking for an apartment. I saw a "For Rent" sign at 88th and Exchange in South Chicago. There were many Polish people in that neighborhood. The landlady says, 'What nationality are you?' I said, 'Mexican.' She says, 'Oh, I don't rent to Mexicans.' Oh, my gosh, I couldn't believe it. I'll never forget that." But Dolores also held fond memories of her years in South Chicago. "I thought my childhood and teen years were great. I was always at Our Lady of Guadalupe Church. We had social clubs there. We had banquets. They had a church-sponsored volleyball team for women. We had picnics and meetings. The priests would take us on outings. We had dances in the church hall. This was the early 1940s and 50s. There were dances every Friday night at the South Chicago Community Center and the Croatian Hall. Mexicans from other neighborhoods and from Indiana would come to these dances. That's how I met my husband. He's from Indiana. We met when we were 16, and married at 22. We also had many social events at the Bird Memorial Center."

The Bird Memorial Center was a settlement house run by the Congregational Church. It provided recreational, cultural, and social activities for Mexicans and other immigrants. Mexican steel workers and their families shopped on Commercial Avenue, the main business district of South Chicago. Lining Commercial Avenue were banks, small novelty stores, fancy men and women clothing stores, and large department stores like Goldblatt Brothers. Mexican-owned businesses like bakeries, grocery stores, barber shops, corner taverns, restaurants, and pool halls flourished. "Walking down Commercial Avenue with the girls was fun," says Dolores. "We would go to the Commercial theater, the Gayety theater, and the Gayety ice cream store. I went to Bowen High School. It was about one-third Mexican. Students got along fine with each other. I remember participating in the Mexican Independence parades as a teenager. The Mexican Patriotic Club started the parade. The club sponsored my sister Ernestine, who was the first Mexican parade queen of South Chicago."

In 1960, Dolores and Emilio bought their brick bungalow home on the East Side, adjacent to South Chicago. Mexicans saw the East Side as a big step up. It was like a small, quiet suburb with better housing and schools. For many years the East Side was mainly white. Today it is mostly Mexican. Upon becoming economically successful, some second and third generation Mexicans became culturally assimilated to mainstream American values. They spoke English and saw no need to maintain a Mexican identity. For example, Dolores' son and daughter married white spouses. Another daughter married a Mexican. Dolores lamented the fact that her children and grandchildren did not speak Spanish.

Other Mexicans, assimilated culturally to American ways but still held onto a strong sense of Mexican identity. Dolores and Emilio were obviously proud of their Mexican culture. In addition to English, they both speak fluent Spanish. They enjoyed watching Spanish-language television. They loved Mexican music, especially rancheros accompanied by mariachi. "Latin music is the best. I like Mexican rancheros like the ones Juan Gabriel and Lola Betran sing," says Dolores. "That's the type of music I grew up with. Mariachi music, now that's music. Last year we went to the mariachi festival in Tucson, Arizona. We're going to try to make it every year."

A stone's throw from Dolores' house is Calumet Park, with its sprawling acres of green grass, and its large beach. For decades, dark-skinned Mexicans and Puerto Ricans were chased out of the park by groups of white men threatening physical violence. However, Dolores says her children were never bothered. "When my kids were growing up, they loved Calumet Park. That's why I never wanted to move from here. They loved it, the beach, the sports, the games, all the activities they had there. Before it was mostly whites in the park. Now, on a summer Sunday, it's packed with Mexicans. In the summertime, the water looks so pretty from my kitchen window."

Dolores was worried about changes she saw in her neighborhood. Two years ago, a gang drive-by shooting occurred four blocks from her house. No one was hurt. Now retired, Dolores looked forward to her yearly get together with friends who grew up in South Chicago "I have six girlfriends from childhood, and although we all live in different states, we get together once a year. This year they all came to Chicago to stay at my home." Dolores says her life in Chicago has been fulfilling. She was very proud her three children have their families, own their own homes and have steady jobs. Her only regret about life: "I thought maybe I would have had a bigger home. All my friends have big, beautiful homes."

Death of the Mills

Yet the unthinkable happened in South Chicago. Most of the steel mills were shuttered in the 1980s and 1990s. Industrial decline, economic recessions, foreign competition, a changing American economy, and poor planning wreaked havoc on the steel mills. In 1980, the Wisconsin Steel Works mill unexpectedly shut down, throwing about 3,500 people out of work. Republic Steel closed shortly afterwards. And after more than a century of operation, United States Steel South Works ceased operations in 1992. More than 15,000 jobs were lost with the closing of the three mills. Many smaller firms, dependent on the steel industry, also failed throwing even more workers onto the unemployment lines.[34] The closing of the steel mills devastated the community. Former steel workers had a hard time finding new jobs. They had little education and few marketable skills. Many homes fell into disrepair. Older, rusted cars lined the streets. Catholic elementary schools sat closed. Once thriving stores, taverns, and restaurants were closed and boarded up. Discount dollar stores, public health clinics, and temporary, day labor offices dot the once bustling Commercial Avenue. Over thirty percent of Latino residents were unemployed and lived in poverty.

Abram Jacinto, 66, and his wife Rosa, 64, lived in South Deering for over 50 years. Abram and his two brothers lost their jobs when Wisconsin Steel folded. "My parents immigrated from Mexico in the early 1940s and came directly to Chicago," says Abram. "I was born in the old Hull-House neighborhood. In 1959, after graduating from high school, I got a job at Wisconsin Steel. I come from a long generation of steel mill workers. My father and six brothers all worked at Inland and Wisconsin steel mills. My father worked for over 25 years at Island Steel."[35] Abram remembered the fateful day Wisconsin Steel shut down. "I worked that day and started at 7:00 a.m. I worked in a skilled trade as a crane machinist. Around 2:00 p.m., my boss asked that I work overtime. I couldn't do it and I went home. Then I got a call from my brother. He tells me, "did you hear the mill closed?" I said, 'well, that's news to me, I just left there and there was no sign of anything.' On the ten o'clock news they showed the company locking the gates for the last time. I put 21 years in that mill and thought I was going to retire early from there. I felt so bad."

Wisconsin Steel workers were shocked. "We thought the closing was temporary, and that they might reopen," says Abram. "Slowly we realized it was permanent. We were out of our jobs but the bills kept coming. We had house, car, and private school payments." Abram believed Wisconsin Steel cheated the workers out of hundreds of millions of dollars. "Our last check that Wisconsin Steel gave us bounced. They cheated us out of pensions and benefits. They cheated me out of 19 weeks vacation. I was three years shy of getting a pension that paid me 100 percent of my last salary."

Former steel workers sued the owners of Wisconsin Steel, hoping to win back their benefits. After years of pressure and court battles, Wisconsin Steel settled with the workers and paid some benefits. "For my 21 years of work at Wisconsin, they paid me only $7,800," says Abram. "That is nothing. Easily they owe me more than $30,000. The workers were seeking something like $90 million in benefits, but they paid us only $14.8 million. They cheated the workers out of millions of dollars. But many workers felt some settlement was better than nothing." After their savings and unemployment compensation were exhausted, families had to go on welfare. "I was unemployed for a year after the mill closed. My family had to go on public aid for six months," says Abram. "I had always looked down on people on public aid, until I got to that point. I thought, my back's up against the wall, and my family has to survive. We have to eat. I realized that people were on public aid for the same reason I was. It gave me a different outlook."

The dreams of steel workers were shattered and families experienced emotional stress. Families lost their cars and homes. Some men took to drinking heavily. Domestic violence increased. Some families divorced. Some men committed suicide. Families moved away searching for jobs in other cities. Some found jobs in retail or small factories. But workers in the steel mills were making $23,000 a year. The new jobs they found paid only about $12,000.[36] Abram and Rosa refused to leave South Deering. Life for them was hard. They struggled to pay the mortgage on their modest, frame bungalow. They worried about the future. "I took training classes to drive an 18-wheeler truck," says Abram. "I took welding classes. Yet despite the training, the jobs did not materialize. The first thing employers ask for is experience. How do you get the experience if you're not given the opportunity to do the job? I've worked at five different jobs over the years. I'm currently working in a factory, but the factory will be closing down soon. I will be unemployed again."

Abram's wife, Rosa, also put in long hours at work. "I have been a homemaker all my life," says Rosa. "After the mill closed, I felt terrible. What were we going to do? I decided to go to work. I worked in a photo factory for five years. Then that place closed down. I worked in a lamp company for several years then that place closed down. Now, I've been working at the Nabisco factory for seven years. I work third shift and it's very hard. And we don't work the entire year due to layoffs. Last year I only worked seven months." The old mills stand silent and rusting away, reminders of a bygone era. Poverty and unemployment have now changed the character of South Chicago. Crime and gang shootings have increased. In 1997, Arnold Mireles, 35, a community activist, was shot and killed by two young gang members. Roel Salinas, 64, a local land-lord, paid the two gang members to kill Mireles. Because of Mireles' activism, Salinas had been fined and briefly jailed for failing to maintain his buildings. Salinas and the two gang members were sentenced to life in prison. A local elementary school was renamed in Mireles' honor.[37]

Tears rolled down Rosa's face as she talked about how her twenty-year-old son was accused by police of participating in a drive-by gang shooting. Police alleged he was in a car that fired several shots at a group of young gang members. No one was injured, but her son was sentenced to eight years in prison in downstate Illinois. "My son was not in a gang," says Rosa. "He just got involved with the wrong crowd. I feel the sentence was too harsh. He was never in trouble with the law before. I feel so bad working so many hours and not spending more time with him. He's taking college classes in jail, and trying to get his life together. He is a very smart kid, with a lot going for himself. He's very sorry about what happened." Rosa's son served seven years in prison. Abram and Rosa were happy their two other children were doing well. Their oldest son is a journeyman electrician. Their daughter worked as a legal assistant. Both are married with families of their own.

Building Community Organizations

Early Mexican immigrants in Chicago formed organizations that fostered a sense of community among its members. The earliest organizations established by Mexicans were mutualistas or mutual aid societies. In 1928, there were about twenty-three such societies in Chicago. Most mutualistas were small working-class organizations. From monthly membership dues of a dollar or two, the groups raised money and provided food, clothing, shelter, and heating fuels to newly arrived immigrants and those who were sick and needy.[38] The earliest Mexican mutualista in Chicago was the Benito Juarez Club. It was organized in 1918 by Mexicans working for the Rock Inland Railroad. The club offered financial assistance and recreational services. However, in 1921, the Juarez Club was reorganized and experienced internal class conflict. Middle-class Mexican doctors, lawyers, and professionals assumed leadership positions in the club. The working-class members saw the club as only interested in holding social events instead of helping poor Mexicans. The laborers broke away and formed their own club.[39]

One active mutualista during the mid-1920s was El Circulo De Obreros Catolicos "San Jose" in Indiana. Its members were mainly middle-class Catholic Mexicans who were refugees from the violence and religious turmoil of Mexico during the 1920's. Besides providing funds and religious and cultural events, this group engaged in civil rights issues like boycotting local theaters that segregated Mexicans.[40] Various settlement houses also helped Mexicans. The three neighborhoods with sizable Mexican residents had long-established settlement houses: Hull-House on the Near West Side, the University of Chicago Settle-

ment House in Back of the Yards, and the Bird Memorial Center in South Chicago. The settlements provided meeting rooms for Mexican community organizations. They offered sports activities, dances, music, art, and English and
citizenship classes.[41] Mexicans also formed Catholic worker groups, independent labor clubs, and radical unions. They created their own artistic societies. The
societies offered performances with musicians, dancers, and artists. They offered
literary and artistic shows highlighting Mexican culture. For instance, the Mexican Band of South Chicago played to big audiences wherever it performed.[42]

In addition to civic organizations, Mexicans established small mom-and-
pop businesses in the neighborhoods where they settled. They were usually pool
halls, restaurants, barber shops, groceries, tailor shops, and bakeries. Also, a
handful of Spanish-language newspapers were published in Mexican neighborhoods.[43] The highlight event in the social life of the Mexican neighborhoods was
the celebration of the fiestas patrias, or the Mexican national holidays. Mexicans
formed committees to organize parades to celebrate Mexican Independence Day
on the 16th of September. The parades fostered a sense of culture and community among Mexicans.

The family of Carmen Martinez Arias, 85, helped organize the earliest celebrations of Mexican Independence Day in South Deering in the late 1930s. "My
father Lucio Martinez and mother, Pasquala, immigrated to South Deering in
1923. They came from Mexico. Lucio worked for the Santa Fe Railroad and
then for Wisconsin Steel for 42 years, until he retired in the early 1970s. My
mother worked at the South Works steel mills during World War II. My father
belonged to a social club that met in a tavern. That's where they planned the big
social event of the year, the Mexican Independence Day parade. Nobody had
money. We had to make everything. The women sewed traditional dresses and
costumes. We dressed up in costumes and carried the Mexican flag. The men
would put on their white shirts. It was a little dinky parade." [44] The Comite Pa-
triotico Mexicano, or Mexican Patriotic Club, organized the first Mexican Independence parade in South Chicago in the early 1950s.

Individual Mexican families dedicated themselves to helping needy Mexicans. During World War II, the family of Carmen Martinez Arias helped hundreds of Mexican braceros in the South Deering neighborhood. "My mother
would feed Mexican braceros a meal of beans and tortillas for 50 cents. The men
had broken their work contracts and were staying in Chicago illegally. She
would lend the men carfare. Since the transient men could not use banks, my
mother kept their savings in shoe boxes. She returned the cash at no cost when
they moved on. I don't know how the braceros knew about my mother, but
many of them ended up at our house asking for her assistance. My mother referred them to social, political, and religious organizations in the city."

Some Mexican families took in boarders to earn extra money. But while
Pasquala Martinez helped braceros, she never took in boarders. "My mother
never let any of the braceros stay in our apartment because we had too many
females in the house," says Arias. "My father never said a word to my mother
for helping so many people. My father would go out and buy ten pounds of

beans and flour. And as young girls, we would help cook them and make tortillas for the braceros. My mother died in 1949: she was 49 and had cancer. My mother was well-liked. When she died, there were hundreds of people at the funeral. We didn't know many of the people." Arias' deceased husband worked at Wisconsin Steel for many years. She still lives in South Deering in a small, brick ranch home. One of her important, lifelong dreams was fulfilled: she is proud that her five children are all college educated.

Community Activism and Culture in Pilsen

Since the 1800s, the Lower West Side, known as Pilsen, was a port of entry for various European immigrants. In fact, Pilsen takes its name from a Czech Bohemian city. Today Pilsen is a port of entry for Mexican immigrants, especially many who are undocumented. The neighborhood has the highest concentration of Mexicans in the city. Over 88 percent of Pilsen's 45,654 residents were Latino. More than 38,000 Mexicans reside in Pilsen.[45] Pilsen has an unmistakable, dynamic Mexican flavor. Spanish-language store signs were everywhere. The neighborhood's main commercial streets, 18th Street and Blue Inland, were lined with Mexican-owned, mostly mom-and-pop bakeries, tortilla factories, barber shops, music and clothing stores, and super mercado grocery stores. There were many restaurants, taco stands, and sidewalk vendors. Mexican music blared loudly from the music stores, and open apartment windows.

In the 1960s and 70s, many younger, second and third-generation Mexicans in Pilsen asserted themselves. Pilsen exploded with manifestations of Mexican culture, identity, nationalism, and political activism. Mexicans stressed brown power, and began calling themselves Chicanos, attesting to their pride in Mexican culture and their new political consciousness. A new generation of community leaders emerged. They were opposing assimilation into mainstream American culture. Instead, local Mexican activists, writers, poets, painters, and authors began reclaiming and expressing their Mexican heritage. Mexican pride was clearly evident in the large murals that began to adore the walls of many buildings in Pilsen. Mario Castillo, 60, was credited with launching the Mexican mural movement in Chicago. He is a well-known Mexican painter, and college professor of art. In 1968, Castillo led a group of Mexican youths in painting a mural on a building in Pilsen at 1935 S. Halsted Street. "The mural was entitled "Peace," a work paying tribute to the Indian cultures of the Northwest, and against the Vietnam War," says Castillo. "The peace symbol was the center motif. It was the age of the hippie and flower power movements, so it had a lot of flowers. It had a person holding a flower in front of a military tank. My mural was the first done by a Mexican in Chicago since the 1940s. In the 1960s, Chicago's Art Institute and other major museums didn't exhibit Latino work. Contemporary, young Latino artists were not being showcased. Nothing was being done with us. So we had to do it ourselves.... "Peace" began a mural movement across the city."[46]

Mexican artists used the walls of buildings, schools, churches, and restaurants to paint their large, colorful murals. The murals contained indigenous Mexican motifs, and cultural and political messages of the Mexican immigrant experience, Latino unity, racism, and world peace. There were more than 100 indoor and outdoor murals in Pilsen and Little Village. "Murals are an affirmation of who we are. Some of the greatest muralists in the world have been Mexican," says Castillo. "I have painted murals in Chicago high schools, colleges, and in East Los Angeles. I enjoy painting murals with teams of high school and college students. I enjoy teaching students about art. I've taught some young, creative, Latinos students who are up-and-coming artists."

Castillo lived in South Chicago. "My parents were migrant farm workers. They came to Chicago and the Pilsen neighborhood in 1962. In Chicago, my mother worked as a beautician. My mother, Maria Enriquez Allen, was a prominent, self-taught painter. Her works were exhibited in places like Chicago's Museum of Contemporary Art. She gave painting and arts and crafts workshops to many children in Pilsen. She passed away at the age of 92." Other noted Mexican muralists and painters from Chicago include Marcos Raya, Alejandro Romero, Carlos Cortez, Aurelio Diaz Tekpankalli, Oscar Romero, and Hector Duarte.[47]

During the 1960s and 70s Mexicans in Pilsen formed organizations to promote their civil rights. Mexicans became angry that white city officials and politicians ignored their community. Mexicans increasingly got involved in community activism and confrontation politics. They took to the streets protesting against police brutality, insensitive immigration officials, inferior schools, and the lack of city services. In 1970, Mexican activists took over the Howell Neighborhood House in Pilsen, a former Presbyterian facility for Bohemian youngsters. They renamed the group Casa Aztlán the mythical original home of the Aztec Indians. Casa Aztlán became an active cultural center for Mexican artists and painters. The inside and outside walls of the center were adorned with murals depicting Mexican revolutionaries, labor struggles, and working-class people. Casa Aztlán also helped those wanting to become permanent residents or American citizens. The group repeatedly protested at the Immigration and Naturalization office (INS) office in downtown Chicago. They, and other immigration groups, complained that INS officials provided bad service and dragged their feet regarding naturalization efforts. People had to wait up to three years to become citizens. They also complained that INS officials selectively targeted undocumented Mexicans for arrests and deportations.[48]

Mary Gonzales, 65, has a long history of community activism in Pilsen. She is a noted community organizer and member of the Pilsen Neighbors Community Council. The organization was founded in 1954 by white ethnics, but was dormant for many years. In the early 1970s, Mexican women like Mary Gonzales assumed leadership roles in the organization. They organized residents and used protests and demonstrations to force city officials to provide employment opportunities, improve schools, and provide better city sanitation services. "Many people I've organized in Pilsen over the last 30 years are wonderful and courageous," says Gonzales. "They had a lot to lose because many were un-documented immigrants. But we fought for many important things. They weren't afraid to fight. They really believed they had a right to have their children in good schools, have a job, and to have clean neighborhoods. They were people with solid values."[49]

Gonzales came from humble beginnings. "My father immigrated to United States in 1925 from Michocan, Mexico. My mother was born in Oklahoma. My parents were migrant workers. They followed the harvest north to Midwestern states. My mother came to Chicago in the 1930s. She met my father here, married and had eleven children. I am the youngest child. My parents worked in factories and struggled financially. We had a lot of meals of frijoles and tortillas." Gonzales got her first taste of community organizing in the late 1950s when she tagged along to meetings with her mother, Guadalupe A. Reyes. Despite putting in long hours at the factory, Reyes found time to become an active volunteer in Pilsen's social service agencies. One of Reyes' children contacted spinal meningitis at eight months, and was partially paralyzed. Thus, Reyes dedicated her life to helping him and others with developmental disabilities. In 1972, Reyes founded the Esperanza School. The school served children and adults with physical and mental disabilities. "My mother decided that my brother would learn to walk and talk," says Gonzales. "She helped him a lot and he walked, talked, ran, and jumped. He went to Esperanza school. He passed away about 14 years ago." Years later, Reyes founded El Valor and the Guadalupano Family Center, which served physically and mentally challenged children and adults. These two organizations are in Pilsen. In 2000, Guadalupe A. Reyes passed away at age 83. Gonzales is married to Gregory Galluzzo, a former Jesuit priest. They founded the Gamielo Foundation, and the Metropolitan Alliance of Congregations. The two organizations trained community organizers throughout Illinois.

Since the 1970s, community residents have worried about gentrification in Pilsen. Residents feared private developers were turning the neighborhood into an artists' colony for middle-class, white professionals who were displacing working-class Mexicans. Pilsen is located on prime land close to downtown, with old buildings ripe for redevelopment.[50] On Pilsen's east end, developers and real estate brokers continued to renovate dozens of older houses and industrial buildings as artist studios and upscale apartments. The University of Illinois expanded into Pilsen. And the city of Chicago designated a large section of Pilsen as a tax-increment financing district (TIF). City officials argued that TIF financing was a crucial tool to redevelop "blighted" areas. In effect TIF districts freeze property tax revenues for years. Critics argued that TIF districts robbed schools, public parks, and other city services of needed tax revenues.[51]

Mary Gonzales and the Pilsen Neighbors Community Council, were strongly against gentrification. "Gentrification is the only issue in Pilsen these days. My taxes went up 30 percent," says Gonzales. "There are families along 18th Street whose property taxes went up 200 percent. They're going to be priced out in six years. TIF is not bad if it benefits everyone. But whom does it usually benefit? It benefits the big developers who build upscale housing. They displace poor and working-class people. They displaced poor Latinos in other neighborhoods. Why would they not use the same methods here?"

Gonzales liked the fact that Pilsen has working and middle-class Mexicans living together. She hopes the community remains predominately Mexican. "I've lived in Pilsen for the last 40 years. I love the neighborhood. Pilsen gets a bad rap. Outsiders and the media focus on gangs and crime in the neighborhood. But the community is not that bad. It's one of the best kept secrets in the city. I've never been touched by the gang problem. Of course, I have four daughters, and gangs usually bother young boys. But people believe this neighborhood is very poor. Baloney, it is not. There are a lot of middle-class Latinos here."

Danny Solis, alderman of the 25th ward that encompasses Pilsen, supported Pilsen's TIF designation, and the University of Illinois and middle-class residents moving into the neighborhood. He believed the changes would bring jobs, tax revenues, and better housing to the area. Solis was a former community organizer for the United Neighborhood Organization (UNO). The organization was founded in 1980 by Mary Gonzales and her husband. UNO established Catholic church-based, grass-roots chapters in Mexican neighborhoods. In its early years, UNO mobilized residents and used protests against city officials to win millions of dollars of neighborhood improvements in education, health, and city services.[52]

But in 1989, Danny Solis and Mary Gonzales had a major falling out over the direction of UNO. Solis took over UNO. In the past UNO kept at arm's length from politicians, fearing it might be taken for granted. Many felt Solis used UNO to further his political career and to develop a close relationship with Mayor Richard M. Daley.[53] Indeed, in 1996, Mayor Daley appointed Solis as 25th ward alderman. Many saw Solis and his allies, including UNO, the Mexican American Chamber of Commerce, and the Hispanic American Construction Industry Association as representing a conservative political viewpoint among Mexicans. Juan Rangel, 40, the new executive director of UNO disagreed.

"I believe Mary Gonzales, some Mexican American politicians and even the Puerto Rican U.S. Congressman, Luis Gutierrez (D. ILL.) are out of touch with the values of neighborhood residents," says Rangel. "They always represent Hispanics as victims. Hispanics do not see themselves as victims. Police brutality, discrimination, bilingual education, and gentrification are not the real issues. If you talk to people, the most important issue is crime. People want safer streets. They want the gangbangers out of the community. Crime, education and jobs are the real issues. There is nothing wrong with being pro business. We need jobs."[54]

Rangel lives in Little Village. He says his immigrant parents progressed in Chicago through their own hard work and did not look to government for handouts or assistance. "My parents were undocumented and worked in Texas picking crops. They did not speak English. My father came to Chicago in the mid-1950s. My parents wanted to make some money. They wanted to buy a home. My dad is a hard worker. He worked in various small factories and restaurants.

He worked on weekends. My mother stayed in Texas taking care of her children. My dad would send money and return to Texas on weekends. That went on for 12 years. Then in 1970, my mother and us came to Chicago to join my dad. My dad was fortunate to get a job at Coca-Cola. They sponsored my dad and mom and helped them become legal residents. There are seven in my family."

These days, Mary Gonzales, and other Latinos see UNO as nothing more than a clout-heavy political group aligned with Mayor Richard M. Daley and his new political machine. UNO abandoned confrontation politics. The group regularly gave awards to Mayor Richard M. Daley and other influential politicians. UNO received large, yearly contracts from the city of Chicago to renovate housing and provide immigration services. But Rangel disagreed that UNO was currying favors with politicians. He says his group helped immigrants. "In the last six years UNO has helped about 50,000 people, mostly Mexican, become American citizens.... We helped my parents become American citizens. In the 40 years they were here, they always believed they were going back to Mexico. The majority of immigrants have this belief of going back someday. By becoming a citizen, you already made a conscious decision that you are going to be staying here. So why not reap the benefits of citizenship. My parents bought a home in Little Village. They learned English. My brothers and sister have all become American citizens. They all know America has been a great country for them."

Mexican Culture

A highly popular cultural event in Pilsen is the annual Fiesta del Sol (Festival of the Sun), sponsored by the Pilsen Neighbors Community Council. The Fiesta, held in August, highlights Mexican heritage and identity. The festival began in 1972 as a small corner party. It is now a four-day, outdoor festival and one of the largest ethnic festivals in the Midwest. Fiesta del Sol was Pilsen Neighbor's main fund raising activity, and brought in about $50,000. About 1.5 million people from throughout the city visited the festival. Hundreds of vendors in booths prepared and sold Mexican food. Hundreds of other vendors sold Mexican arts, crafts, and paintings. Three stages provided Mexican music including norteño, ranchéra, tex-mex, and mariachi. In 1999, Pilsen Neighbors leaders charged that Alderman Danny Solis was playing petty politics and trying to kill the Fiesta by denying them a city permit to hold the festival at its regular location at Blue Island and 18th Street. This area was remodeled into a Mexican-themed plaza, complete with new streets, sidewalks, benches, street planters, and parking space. City officials finally issued a permit for a new location on Cermak Road. Planners of the Fiesta argued that this was an inferior location offering less visibility and less access to 18th Street businesses.[55]

A neighborhood institution that was putting Mexican culture on the map in Chicago was the Mexican Fine Arts Center Museum. The museum, located at 1852 W. 19th St. was housed in a small, Chicago Park District building in Harrison Park in Pilsen. In 2006, to celebrate its 20th anniversary, the museum changed its name to the National Museum of Mexican Art (NMMA). In fact, the museum is indeed a national success story. Each year hundreds of thousands of people visit the NMMA. "The museum showcases the rich, artistic Mexican culture through exhibits, performances, readings, a radio station for youth, art classes, youth concerts, and collaborative projects with other major institutions," says Carlos Tortolero, 52, the museum's executive director. "People come from all over the city, country and the world to visit our museum. We had some people from Japan. Busloads of white, African American, and Latino children come to the museum from the city, the suburbs and other states. We Mexicans have a story to tell and we want people to know who we are. Some people only know Mexicans from television."[56]

The NMMA was founded in 1987 by Carlos Tortolero and Helen Valdez. "We were teachers at Bowen High School in South Chicago," says Tortolero. " I remember some second and third-generation Mexican kids at the high school calling other Mexican kids wetbacks. I said wait, that's not right. I began to see that kind of rift. It was also disturbing that the kids didn't speak Spanish. They were very Americanized. They were beginning to lose their culture. I believed that preserving Mexican culture was important."

With no experience in running museums, Tortolero and Valdez put together exhibits and programs on Mexican culture throughout the city. Then in 1987, they persuaded Chicago Park District officials to let them use an old boat craft building in Harrison Park to house the NMMA. Tortolero says he got his clue from Puerto Ricans across town who were asking the Park District for a building for a Puerto Rican museum. Tortolero made no apologies about promoting a Mexican museum instead of a Latino museum. "Of course we're proud to be Latino. But to us, being Mexican, Puerto Rican or Cuban, is different. We can't lose that. Every culture has something that they bring to the table.... If you look at the areas of housing, health, education, politics, and the media in Chicago, Mexicans are not where they should be in terms of their percentage of the Latino population. The people from Central and South America, the ones who are educated, they're getting the jobs. Mejicanos don't want to raise this issue because they become the bad guys. We have to work together, but we have to admit there are these problems."

In its early years, some Mexicans criticized the NMMA as elitist for not showcasing the works of local artists. Now the museum regularly exhibits the works of local, national and international Mexican artists. In April 2001, the museum opened its new $5.3 million, building adjacent to the current facility. The new building tripled the museum's gallery and administrative space to 48,000 square feet. Funds for the new wing were raised from public and private donors. The NMMA also operated a satellite youth museum and radio station in Pilsen. Altogether, NMMA has more than 70,000 square feet of space. "We are the largest Latino art organization in the U.S. When we opened in 1987, we had a staff of three people and a budget of $200,000. Now we have 32 full-time staff and a budget of $4 million," says Tortolero. "We will have a classroom for live arts and more major exhibitions. In the new building we're doing a plaza to honor Mexican veterans who fought in all the wars of the United States."

The NMMA annually honored Mexican women for their varied contributions to Chicago. Among those honored in 1998, were two widely recognized Mexican authors from Chicago, Sandra Cisneros, and Ana Castillo. Sandra Cisernos, who lived in San Antonio, Texas, is the author of popular books of poems and novels such as The House on Mango Street. Ana Castillo, lives in Chicago, and has published widely read works of fiction like So Far From God and Peel My Love Like an Onion.

Struggling to Make it in La Villita

Traditionally, Mexicans from Pilsen moved into the nearby South Lawndale neighborhood, or what is called Little Village. Mexicans endearingly called the neighborhood La Villita. They saw it as a suburb in the city and a step up toward the middle class. After Pilsen, South Lawndale had the second highest concentration of Mexicans. In 1990, more than 64,000 Mexicans lived in Little Village, almost 80 percent of the community's total.[57] The homes were brick, bungalow, and single-family homes, in addition to numerous graystone and brownstone three-flats. While many housing units were old and overcrowded, they were well maintained. The homes have small, front yards with flowers, grass, and often vegetable gardens.

Norma Seledon, 44, lives in Little Village with her husband and three children. She moved to Little Village when she was 10 years old. "My father immigrated from Monterey, Mexico in 1967 to an Illinois suburb called Argo Summit. He found a job, established himself and found an apartment. A year later my mother and four siblings joined him. My father came looking for work. He was very fortunate, he got a job at Reynolds Metal Company in Argo, and he has been working there ever since. It is unskilled work. Four years later, we moved to Little Village. My father bought a building. We lived upstairs and downstairs he opened a bar. He worked all the time. In Little Village we were able to keep in touch with Mexican culture. There were some gangs in the area. But this is a good community."[58]

Like other Mexicans who come to Chicago, Seledon's parents dreamed of someday returning to live in Mexico. However, many Mexicans realized that opportunities were better in the United States, and they never did return to live in Mexico. Instead, Mexican families made yearly, short visits back to Mexico to see families and friends. This back and forth migration helped many Mexicans retain their Spanish language and a strong sense of Mexican identity. "My mother wanted to return to Mexico. Maybe even ten years ago she wanted to return. She hates the winter here. She hates that she does not have many friends. She is very secluded here and doesn't go out much. In Mexico, we would go out and talk to the neighbors. She found the culture here a little strange. My dad always talked about returning. He wanted to own a business in Mexico. But as time went by, he realized that he could not give us in Mexico what he could give us here."

After many years of living in Chicago, Seledon's parents fulfilled their dream of becoming American citizens. "My dad eventually became an American citizen. My father self-taught himself English. And recently my mother became an American citizen. My mother took English classes and learned English. She speaks with an accent is very self-conscious."

Another dream of Seledon's parents was that their children would obtain a college education. They paid hefty tuitions for their children to attend Catholic grammar and high schools. They also paid for their college education. "It was a huge sacrifice for my parents to put us through Catholic schools, and pay for our college education. My father worked two jobs for a long time to put us through school, his regular factory job and running his bar....There was a little of a double standard with my dad. He wanted a housewife at home, but he wanted his daughters to be strong, educated, and influential. Four of us graduated from college. My mother is disappointed that one of my brothers didn't finish college. My mother wants my brother to return and get a college education."

The job Seledon's father held for many years was uncertain. "The Reynolds company is going through downsizing now. They were bought out, and so he's worried about losing his job. I know he took a huge pay cut recently. But he's holding out because he's going to be up for retirement soon." Seledon was the executive director of Mujeres Latinas En Acción (Latina Women In Action), a social service agency on 17th Street in Pilsen. She left the agency but hoped to continue working in women services. The agency was founded by a group of Mexican and Latina women. The agency served women from Pilsen and Little Village mainly in domestic violence prevention. Over 800 women annually came to the agency for assistance with this problem. Most were first and second generation Mexican women ranging in age from 15 to early 40s.

"Latino men certainly don't have the market on machismo," says Seledon. "Domestic violence is a behavior that runs across cultures, and across economic, racial, ethnic, and social backgrounds.... I think the difference with Latinas is that we don't have access to services as much as other populations. There is physical, emotional, psychological, and sexual abuse. Violence is not healthy behavior. We have individuals who lock their women at home, sell their dresses, take the phone away, or threaten to take the children away. It's something men do to manipulate and control their women. Abusers abuse because they can get away with it." Seledon says some in the community often see Mujeres Latina En Acción as an agency that breaks up marriages by encouraging divorce. "That's not the case. Women who leave our program come out powerful, and in more control of their lives. Most women do not want to leave their husbands. They just want the abuse to stop. We present information and lay out options. We offer support groups for women and the legal venue, which is to get a court order of protection. Some women decide to get a divorce. Not because the agency's pushing them, but because they realize things are not going to change. They have to make a choice."

In a 1996 report, Mujeres Latina En Acción found that Latinas had crucial needs like affordable child care facilities, access to jobs, obtaining a better education, and employment. The report concluded that while 57.2 percent of Latinas worked, 28 percent worked in low-paying jobs as operators, fabricators, and laborers, compared to 28 percent for all other women. Moreover, only 14 percent of Latinas held professional or managerial jobs compared to 28.1 percent of all women.[59]

A distinguishing feature of Little Village is a Mexican-style arch gateway at 26th Street and California. Ron Baltierra, a Mexican contractor and Vietnam veteran, constructed the arch in the early 1990s. The arch has a sign saying "Bienvenidos a Little Village."[60] The neighborhood's main, bustling commercial district runs along 26th Street for over 25 blocks. There were over 1,500 stores along 26th Street. Over 95 percent of the businesses were Mexican-owned. The businesses included restaurants, bakeries, laundromats, currency exchanges, banks, clothing stores, and jewelry stores. According to the Little Village Chamber of Commerce, this 26th Street retail corridor generated the second largest sales tax revenues in the city, after the big stores downtown. Another bustling business district in Little Village is along Cermak Road and 22nd Street. There were over 200 Mexican-owned, small businesses along this strip. Some viewed the many Mexican-owned businesses as a clear indication that the Mexican community was thriving in Chicago. Others insisted the stores were mostly small, mom-and-pop operations, and it was easy to overstate the success of Mexican businesses.

"I think it's great," says Juan Ochoa, 36, the former executive director of the Mexican American Chamber of Commerce. "Most are ma-and-pa establishments. These are people who have the entrepreneurship spirit. There isn't any other ethnic group in this city that opens as many businesses as we have per capita. Most Mexican Americans in this city are first and second generation. And when you look at all those businesses on 26th Street, I think we're doing a tremendous job. I think our businesses are at a point where they realize they need to get those Harvard and Northwestern graduates to help them to the next level which is owning larger chain stores and franchises like McDonalds."[61] In 2007, Governor Rod Blagojevich appointed Ochoa chief executive to run McCormick Place and Navy Pier.

Ochoa sees Chicago as a good city for Mexicans to start up businesses. He believes city and state officials are reaching out with grants and assistance to help Mexicans establish and improve their businesses. "Many businesses on 26th Street are members of the Mexican American Chamber of Commerce. Our group was founded about 28 years ago, but for whatever reasons, it broke off. A group of businessmen brought it back to life in the early 1990. They wanted to develop a vehicle that would help them bid on city and state contracts. We seek opportunities for Hispanic businesses across the city and suburbs. We have about 184 businesses in our group.... Many of our Hispanic elected officials traditionally focus on liberal issues like illegal immigration, police brutality, bilingual education, and discrimination. Business development, unfortunately, has not been a priority for them."

Mexican business owners regularly met with police to complain about gangs and drug dealing in Pilsen and Little Village. "In the south end of Little Village, the biggest problem is gangs and drugs," says Dennis Prieto, commander of the Chicago's Police Department's tenth district, which includes Little Village. "I don't know how many gangs there are, but there are pockets of gangs on one side and pockets on the other side. The gangs are always feuding with one another.... We have 16 officers in the gang's unit. They concentrate on gang problems. When I hear shots fired in a gang territory, I inundate the area with a lot of police presence. I deal with it so there is not further escalation of the gang problem. I say, 'let's go out there and make some arrests.'"[62]

During the summer months, community residents regularly organized marches through 26th Street in efforts to "take back the streets" and denounce gangs and drug dealing. Police and local politicians often participated in these highly publicized marches. Community leaders were at a loss to explain why young teenagers joined gangs. They pointed out that lack of meaningful employment and educational opportunities caused some teenagers to join gangs. Ochoa, who served in the United States Marine Corps, reaching the rank of corporal, expressed an unpopular opinion as to why teenagers joined gangs: he blamed the parents and their kids. "I absolutely blame the parents and the kids," says Ochoa. "Those gangbangers have parents. Those parents, they're accountable to their kids. When these kids reach the 14 and 15 age bracket, they know what you're doing. I certainly made the choice not to do that. Why can't they make those choices? I am no different from anybody....The majority of people in our community, the kids and adults are good people. But the ones who stick out the most are those gangbangers. You have parents and leaders in our community making excuses for them, saying it's not their fault, it's society's fault. When you make excuses, it no longer holds parents accountable."

Ochoa says that Ricardo Munoz, the alderman of the 22nd ward, which includes Little Village, was soft on crime and gangs. But community residents disagreed. Munoz was very popular with residents and has served as alderman since 1993. In 1999, Ochoa, an ally of Mayor Richard M. Daley, ran against Munoz as alderman. Many saw the contest as Daley's loyal Latino allies trying to unseat the more independent Munoz, who sometimes publicly disagreed with the mayor on certain issues. In the five-way aldermanic race, Ochoa and the others were defeated, and Munoz won.

Sidewalk Entrepreneurs

In addition to established businesses, Little Village has many sidewalk entrepreneurs. Paleteros, or vendors of ice cream and frozen treats, pushed their small carts up and down the streets and sidewalks, ringing bells to attract customers. On almost every corner along 22nd and 26th Street stand the eloteros. From their rickety, brightly-painted wooden pushcarts, they hawked corn-on-the-cob, fruit juices, sliced watermelon, and cucumbers. They sold sweet mangoes in plastic cups, sprinkled with salt, lime juice, and cayenne pepper. Some sold snow cones, pork skins, and tamales. Most eloteros were poor, undocumented and recent arrivals. They spoke little English.

Six days a week, rain or shine, Esperanza Torres, 67, and her wooden pushcart were on the corner of 26th and Christiana. She is an elotero and has claimed this corner as her space. Torres came to Chicago in 1979 from Cuernavaca, Mexico. She says she is a legal resident. "I'm a pushcart vendor because I have to survive and pay my apartment rent," says Torres. "I get up early every morning to boil my corn. Then I hurry to the store to buy large quantities of cucumbers, watermelons and mangos. I am on my corner working from early noon until nine or ten at night. I've been selling for about 15 years. My husband died two years ago from diabetes. He was 59 years old. I have six children, three daughters and three sons. I have 16 grandchildren and one great-grandchild. They are all grown with their families. I don't want to impose on my daughters or sons for help. I don't want to bother anyone."[63]

There were easily over 500 food vendors in Latino neighborhoods, and their numbers multiplied everyday. In the freezing winter months, some food vendors were wrapped like Eskimos as they hawked hot, homemade tamales. Food vendors have long been part of Chicago's urban fabric. Previous immigrants began as food vendors as they slowly made it into a middle-class lifestyle. However, a few Chicago aldermen have tried to put the eloteros out of business. Some aldermen argued that the food vendors were noisy, a nuisance, and their food was unhealthy. They said the vendors did not wash their hands and often urinated in alleys. In 1999, more than 30 eloteros protested at City Hall temporarily stopping aldermen from passing legislation shutting them down.[64] But aldermen have passed ordinances banning the peddlers from sixteen, mostly white city wards, and from parks, beaches and Chicago's downtown.

"I don't know why the city is making up all these new rules. I think it's because we're Mexican," says Torres. "They don't like us. But I'm an older person. No one is going to give me a job. The politicians think we're getting rich selling from our little carts. We're very simple people. We barely make enough to pay our rent and utilities. On a good Saturday I can make about $150.00, which is good money. On a slow day I make only about $50.00. It's not true that we urinate in alleys. I live down the block. When I want to use the washroom, a friend of mine takes over while I go to my home. No one has ever gotten sick from eating our food."

Some 26th Street Mexican restaurant owners also complained about the food vendors. They complained that while they had to pay rent and property taxes, the vendors did not. The owners felt the vendors took away their customers. Ironically, some of the restaurant owners once started out as pushcart vendors, and then moved up to owning a small taco stand, then later a fancy restaurant. Ed Campos, president of the Little Village Community Council, has organized the vendors into an informal union. The vendors opposed Chicago ordinances that limited their hours of operation, and restricted their sales to designed corners. But they have agreed with the city to purchase vendor licenses. Yet many vendors operated without licenses. "I understand it. The food vendors are doing what my father did 50 years ago when he opened a stand at Maxwell Street," says Dennis Prieto, police commander. "But we're enforcing the law. We have to see if they are properly licensed. If they do not have a vendor's license, they have to pack it up and go. We're not taking their carts away right now. We just issue them a citation and tell them to stop. Then they have to go to court."[65]

"I have to pay $95.00 each year to renew my license," says Esperanza. "Many times police stop by my cart to buy corn, mangos, and fruit drinks. I never charge police. They perform an important duty by protecting the public. Now the city says we have to wear plastic gloves whenever we serve food. But the gloves are expensive. We don't really need gloves because I never touch the food with my bare hands. The city wants us to carry soap and water to wash our hands. Now the city is saying we need two people behind every pushcart, one to serve food and another to collect money. I don't make enough money to support myself, how can I hire someone else? I feel frustrated with all the rules the city is coming up with. I feel like I should do something else to support myself. But you tell me, what else can I do?"

City officials have also discussed an ordinance that may force vendors to purchase a one-of-a-kind, stainless steel cart equipped with hand-washing sinks, and hot and cold running water. The carts cost between $3,000 and $5,000 each. Esperanza hoped she does not have to buy a new cart. "I paid a man $400.00 to make my pushcart. What's wrong with it? I cannot afford $5,000 to buy a new cart. I don't make that kind of money.... I don't ask for welfare. I'm a hard-working person. I only work during the summer months. I don't sell during the winter months. Other vendors do but I have arthritis and the cold aggravates it. I usually baby sit children in my apartment during the winter months. My baby-sitting barely brings in enough to pay my bills. I don't like to complain.... My children are well-mannered. They don't drink or bother anyone. My sons have good jobs. They paint houses in the suburbs. I love Chicago. You don't have to go on welfare here. There are opportunities to work in this city."

Cultural Celebrations

Mexican pride and culture were on display throughout Chicago in September and October. September 16th to October 16th is Hispanic Heritage Month in the United States, a time set aside to recognize the contributions of Latinos. September 16th is also Mexican Independence Day, which commemorates the anniversary of Mexico's independence from Spain in 1821. In Chicago, community and civic organizations sponsored carnivals, beauty pageants, and parades celebrating Mexican Independence Day. Since 1967, the Mexican Civic Society sponsored the annual September 16th Mexican Independence Day Parade in downtown Chicago. Thousands of spectators enjoyed over 120 colorful floats and marching bands. Men and women dressed in traditional and folkloric Mexican costumes. Shouts of Viva Mexico were everywhere.

The Little Village Chamber of Commerce also organized a popular Mexican Independence Day Parade along 26th Street during the second week of September, along with an all-day festival. The Little Village parade and festival were becoming even more popular than the downtown Mexican parade. The sidewalks were jam-packed with thousands of people proudly waving the green, white, and red Mexican flags. About 200 floats participated in the parade. In 1980, the 26th street parade underscored the ideological and generational differences among Mexicans. That year, police ordered 200 members of the People's Contingent, a coalition of Mexican social activists to leave the parade. Contingent members were passing out literature protesting the oppressive working conditions of undocumented workers. Parade sponsors complained to police that the parade was supposed to be enjoyable not political. Police arrested seven Contingent leaders, including Rudy Lozano, a young up-and-coming Mexican leader. They were charged with mob action and disorderly conduct.

Another popular Mexican cultural event on Cermak Road was the Cinco de Mayo (May 5) parade and four-day festival, sponsored by the Cermak Chamber of Commerce. Cinco de Mayo, a national holiday in Mexico, commemorated the Battle of Puebla, Mexico in 1862, when an ill-equipped Mexican army defeated occupying French forces. Over 100,000 Mexicans gathered at Douglas Park in Chicago to participate in the festival. The audience was treated to an exciting 16-team soccer tournament involving teams from Mexico playing against favorite teams from Chicago.

Chapter Two: Mexicans

Is God in the Basement?

Rev. Peter Rodríguez was born in Spain and joined the Claretian Missionary Fathers at age 19. He came to Chicago in 1960, and worked as a Roman Catholic priest serving Latinos for over 40 years. He was the pastor at Holy Cross-Immaculate Heart of Mary parish for 13 years. The church sits on the corner of the 4500 block of South Wood, in the New City area, better known as the Back of TheYards. In 2004, Rodríguez, 72, passed away. But shortly before his death Rodríguez recalled with indignation, the prejudice Mexican immigrants faced from fellow Catholics as neighborhoods experienced racial change during the 1960s and 70s. "Some whites in certain churches in the Back of TheYards and other neighborhoods did not accept Mexican Americans," said Rodríguez. "They didn't want to have anything to do with Mexicans. I know of churches where Mexicans tried to attend and some white pastors and parishioners told them, 'why don't you go to your own church?' When Mexicans were admitted to white churches, they sent them to the basement to have mass there. We, the Claretian priests, complained to the Cardinal about how churches were not accepting Mexicans and how they were putting them in basements."[1]

Holy Cross is an ornate church with a tall dome ceiling, and intricate, stained-glass windows. The area's Lithuanian community built the church in 1904. On Sundays the church was packed with about 1,600 parishioners sitting in wooden pews. These days, however, the parishioners are not Lithuanian, they are mainly Mexican. On Sundays, the church offered three Spanish-language masses. Mexicans began moving into the Back of The Yards after World War I. The neighborhood was home to Irish, Poles, Lithuanians, and Ukrainians. It was here where the famous Union Stock Yard opened in 1865. After World War I, over 40,000 people worked in the stockyards, meat-packing houses, and ancillary industries.[2] In his 1906 novel, Upton Sinclair called the place "The Jungle." Sinclair's portrait of the horrific working conditions at the stockyards led to the passage of the Pure Food and Drug Act. Meat-packing executives used Mexicans as strikebreakers. Several hundred Mexicans began working in the meat-packing industry during the major 1921 packinghouse strike. After labor disputes were settled, many of the Mexican workers were fired.

Years later, Mexicans became an accepted presence in the packinghouses. By 1928 over 5.7 percent of both Swift's and Armour's employees were Mexican. Mexicans worked mainly as laborers in the packinghouse freezers. They received few promotions. By 1930, some 3,000 Mexicans lived in the neighborhood.[3] In the 1930s and 40's some prejudiced white ethnics did not want Mexicans as neighbors. Thus, Mexicans settled on the west side of the stockyards.

They lived in dilapidated and overcrowded apartments where they paid high rents. Poles were the largest white group in the area, and there were often fights between Poles and Mexicans.[4] Early Mexican newcomers to Back of the Yards found over a dozen, large Catholic parishes, often just blocks from each other. But the churches, both Catholic and Protestant, either neglected or rejected Mexicans. One institution that accepted Mexicans, even undocumented ones, was the University of Chicago Settlement House, founded by Mary McDowell. The Settlement House offered Mexicans health services, dances, music, art, English lessons, citizenship classes, crafts, homemaking, and movies.[5]

The Cordi-Marian Sisters Missionary Congregation provided the first catechism classes for Mexican children. These missionary nuns were exiled from Mexico in 1927. They came to Chicago to work with Mexican immigrants. For years, they held catechism classes and mass in the homes of Mexicans. Finally, in 1940, Mexicans established a church of their own in a cheap storefront at 4330 South Ashland Avenue. The store was formerly a butcher shop and was falling apart. Mexican men completely repaired it. An old icebox served as the altar. This was the humble beginnings of Immaculate Heart of Mary Vicariate. The Claretian Missionary Fathers, a Spanish Order from Mexico, provided mass in Spanish.[6] Holy Cross and Immaculate Heart of Mary were merged in 1981. During the 1960s and 70s, the racial makeup of the Back of the Yards changed. White ethnics moved to the suburbs while Mexicans moved in. Some white ethnics that remained in the neighborhood resented that Mexicans were taking over Catholic parishes they had considered as their own for generations.

Rev. Rodríguez recalled one painful episode. "For a time Holy Cross was a Ukrainian church. A young Mexican American girl came to get married here in the early 1970s. The pastor told her, 'no, you go to the Mexican church, Immaculate Heart of Mary.' She was so hurt she abandoned the Catholic Church. Years later she came back to the church and I heard the story from her." Some pastors and parishioners resented that Mexicans were asking for Spanish-language masses. "In the 1970s, Cardinal John Cody put the last Ukrainian pastor here at Holy Cross so he could start a mass in Spanish. That pastor was a professor of Spanish at the seminary," recalled Rev. Rodríguez. "A Mexican American deacon asked the pastor to begin a Spanish mass because many parishioners were Mexican. The pastor, replied, 'over my dead body.' Finally, they gave Mexicans Spanish-language masses in the basement, while whites had English masses in the main church. Another time that Ukrainian pastor told parishioners that 'those people,' meaning Mexicans, 'were taking over our church and that they would destroy it.' When Cardinal Cody told the Ukrainian pastor that they were merging Holy Cross with St. Mary's in 1981, the pastor cried. He said it was so unfair. The first thing we did when we merged, was to clean and paint Holy Cross. It had not been painted since it was build. It was dark and in bad condition. Now it's clean and beautiful."

In 1971, the Union Stock Yard closed its gates ending an era in the industrial life of Chicago. The only physical remnant of the stockyards is a gate built in 1875. The community is now largely minority. By 1990 Latinos were 39 percent of the population of Back of the Yards, African Americans comprised another 42 percent.[7] Yet the two groups lived in different sections of the neighborhood, and had little interaction with each other. An indication of the community's growing poverty was that Holy Cross no longer operated its elementary school. "We rent the school to the public schools. The poor people cannot attend Catholic schools because they are very expensive. In a way Catholic schools have become elitist," said Rodríguez. The poverty in the community caused other problems: "One big problem in the neighborhood is gangs," said Rev. Rodríguez. "There are a lot of gangs. There is rivalry between young people in gangs who shoot and kill each other. A month ago Holy Cross had a funeral for a 17-year-old boy killed by gangs. These kids come from dysfunctional families. Other problems are drugs and alcoholism among young men and adults. To help the youth we are establishing an alternative high school for dropouts." The alternative school was named the Sister Irene Dugan Institute. Sister Dugan helped youths avoid gang involvement. She died of cancer in 1997. Holy Cross' new young pastor, Rev. Bruce Wellems, continued steering youth away from gangs and violence. He brought neighborhood kids to the church where he taught them music. He formed a noted parish Marimba Ensemble, composed of Latino youth who performed throughout the city.

Our Lady of Guadalupe

Since the mid-1800s, the Archdiocese of Chicago encouraged the building of large Catholic parishes throughout the city. These elegant national parishes served white ethnics like the Irish, Poles, Italians, and Germans. These parishes became sacred public spaces where immigrants received mass and spiritual care in their own language.[8] Parish priests spoke the immigrants' language, defended them from outside hostilities, and helped immigrants make the difficult transition from one culture to another. When Mexicans began arriving in Chicago in 1916, however, Cardinal George William Mundelein was discouraging the building of ethnic parishes. Church officials believed ethnic parishes hindered Americanization. They wanted to rapidly assimilate Mexicans into mainstream American Catholicism and culture. The Catholic church did not welcome Mexicans as openly as it had previous immigrants from Europe.[9]

However, Cardinal Mundelein was pressured to give Mexicans a few national parishes. Cardinal Mundelein knew he had to compete with the proselytizing efforts of Protestant churches. Thus, Cardinal Mundelein sanctioned the construction of Our Lady of Guadalupe in Chicago's steel mill colonia.[10] Cardinal Mundelein, along with Rev. William Kane, a Jesuit, secured a $12,000 donation from the head of the Illinois Steel Company to construct a one-room wooden chapel at 9024 Mackinaw Avenue to serve Mexican steel workers and their families. The chapel was constructed in 1924 and named Our Lady of Guadalupe, after the patron saint of Mexico. Claretian Missionary Fathers became priests in the new chapel. As the Mexican colony in South Chicago grew in the late 1920s, a larger church of the same name seating over a thousand persons replaced the wooden chapel in 1928.[11] Residents pitched in their hard-earned dollars to pay for the church's construction. The parish still sits on the corner of 91st Street and Brandon Avenue, in the shadow of the shuttered steel mills. Thousands of Mexicans came out for the dedication of their new parish on September 1928.

Our Lady of Guadalupe parish has been a haven and lifeline for Mexicans. The parish helped generations of Mexican immigrants find jobs, decent housing, and provided them with food and clothing. The parish also held the National Shine of St. Jude, honoring the 'patron saint of difficult or hopeless cases.' The shine was established in 1929 during the Depression, when the steel mills closed and many Mexicans lost their jobs. Devotion to St. Jude became nationwide. Over 400 members of the Chicago Police Department formed a branch of the St. Jude League in 1932. The church became the police officer's shine in Chicago. In 1998, Mexicans celebrated the 75th anniversary of Our Lady of Guadalupe parish. Parishioners marched in a parade along Commercial Avenue to mark Mexican Independence Day. The parade was organized by the Mexican Patriotic Club of South Chicago. Parishioners then walked back to the church where Chicago's Cardinal Francis George gave an outdoor mass. "Naturally, this church has been an important institution in this community over the last 75 years," says Rev. James Maloney, the church's pastor. "It has served the religious, social, educational, and cultural needs of Mexicans. Our Lady of Guadalupe has bought a sense of communitarian faith that has helped Mexicans have a sense of belonging in this society. Unfortunately, a detailed history of the church has never been written. That kind of history is very much needed. But this church continues to play an important role in the lives of Mexicans and other Latinos in this neighborhood."[12]

Protect Me Virgin of Guadalupe

The Virgin of Guadalupe image is a popular and powerful religious and cultural symbol among Mexicans. The image is found in most Mexican homes, framed on the wall or on glass-encased candles of home altars. It is found in restaurants, on outdoor wall murals, T-shirts, hats, on cars, bracelets, and gold chains. Anywhere Mexicans gather, the image of their patron saint is not far away.[13] Mexican young men going off to war looked to the Virgin of Guadalupe for protection. They often tattooed her image on their arms or chests. During the Vietnam War, Our Lady of Guadalupe parish suffered more war dead than any other Catholic parish in the United States. In 1970, the church built a simple marble headstone in honor of 12 young parishioners who died in Vietnam. The headstone is in a parking lot across the street from the parish. It lists the names of the young parishioners, the dates of their short lives, and an inscription that reads, "We owe so much to so few—Vietnam." The faces of the 12 young men were painted on the side of a building in the parking lot.

One name on the headstone is that of Joseph A. Quiroz, a 21-year-old Army private killed in Vietnam on January 1966. "Joseph was an outgoing person, really carefree. He was well liked by everybody," recalls his sister, Mary Quiroz Flores, 70. "He had charisma and was a joker. He had a good sense of humor. He went to high school, but dropped out in his third year. Then he went to work as a laborer in the steel mills.... He was a free spirit. He dated and had many girlfriends, but nothing serious. He attended Our Lady of Guadalupe Church. We all did. Then they drafted him. Joseph didn't feel right being in Vietnam. He said it was a political thing, and we shouldn't really be there. He said they were killing young boys daily.... I had sent him a picture of San Juan De Los Lagos, a saint from Mexico. I told him to keep it with him, and I'll take it back when he came home from the war. They sent it back to me with his blood on it."[14]

Flores has lived in South Chicago most of her life. She is a homemaker. Her father was a lifelong worker in the steel mills. Her husband, Silverio, 75, retired from the Chicago Police Department as a lieutenant after 31 years. They had five children. She comes from a long line of relatives who served in the United States armed forces. Her husband, Silverio, served in the Korean War. Her nephew was a Green Beret in the U.S. Army. Her son served in the U.S. Marines as a private. Her daughter retired from the U.S. Army as a lieutenant. Besides her brother Joseph, a couple of her other relatives have also made the supreme sacrifice for the United States. "My cousin, Jonias Flores was a U.S. Marine who fought in World War II. He was killed at Iwo Jima, when he was in his early 20s. They killed my other brother, the second to the oldest, John Allen Quiroz, in the Korean war. He joined the Army at 15, and was 17 when he was killed."

Flores vividly remembered the day her brother Joseph died. She had a premonition. She cried as she recalls the day. "It was a Sunday and I was sewing a dress for myself. For some reason or another, I kept sewing it wrong. Then I decided to stop sewing. I had a little altar for my brother Joseph with his pictures and candles. When I tried to light the candles, the glass containers that hold the candles kept breaking. I told my husband, I don't know what's wrong, my candles keep breaking.... My mom went to Our Lady of Guadalupe Church and bought a candle. She brought it home and the same thing happened, it cracked. So that afternoon, about three o'clock, military officials arrived with a telegram telling us my brother had been killed." Flores treasured the Purple Hearts and Bronze Stars her decreased cousin and brothers earned. She designed an altar on her dining room table in their memory. "On Veteran's Day and Memorial Day, the American Legion and Vietnam veterans hold a special mass at Our Lady of Guadalupe Church to honor the dead. Right after mass they go across the street and hold a ceremony at the memorial. They have a gun salute. Families leave flowers. It's beautiful and touching. Then they go to the memorial at Lansing, Illinois to hold another ceremony for deceased veterans."

Mexicans have a distinguished record of service in U.S. wars. They have won more Congressional Medals of Honor than any other ethnic group. Mexicans in the Midwest won five Congressional Medals of Honor for heroism in

wars, including Manuel Perez from Chicago who fought and died in World War
II. An American Legion post and an elementary school are named in his honor.
Mexican patriotism is evident in the small town of Silvis, Illinois, where 130 of
its young Mexican men have fought in World War II, Korea, and Vietnam. A
main street in the town was renamed "Hero Street," in memory of these young
men, including eight killed in action.

Searching for a House of Worship

As Mexicans moved into Pilsen and Little Village in the 1960s, they too
searched for a house of worship. Both neighborhoods contained many large,
magnificent Catholic parishes often a stone's throw from each other. Yet some
European ethnics did not want Mexicans to attend their churches. Rev. David
Staszak, a Polish priest, worked at St. Pius church in Pilsen. He served Mexicans
for many years. Rev. Staszak passed away in 1998 at age 72. Shortly before his
death, he spoke about how Mexicans were often not welcomed at some Catholic
parishes. "Pilsen started changing in the 1960s, from Polish to Mexican," recalled Rev. Staszak. "Mexicans were laborers looking for work. Many were
undocumented, but they were hard workers. There was tension between Mexicans and Poles. Lack of communication, prejudice and stereotypes were part of
the problem. Parishioners would tell Mexicans, 'you don't belong here, go to
your own church,' Tension would also arise when Mexicans began asking for
Spanish mass. The Poles felt they were taking over my church."[15]
Some white priests like Rev. Staszak learned to speak Spanish and welcomed Mexican parishioners. "This church was the first in Pilsen to start masses
in Spanish," said Rev. Stascak. "The pastor tried to compromise between Mexicans and white ethnics. With good intentions he put Mexicans in the basement.
They had Spanish masses in the basement for eight years. Mexicans resented
that. They felt they were second-class citizens here. Slowly the Mexican presence in the church got bigger. The Poles left to other Polish parishes nearby. I
gave Spanish mass to Mexicans in the main church." Rev. Staszak was a priest
at St. Pius for forty-one years. Mexicans remembered Rev. Staszak as a warm
man comfortable in jeans and T-shirt. He obtained grants and founded two
homeless shelters in Pilsen. One shelter was for homeless men, the other for
women and children. The centers served about 30,000 persons a year. Many
were undocumented immigrants new to the city.
Rev. Staszak believed that Mexican immigrants would eventually achieve
the American dream of finding good work, buying homes, and building a bright
future for their children. "Mexicans are struggling. They work hard, save
money, and are very thrifty. Polish immigrants went through the same things.
The Poles have moved farther west to places like Niles, Illinois. The Mexicans
have not reached that yet, but they will eventually make it like all the other
groups. Once they learn their English and go to school. That's why the schools
are very important. Mexicans are already moving out of Pilsen. They're going

west to Cicero, the suburbs. They like a nice little house, where it's quiet with no shootings or killings. Their dream is coming true, but it's a struggle. It's not easy."

Today, there are 714,000 Latinos or 31 percent of the 2.3 million Catholics in the Archdiocese of Chicago, which includes Cook and Lake counties. And their numbers continue to swell.[16] Mexicans make up two-thirds of that 31 percent. About 80 percent of Mexicans in Chicago and the suburbs were devoutly Roman Catholic. A small number were converting to evangelical Protestantism.[17]

Relations between the Archdiocese of Chicago and Mexicans have not always been heavenly. In the early 1990s, the Archdiocese, due to financial considerations, closed thirty-seven churches and schools in the city. A good number of the shuttered churches and schools were in Mexican neighborhoods. The closings angered Mexicans, who felt Archdiocese resources were not always allocated evenly. The anger peaked in 1993, when the Archdiocese tried to close and demolish St. Francis of Assisi parish on Roosevelt Road and Newberry Avenue. The church was very special to Mexicans. The church was once German and later Italian. But in 1927, under the direction of Spanish-born Father James Tort, St. Francis officially became a Mexican parish. The Archdiocese wanted to merge St. Francis with Holy Family parish a few blocks away. Mexican parishioners objected, and argued that church membership and finances were strong. In protest, Mexicans set up living quarters inside the parish and maintained a 24-hour vigil to prevent its demolition. Finally, after 25 months of resistance the Archdiocese decided to keep the parish open. Over 3,000 worshipers attended mass at St. Francis to celebrate the church's reopening.[18]

Mexicans lamented the woeful lack of Mexican priests. Unlike the Poles or Irish, Mexicans came to the United States without their own priests. Of 895 Archdiocesan priests in Chicago, only 16 were Latino.[19] Mexicans wondered if the Archdiocese was really interested in recruiting and training Mexicans as priests. Yet others believed Chicago's Catholic Church was genuinely reaching out and helping Mexicans. In 1998, the Archdiocese of Chicago appointed Rev. Esequiel Sanchez, a Mexican, as director of Hispanic ministry. The Archdiocese also started a program, Casa Jesus, to recruit Latino seminarians. They were recruiting candidates from Mexico and Central America. However, only a handful were recruited. The Archdiocese had Latino ministry programs teaching white priests how to speak Spanish. Of 377 parishes in the Archdiocese, over 100 offered Spanish-language masses.[20] "I think the assistance and services the Catholic Church offers Latinos are more than generous," argues Jesus Zeferino Ochoa, 70, director of Immigrant and Refugee Services for Catholic Charities of Chicago. "It is not just Catholic Charities that helps people. Many neighborhood Catholic churches are helping people. Many churches have programs like food pantries and emergency clothing. Churches serve new immigrants who are mostly Latino. Latinos see the church not only as a place of worship, but also as a place to meet their needs. We don't ask if they have legal documents."[21]

Ochoa insisted the Catholic Church has a long tradition of helping Latinos.

"The church has helped Mexicans, Puerto Ricans, and Cubans. We have a tendency to ignore and forget what the church did for Latino groups....There are many good things Latinos have gone through with the Catholic Church and some things not so good. It's true some people openly refused to let Latinos worship at their churches. But we have come a long way. All the priests know they must serve newcomers. We don't ask whether they are Catholic or not." Some Catholic parishes were helping residents by building affordable housing. In 1990, six Catholic churches in Pilsen formed the Resurrection Project, a nonprofit community development corporation. With city funds, the Resurrection Project built single-family affordable rental units in Mexican neighborhoods.s.[22]

Rev. Juan Huitrado was the Mexican pastor at St. Roman's Catholic parish in Little Village for many years. He passed away at age 51 in 2004. Rev. Huitrado agreed the Catholic Church is an important institution in the daily lives of Mexicans. "The Mexican community sees the Catholic Church as a trusting institution. They see it as an institution that will help them in their hour of need. Many Mexicans who come here to St. Roman's are undocumented and often recent arrivals. Some come and say, 'father, pray for me.' Others come and say, 'father, I just got off the train and I need help.' Usually they ask for food. They ask for leads where to find jobs or apartments....During times of crisis, people look for safety and understanding. They look to the church. Undocumented immigrants really do not impose on us. They just ask for something and move along. It helps that I'm Mexican and speak Spanish. They say I understand them better than other priests."[23]

Rev. Huitrado came to Chicago from Mexico in 1976. He recalled how some undocumented, single Mexican men complained to him about police harassment. "Unfortunately, that is a common thing. Once I was speeding and the police stopped me. They said, 'why are you in a hurry?' I said, 'I'm a priest and have to give mass in a church.' The one cop says to the other, 'he says he's a priest.' They started laughing in my face. So I had to pull out my I.D. from the Archdiocese. They were horrified. I didn't make a big deal about it. But to tell you the truth, how many Mexican priests are there?" Undocumented Mexicans would seek out Rev. Huitrado to ask forgiveness of their sins. One sin, for instance, was that some undocumented men abandoned the wives and children they left back in Mexico. They remarried and began new dreams with new families in Chicago. "I wouldn't say it happens a lot, but it does happen. Those situations do not have a simple answer," recalled Rev. Huitrado. "They usually break with the family in Mexico. They move along. Another thing that happens is fraud marriages to fix their papers. This arrangement of fraud marriages was even a little business for some people. The businesses would find an American citizen to marry an undocumented person. After the papers were fixed, the couple would get a divorce. That's why the immigration department now requires a lot of information if you want to fix your papers."

The Catholicism practiced among Mexicans in Chicago was of a popular type. Popular religion was that practiced by laity in contrast to clergy. It was a kind of folkloric religion practiced through popular traditional expressions. For instance, the rosaries, devotions to saints, pilgrimages, and processions, were examples of popular Catholicism among Mexicans. Often the official church rejected popular expressions of Catholicism.[24] One popular religious practice among Mexicans was the yearly Via Crucis, or Living Way of the Stations of the Cross. This procession along 18th Street in Pilsen, occurred on Good Friday. It was a re-enactment of the crucifixion of Jesus Christ. Eight Roman Catholic churches participated in the event. An individual dressed as Jesus Christ carried a large wooden cross. Other parishioners dressed in costumes as shepherds and Roman soldiers of biblical times. Thousands of spectators solemnly watched the procession portraying Jesus' walk to Calvary. The procession ended with the enactment of Jesus' crucifixion on a hill in Harrison Park, and a closing prayer.

Another popular religious tradition among Mexicans was the quinceañera, or celebration of a young girl's 15th birthday. This custom, dating to the Aztecs, was a rite of passage for young women in Mexico and Latin America. It marked a young woman's coming of age party. The quinceañera began at the Catholic parish with a full mass and a blessing by the priest. It ended with a party much like a wedding reception, in a hall, a hotel or a home. Fifteen girls, damas, and fifteen boys, chambelanes, dressed up in elegant, expensive evening dresses and tuxedos. Quincerañeras can cost over $20,000. Working-class families often relied on padrinos and madrinas, or godfathers and godmothers, to pick up some of the costs. Some Catholic priests believed the quinceañera has lost its religious and cultural significance, and they refused to celebrate them in their parishes. Some priests believed it was just one big bash that costs a lot of money, created indebtedness, and brought no one to the churches. Other priests celebrated quinceañeras. They saw them as a way to bring back Latino teens that were rapidly drifting from the church.[25]

A Neighborhood High School

Teresa Fraga, 64, was seven-years-old when she immigrated to Donna, Texas in 1949 with her parents. Her parents entered the United States illegally from Jalisco, Mexico. The family almost drowned crossing a dangerous section of the Rio Grande River. Fraga was a precocious child, eager to start school. She attended a public elementary school in Texas. She was a good student, learned English quickly, and dreamed of someday attending college. She liked school but felt uncomfortable. "I went to school with Anglos and with fourth and fifth-generation Mexican Americans, who did not speak Spanish. I didn't fit in. I was poor, from a rural area in Mexico, and undocumented. In those days, the principal would spank you with a wooden paddle if they caught you speaking Spanish on school grounds. The teachers would tell us, 'Speak English, you're in America.' One teacher told me, 'Teresa, tell me who speaks Spanish on the playground.' Five girls spoke Spanish, but I never turned them in. I never felt that speaking Spanish was wrong."[26]

Fraga's education was cut short. After 7th grade she had to leave school to work in the fields. Her parents were poor migrant workers. They were constantly on the road following the harvests from the Southwest to the Midwest, to the North and back to the Southwest. "Children were expected to work, and help their parents in the fields. Working in the fields is hard, filthy, backbreaking work. We picked cotton and crops in Texas. We picked crops in Idaho, and tomatoes and strawberries in California and in Michigan. After work you were so dead tired you didn't even want to eat. You somehow walked back to the barracks, and dropped yourself onto an old mattress on the floor and immediately fell asleep."

Up through her teen years, Fraga picked crops. The heat from the hot sun was often over 115 degrees. In 1959, Fraga met Refugio, a young undocumented migrant worker. That year they married in Texas. The Fragas continued working as migrant workers. Then, a relative told them about better-paying factory work in Chicago. In 1966, they came to Chicago searching for steady work. They settled in the Pilsen neighborhood. "My God was Chicago cold when we arrived. I was eight months pregnant with my third child. We lived in a cold basement apartment for six years. We shared a washroom in the hallway with other tenants. But at least we had hot running water. My husband found a job in landscaping. My husband knew a little English. He then found a better job in construction. It was physically demanding work but the owners of the company liked that my husband was very hard working. They hired many of my husband's relatives there"

Despite her lack of education, Fraga hoped her six children would receive a quality education in a large city like Chicago. In 1972, she eagerly visited Froebel High School where her son attended. She was shocked at what she saw: the school was unsafe, overcrowded, and dilapidated. "I stayed in Chicago because I thought my children would have better schools," recalls Fraga. "Yet when I saw the school, it angered me. Froebel was for 9th and 10th grade only. It was a branch of Harrison High School. But it was in a condemned building. It was not a facility meant to be a high school. It was dingy and dark. The bathrooms were in the basement and there were no lights. The walls had holes. The school was cold. Our kids didn't want to go to Harrison. The school was mostly black and they had many racial problems. So about 77 percent of Mexican kids were dropping out of high school after 10th grade."

Fraga channeled her anger into community activism. She became a member of the Pilsen Neighbors Community Council. Fragra began organizing other Mexican parents, especially mothers. The parents demanded that the Chicago Board of Education build a new high school in Pilsen. But school officials argued that the school system was in a financial crisis, and they did not have funds for new schools. To relieve overcrowding, school officials suggested that Mexican parents bus their children miles away to underutilized African American high schools. Mexican parents, however, wanted their own high school in their own neighborhood. The parents put more pressure on school officials. "We had a petition drive for a new high school. We had marches with over a thousand parents. We marched downtown to the Board of Education. We had candlelight ceremonies. We called for a boycott. Parents from seven grammar schools in Pilsen kept their kids home for three days. The boycott was 85 percent effective. School officials began losing state monies because kids were not attending school. It was a national news story."

The battle for the new high school raged on for five, long years. Finally in 1977, Fraga and the parents won. School officials built the new, modern Benito Juarez High School in Pilsen. The school was named after the Mexican president who began public education in Mexico. A Mexican architect designed the school. The campaign to build Juarez high school dispelled the myth that poor and working-class Mexican women were passive and complacent. The campaign propelled some Mexican women into visible, community leadership roles. Fraga was one of them. In 1979, Fraga became an American citizen. She became president of the Pilsen Neighbors Community Council. As a community activist, she spearheaded other protests to bring reading programs, hot lunch programs, smaller class sizes, and bilingual education to elementary schools in Pilsen. Fraga also pursued her dream of educating herself. "I enjoyed learning when I was little. I rekindled my desire to learn. People would tell me, 'you're college material.' I went back to school. I earned my bachelor's degree and my master's in counseling."

Fraga is a public elementary school teacher at Orozco Academy in Pilsen. Fraga was against the gentrification of Pilsen, and feared expensive housing and high property taxes would displace poor and working-class Mexicans. "I care about poor people. You think I am going to forget 1966 when I first came to this neighborhood? Just because I have a master's degree, a home, and I've made it this far, am I supposed to forget where I came from? I don't mind having neighbors who arrived yesterday from Mexico. I tell my kids, 'Look at that family that just arrived. That is us 30 years ago.' Why can't we have great housing, schools, and good city services for the people who live here now?"

Education for the Children

Most Mexican families historically looked to the Chicago public schools to educate their children. Chicago was the third largest public school system in the country with over 430,000 students. Over the past two decades, Latino enrollment in Chicago's public schools skyrocketed. By 1997, Latinos were 33 percent of students in Chicago's public schools, African Americans were 53.7 percent, and whites were 10 percent. Of Latino students, Mexicans were 25 percent and Puerto Ricans six percent. The number of Latino children in the city's public schools continues to steadily climb.[27] Mexican children attended Chicago public schools that were literally falling apart. Most had been built before 1930, and school officials deferred maintenance on buildings. The schools had chipped paint, rotting floors, crumbling roofs, and leaky windows. By 1991, two-thirds of the city's schools needed more than $1 billion for repairs and new buildings.

Additionally, Mexican children usually attended severely overcrowded schools. Kids were learning in closets, hallways, and auditoriums. Instead of building new schools, school officials placed many old mobile classrooms in Mexican schools. These one-room trailers with corrugated metal walls, were dilapidated and dangerous. The mobiles had been used in the 1960s to segregate African American students away from white schools.[28] In 1974, Mayor Richard J. Daley appointed Carmen Velasquez, to the 11-member Chicago Board of Education. Velasquez, 68, served as a board member for six years. She recalls how poorly schools treated Mexican children. "Everybody has the basic right to good health, to good education, and to an environment that allows their spirit to grow. It angered me that they were teaching Mexican children in mobiles, closets, and hallways. Also, many Mexican kids didn't speak English, and it bothered me that they did not have access to bilingual education. I pushed to get more bilingual teachers in the schools." [29]

Carmen is part of the Valasquez family, a prominent Mexican business family in Chicago. Her father, Auturo, was a migrant worker who came to Chicago in 1929. He achieved financial success with his jukebox company, Velasquez Automatic Music Co. Her brother, Arthur R. Velasquez, is also a successful businessman.[30] Carmen is co-owner of the Decima Musa a popular restaurant in Pilsen. She is also founder of the Alivio Medical Center in Pilsen. The clinic provided health care to thousands of low-income families. Carmen is not afraid to say that the future of Mexican children, not Latinos, has been her main priority. "I'm not Latino. I am Mexican. I have a Mexican agenda. Other groups have their agendas. Why the hell can't we have a Mexican agenda? During my years as a board of education member, I was concerned that Mexican schools got their fair share of Chapter One poverty funds that came from the state. I was also concerned that school officials were asking kids for citizenship papers. I told the associate superintendent of schools that school officials did not have the right to ask kids for citizenship documents. Then I got the state Board of Education to put that in writing. Immigrant children who are undocumented are still entitled to an education."

Even today, newly arrived, undocumented Mexicans enroll their children in Chicago's public schools. Martin Jaimes, 42, is Mexican and undocumented. He came to Chicago in 1995 from Guerrero, Mexico. Three years later, his wife and two children came from Mexico to Chicago to join him. "I went to enroll my five-year-old daughter, and fourteen-year-old son in the nearby public school. I heard it's a good school. The principal asked me if they were residents or citizens. I had to tell her they are undocumented. Thank God she still allowed my children to enroll there. My children do not speak English and are in a bilingual program. My daughter is in kindergarten and my son is in eight grade. My dream is for my children to get a good education. I want my children to learn English and learn about the North American culture. I want my children to get a good education so they never have to work as hard as I do."[31]

Jaimes shared his small, sparely-furnished Logan Square apartment with his aunt, sister and brother-in-law. They were also undocumented and recent arrivals. Jaimes, his wife and relatives were day laborers. They worked twelve hours a day in suburban factories for minimum wages and without health insurance. The work was unsteady and often dangerous. "Luckily, I have been working at the same factory for six months now. I work on a machine that cuts paper. It was dangerous when I first started. I almost cut off my finger. I cut off part of my fingernail. A friend of mine was working here for two weeks, when he cut off three fingers. He has a lawyer and is trying to get money from the factory." Jaimes almost lost himself on the streets of Chicago. He was drinking heavily with other undocumented Mexican men. "I used to misspend my money drinking with friends in bars. But I got tired of that life. I stopped drinking and hanging around with those guys. A coyote charged me three thousand dollars to bring my family over. I'm paying him in monthly installments. I'm just so happy to have my family with me now."

Jaimes' fourteen-year-old son, Edgar was struggling to adjust in school. "I only speak Spanish. It's hard learning English," says Edgar. "There are so many new words and sounds. I get the tenses all mixed up. But I'm trying hard to learn. Many of my teachers are very nice to me. My father tells me if I study hard, I will learn English and do well in this country. I want to graduate and go on to high school." Jaimes did not believe he was doing anything wrong by being in the United States illegally, and sending his children to public schools. In fact, he dreamed of educating himself one day. "I know Americans and other Latinos look down on illegal uneducated Mexicans," says Jaimes. "Even Mexican Americans believe illegals make it bad for them; they wish we wouldn't come to the United States. But we do the dirty work here. We only want what everyone else wants. Maybe one day I can get an education. I would like to learn English. I would like to get my GED. Maybe I can become an American citizen. Then I would like to find a better-paying job with health insurance. I want my children to have a better life."

School Reform

In 1988, various Mexican community organizations pressured the Illinois State Legislature to enact the Chicago school reform legislation. The law decentralized authority and established a Local School Council (LSC) in each Chicago public school. The councils, elected every two years, were composed of parents, teachers, students, community representatives and principals. LSCs have the authority to choose their own principals, and wide discretion over how to spend over $261 million in state anti-poverty funds that Chicago schools are allocated annually. School reform appeared to be working well in Latino schools. Before school reform, the school system hired few Latino teachers and administrators. In 1981, only 3 percent of the system's 23,190 teachers were Latino, and only 4 of 515 principals were Latino.[32] The LSCs hired more Latino principals. In 1997, for instance, of 971 administrative positions—including principal—in Chicago public schools, 34 percent were white, 52 percent were African American and 12 percent were Latino. Of 26,000 teaching positions, 45 percent were white, 43 percent were African American, and 10 percent were Latino.[33]

In 1995, Mayor Richard M. Daley persuaded the Illinois Legislature to give him more direct control of the city's school system. The mayor appointed a five-member School Reform Board of Trustees, which has wide powers to implement school policy. He placed his top aides, Paul Vallas, as chief executive officer of the schools, and Gery Chico, as president of the board. Since 1995, many credit Mayor Daley and his school team for significantly improving Chicago's public schools. "Results, not excuses, that's our platform," says former board president Gery Chico, 50. "We have a long list of accomplishments. One, we established a sound financial footing for the school system. Two, we established eight years of labor peace with the teachers; before you had many teacher strikes. Three, we're put in place a core curriculum and a sound education plan, which have led to three years of rising test scores. Four, we have the most aggressive capital improvement program of any place in the United States. We made $2 billion available in the renovation and building of new schools in Chicago. The $2 million raised locally have come from bonds."[34]

In 2001, however, both Chico and Paul Vallas left the school system amid Mayor Daley's dissatisfaction with drooping test scores. Mayor Daley then placed his top aide, Arne Duncan to run the school system. Chico's father is Mexican, and his mother is Greek and Lithuanian. He was Mayor Daley's former chief of staff. Chico walked a thin ethical line by being school board president while lobbying for private companies. The law firm he worked with, Altheimer and Gray, was a City Hall lobbyist. Chico represented many companies wishing to do business with the Chicago public school system. The companies he represented won more than $100 million in business from the school system. Yet Chico did not see any conflict of interest.[35]

Mayor Daley was dubbed the 'education mayor.' He was praised for building new schools and repairing many others. From 1995 to 2000, school officials built 27 new schools, 24 additions, 27 annexes, and more than 100 modular classrooms. "Mayor Daley wants the Chicago Public Schools to be the best in the nation," says Chico. "In trying to fix the schools, it helps tremendously that we got the mayor of Chicago right next to us. President Clinton and I toured one of our new schools. He thought it was the best thing since sliced bread. The kids were so happy to be in a new school." The additional new schools and classrooms were a welcome sight to parents and students. Despite the improvements, however, many Mexican children still attended overcrowded schools. The Mexican American Legal Defense and Educational Fund, issued a report that showed that of 453 Chicago public elementary schools, 149 were overcrowded, and 71 severely overcrowded schools were majority Latino.[36]

School officials hoped to raise another $1 billion over the next six years to build new schools in the city. Yet some questioned whether the city was taking on too much debt, risking the future fiscal stability of the schools and city. Civic groups are urging Mayor Daley and school officials, to lobby state and federal governments for more education dollars. And even with an additional $1 billion, Chicago schools will still need about $2 billion more to meet the challenges of overcrowded schools, rising enrollments and aging facilities.[37] Moreover, Gery Chico and Paul Vallas pushed for construction of two selective high schools to cater to gifted students. Both schools were built and cost over $40 million apiece. Mexican parents were promised that a third new high school would be built to relieve overcrowding in Little Village. School officials later admitted they did not have funds for a third new high school. A handful of Mexican mothers in Little Village staged a highly publicized, two-week hunger strike to persuade school officials to build the new high school. The striking mothers scored a victory in 2001 when school officials declared that funds would be allocated for two new high schools in Pilsen and Little Village. Each school will cost over $30 million.[38]

Some community-based Mexican groups have honored Mayor Daley for improving Chicago schools. Others pointed to continuing problems like the high dropout rate among Mexican high school students, and wondered if school officials were doing anything about it. For instance, 45.1 percent of African Americans dropped out of high school in 1995, compared to 42.3 percent for Latinos, and 38.3 percent for whites.[39] "The dropout rate for Latino students is in the high 40s, and it's something that very much concerns me," says Chico. "I don't know why they drop out. The basis changes that we made overall in the education program are going to benefit our Hispanic children. Better facilities, a core curriculum, after school programs, alternative schools, and better teacher quality. We're planning special initiatives like ACT preparation for Hispanic children. Also, bringing more Hispanic role models into the schools to mentor children." Chico envisioned only good things for the future. "Violence in the schools is decreasing. Reading and math scores are going up. The facilities are certainly going to get better. I think Hispanic children in Chicago are going to get a much better education as time goes forward."

Catholic Schools/College

Many Mexican families believed Chicago's Catholic schools did a better job of educating children than public schools. Many Mexican families desired a Catholic education for their children, yet families could not afford the high cost of parochial school education. Due to low enrollments, Catholic schools in Mexican neighborhoods continued to close. One school that earned praise for making Catholic education affordable was the Cristo Rey High School. Built in 1996 by the Jesuits of Chicago, the $9.7 million high school provided college-preparatory education for about 280 students from Pilsen and Little Village. Cristo Rey was the first Catholic high school to open in the city in the last 37 years. School officials placed students in jobs and then combine family payments with money students earn through work-study to pay the $6,000 annual tuition.[40]

Mexican parents like Ramon Abrego, 86, and his wife, Socorro, 83, praised Catholic school education. "We have the highest regard for Catholic schools," says Socorro. "Kids in public school are often afraid to go to school because the gangs threaten them. In Catholic schools, the kids have a lot more discipline. They don't wear earrings. If your child arrives late or cuts school, they call and tell you. The kids have good values. Since we didn't have education, we wanted a good education for our kids. I always told my kids to study. We have four daughters and six sons."[41] "I came from Monterrey, Mexico to Chicago in 1956," says Ramon. "I came as a legal resident. I came to work. I was a laborer and didn't have any education. Five years later, I brought my wife and seven children from Mexico to Chicago. Three of our children were born here. I worked mostly in small factories. I found work in a factory in Chicago. I worked there for 26 years, until I retired. My wife, Socorro, did not work. She was a housewife who closely watched over our children."

After years of working in Chicago, the Abregos were able to afford a Catholic education for some of their younger children. They insisted that Catholic elementary and high school education contributed to their children's success. Today, two of their sons are medical doctors. One is an anesthesiologist, the other specialized in obstetrics and gynecology. Both worked in reputable Chicago hospitals. Another daughter owned two, large Mexican bakeries in Waugekan, Illinois. In 1971, the Abrego's bought a two-story, brick building in Humboldt Park, where they currently live. Ramon's factory job did not provide a pension when he retired. He collected social security. Their children helped them financially. "I feel our dreams in America have been realized," says Socorro, with tears in her eyes. "Our children have progressed. They have good education. They have their own homes and have good cars. They make good money and have good jobs. We don't worry that someday they may be unemployed."

Says Ramon, "I was always working. I give all the credit to my wife for raising our kids, and ensuring that they received a good education.... Yes, we have realized our dreams. Our kids have education. Our children now want us to move to the suburbs, but we don't want to go. We lived here since 1971. We like being independent. We get along fine with all our neighbors many of whom are Puerto Ricans. We love Puerto Rican food. We love Chicago." Some Mexicans lived and worked all their lives in Chicago, yet when they died, family members sentimentally preferred to bury them in their hometowns in Mexico. Ramon does not wish to be buried in Mexico. "America is my country," says Ramon emphatically. "In 1994 I became an American citizen. Mexico never gave me anything. I had to leave Mexico to find work in this country. It is this country that gave me work and opportunities. It gave my children education and opportunities. I want to die and be buried in this country."

Second and third-generation Mexicans realized that a college education was necessary to climb up the economic ladder. Yet getting their foot into the door of academe was not easy. Colleges required high scores on standardized tests for admission. Also many Mexican students lacked the financial means to attend college. In 1973, a small group of Mexican and Puerto Rican college students and community activists angrily demonstrated against the University of Illinois at Chicago. They were protesting because the university was built on what was once a large Mexican community, yet few Latino students attended the university. University administrators refused to meet with the group. Therefore, the students and activists occupied the offices of a high-level university administrator. Police arrested about 39 members of the group when they refused to leave. The group continued their protests and sit-ins in the following days and weeks.

Arthur R. Velasquez, 67, was the first Latino elected to a statewide office when he was elected in 1974 as a trustee of the University of Illinois at Chicago. He recalls that the students and activists had legitimate concerns. "As a trustee, I was working with top university administrators to open the university, both the Chicago and Urbana-Champaign campuses, to Latino students. We found that out of 6,000 entering students at the University of Illinois at Urbana-Champaign, there were only about 25 Latino students. So the university hired a recruiter and the number of Latino students started going up rapidly. There was a lot of urging for administrators to help Latino students with financial aid. The number of Latino employees at the university also increased. I saw a lot of progress."[42] Arthur R.Velasquez is the owner of Azteca Corn Products Corporation, a multimillion-dollar tortilla and corn chip business in Chicago's Garfield Ridge neighborhood. He has over 130 employees.

In response to the protests, University of Illinois administrators set up the Latin American Recruitment and Educational Services (LARES) program in 1975 to recruit Latino students. The program recruited about eight hundred Latino students each year. But the number of Latino students at the University of Illinois was well below their percentage of the state's population. In 1998, of 24,578 students at the University of Illinois, 13.4 percent were Latino.[43] The growth in Illinois' population during the next 20 years will come mostly from Latinos. Thus, more colleges were recruiting Latino students, and the number of Mexican and Latino students attending college was growing. There were about three hundred Latino students at top-rated Northwestern University, and about 1,296 at DePaul, a Catholic University. DePaul had the highest enrollment of Latino students of any private university in Illinois.[44] A 1998 report by the Illinois State Board of Higher Education, showed that Latino undergraduate enrollment at Illinois public and private universities increased 3.7 percent from 35,112 in 1995 to 36,400 in 1996. Yet few Latino students were earning the doctoral degree.[45]

Increased access to a college education has created a growing Mexican middle-class in Chicago and the suburbs. Yet educational attainment was still a major problem for Mexicans. Newly arrived immigrants from Mexico often came with little schooling. In 1990, 4.5 percent of Mexicans had bachelors' degree or higher, compared to 6 percent for Puerto Ricans, and 18.9 percent for Cubans.[46] Nevertheless, some believed the educational future will improve for Mexicans. "The key to success and progress for the Mexican community is education," says Arthur R. Velasquez. "I am extremely hopeful that a lot of people are working hard to improve the Chicago public school system. And the Catholic schools are putting much money to sustain the Catholic elementary and high schools, where many Latinos attend. More Mexicans are attending college."

Leaving the Gang

Maria Sánchez (not her real name), 26, is a pretty Mexican teenager. She is wise beyond her years. She enjoyed her early years in public elementary school. She loved to read and write poetry in Spanish and English. "My parents immigrated to East Chicago, Indiana from Guanajuato, Mexico around 1982," recalls Sánchez. "They came here for a better life, because they were real poor in Mexico. My parents married young. My dad was 15 and my mom 14. I am the oldest of four children. My parents didn't have a lot of education. In Indiana my dad worked in a restaurant washing dishes. My dad looks Indian, and some white customers called him mojado, or wetback. He later worked in construction. My mother didn't work, she was a housewife." [47] In 1985, Sanchez's parents moved to Chicago's West Town neighborhood. But instead of finding a better life, things quickly started to fall apart. In high school Sánchez began hanging around with girls who were in gangs. "I went to Wells High School on Ashland and Division. I wanted respect and protection in school, so I joined a female gang. It was mostly Puerto Rican and Mexican girls. We were called 'females with attitude.' We started with 14 girls and ended up with 36. I wanted to have some action and fight with people. If girls in school gave us dirty looks, we would go up to them and start fighting. We would smack them, hit them with fists, kick them, whatever. I'm a tough fighter. I didn't care if I hurt people, I didn't have a heart."

In school, Sánchez and her friends cut classes and roamed the corridors. They wanted to fight with rival female gang members. Once, Sánchez got beat up in school. She has a small scar on the left side of her lower lip. "Once I was in the school washroom. These three girls came in and said, 'bitch, what you be about?' I told them, 'I'm folks (a coalition of gangs), what you be about?' One girl pushed me. I was fighting with one girl beating her up when the other two jumped in. They beat me up real bad. They hit me with brass knuckles and gave me black eyes. They broke my tooth. My glasses were broken. I was bleeding. My friends found me on the floor unconscious. But I ain't scared. That's the only time I got beat up. We got those girls back." Some female gangs engaged in drug selling. Sánchez lost interest in school. She wanted rank in the gang by being the best, toughest fighter in the group. Sánchez and her gang hung out on street corners looking for girls to beat up. "If girls trespassed our neighborhood, we would beat them up. We didn't have guns to kill them but we put some people in the hospital. We would hit them with bottles, bricks or whatever we could. A couple of times when I was alone, I got chased home by girls who wanted to beat me up."

Sánchez and her friends regularly cut school and got together with male gang members. "We would go to people's homes and drink and carry on. We would get high drinking beer, tequila, and smoking marijuana. We used to hang

out at the Brickyard mall. Once we got disrespectful to the cops. They took us to jail. They charged us with disorderly conduct. My parents had to bail me out….When I turned 15, I dropped out of high school. I didn't know what I wanted to do in life. My mother was upset. She said, 'Couldn't you do something better with your life?' I was like, 'I don't care.'" Sánchez's female gang friends also dropped out of school, and the gang broke up. "They all dropped out of school. They're all pregnant and having babies. They are young like 15, 16 and 17. One, who is 16, already has three kids. The guy gang members got them pregnant. Some guys stayed with the girls, but the others just left them. They are mostly on welfare. I never got pregnant . . . My mother took me to Mexico for a short visit. In Mexico, at the Lady of Guadalupe Church, she crawled on her knees for three blocks praying that I get out of the gang. Her knees were bleeding. I felt so bad. Later, I started working with my aunt sewing shirts in a factory in a suburb near Chicago. We got paid minimum wage. I regret dropping out school."

Sánchez was trying to pull her life together. She hoped to pass the GED examination. "I need to do something with my life. After I get my GED, I'm planning to go to college. I want to go to a Catholic university. Because no matter what I did, or what I have been through, God was always with me. I want to be a detective with the Chicago Police Department. If you don't get an education, you're just going to be working like your parents in factories." Sánchez has gotten closer to her family. "My mother is so proud of me. She says the saints answered her prayers that I leave the gangs. My father is also proud. I'm more a homebody now. I don't go out much. I help my brother and sister who are in public schools. They're straight A students. I don't ever want them to join gangs or drop out of school."

Saving Lives

More than three dozen street gangs existed in Pilsen, Little Village, and Back of The Yards. And they were often at war with each other. One Catholic parish alone had twelve funerals one summer for teenagers killed in gangs. Residents were concerned about the menacing presence of street gangs. Yet there exist few community programs dedicated to helping youth people leave the world of gangs. On individual who helped pull kids from gangs was Luis J. Rodríguez, 52. Rodríguez is Mexican, and lived in Logan Square for many years. "In 1994, we started our nonprofit youth group called Youth Struggling for Survival. We're trying to save these kids," said Rodríguez. "We have a board of ten people, mostly youth. Most kids we work with are from Humboldt Park, but we have connected with a youth group in Pilsen. We have informal talks and retreats. We take 25 kids to the mountains to get away. We take them to Wisconsin out in the snow and let them play. We have rival gang members interacting. Most of our kids are Mexican, but we have Puerto Ricans and blacks."[48]

Rodríguez came to Chicago in 1985 from East Los Angeles. He traveled all *gang life.*

across the country hoping to stop kids from joining gangs. "Besides readings from my poetry and books, I also do lectures and talks. I go to schools and prisons. I give anti-gang messages, and force kids to think about why they would want to join gangs. I talk about the indigenous cultural values of Mexicans, and try to impart these values in the gang kids. We have sweat lodge ceremonies with the kids. We have talking circles. The kids begin to appreciate the message of how gangs are destructive." In his youth Rodríguez was a gang member. "In East Los Angeles, I got involved in my own gang. Cops were beating us up. Teachers didn't have time for us. Other Mexican gangs were beating us up. It was like we almost had to come together in a gang.... I was involved in gangs from age 11 to 19. Gang members were selling weed, pills, heroin, and then guns. Gang members were strung out on drugs. I was on drugs for seven years. We did some of the first drive-by shootings. Shooting at people and into peoples' homes. You go by peoples' homes and firebomb or shoot them. Twenty-five of my friends were killed by the time I was 18. I was fortunate that while I was shot at, I didn't get hit."

Like most gang members, Rodríguez got into trouble with the law. "I got arrested for a number of things, including attempted murder. But I pretty much beat all my cases. I once served ten weeks in the country jail. I was tired of the gang life. I left the gangs and let go of drugs. I wanted to be active for my people." In 1988, Rodríguez's 13-year-old son, Ramiro, from his first marriage, came from Los Angeles to live with him in Humboldt Park. He was soon lured into the gangs. "He came to Humboldt Park and two years later he joined a gang. He joined a Puerto Rican gang. They called him 'Mexico'. He started getting busted and arrested. They kicked him out of Clemente High School. I took him to Schurz High School, and they kicked him out of there. I realized I had to be a father to him. It overwhelmed my new wife, but she stood by us. We had a little boy, and this crazy teenager."

Rodríguez is an award-winning, nationally recognized poet and author. In 1993, Rodríguez's book about his gang experiences in Los Angeles was a huge success, selling more than 100,000 copies. He appeared on the Oprah Show.[49] Rodríguez desperately tried to steer Ramiro away from the danger of gangs. Ramiro lived with a girlfriend and had two small children. He worked and was taking college classes. But in January 1997, at age 23, Ramiro's world came tumbling down. He got into a traffic altercation with a truck driver. They exchanged harsh words and Ramiro shot the truck driver with a semiautomatic .38 pistol. He also fired shots at two police. "It was road rage. He got out the gang," says Rodríguez. "He was working. He was trying to be a father to his kids. A truck driver got shot. Then for some reason, Ramiro, I guess he just wanted to commit suicide, shot at the cops. Maybe he was thinking they were going to kill him. The cops did not get hit. It didn't turn out the way he wanted. He's at Menard Prison." The truck driver survived, but Ramiro was charged with three counts of attempted murder. He was sentenced to 28 years in prison. He probably will not come out of prison until the age of 45. Ramiro's imprisonment was very painful for Rodríguez. He eventually left Chicago and relocated to Los Angeles, California where he runs a book store with his wife.

Struggles for Political Power

The first Latino alderman elected in Chicago was William Emilio Rodríguez. He was an alderman from 1915 to 1918 in what was then the 15th ward or West Town. Rodríguez was born in Naperville, Illinois. He was part Mexican and part German, and was considered a German socialist. He ran unsuccessfully for mayor in 1911. After Rodríguez's short reign as alderman, it would be about sixty-eight years before Mexicans again sat in the city council. The major obstacle was Chicago's regular Democratic Party. Mayor Richard J. Daley's regular Democratic Organization, commonly referred to as a political machine, called the shots in Chicago. Chicago's political machine shared jobs, city contracts, and power with successive waves of white ethnics like the Irish, Jews, Italians, Poles, and German. In return, the immigrants usually voted for machine candidates. Yet due mainly to racial prejudice, Daley's Irish-controlled, political machine stubbornly refused to share jobs, city contracts, or power with Mexicans.

Second-generation Mexicans in Pilsen and Little Village complained during the 1970s and 80s that white aldermen loyal to the political machine represented Mexican wards. These white politicians, they argued, did little to improve their neighborhoods. Vito Marzullo, was the Italian alderman of the 25th ward, which includes Pilsen. He was alderman for more than thirty years. In his mid-eighties, Marzullo had a knack for publicly insulting and angering Mexicans. When asked by reporters about the growing Mexican presence in his ward, he replied, "Sure, there are Mexicans in the ward. If you're counting the rats of the ward." On another occasion, he said of Mexicans, "For God's sake, these people better learn something about America or go back to Mexico where they belong"[50] Mexicans tried to put Marzullo out of office. In 1983, Juan Velazquez, a young community activist, ran against Marzullo. Marzullo beat Velasquez, capturing about 57 percent of the vote. In 1984, State Rep. Marco Domico, a Marzullo ally, also defeated Velasquez to succeed Marzullo as ward committeeman.[51] The contests highlighted the inexperience and poor campaign organizing of Mexican candidates. Also, although Pilsen was about 65 percent Latino, many Mexicans were below voting age, and a large percentage were undocumented and ineligible to vote. Traditionally, Pilsen and Little Village had the lowest rates of registered voters in the city.

An emerging, charismatic Mexican leader was Rudy Lozano. In 1979, the young Lozano, who was a community activist and labor organizer, founded a group called Por Un Barrio Mejor (For A Better Neighborhood). The organization fought for the rights of immigrants and laborers. Lozano and others realized that Mexicans were outside the circle of power, looking in. "Rudy Lozano, other community activists and I, were against getting involved in electoral politics," says former Illinois state senator Jesus "Chuy" Garcia, 50. "We thought it was corrupt. In 1977, we visited Springfield, Illinois attempting to kill anti-immigrant legislation. We discovered how powerless we were in electoral politics. While growing in numbers, we were voiceless and voteless in the city council....But we began to study how women, and especially African Americans, struggled for the right to vote. We concluded that the struggle for political representation was progressive. We could engage in electoral politics, but not through the regular Democratic Organization of Chicago. That organization always worked against the interests of African Americans, women, and Latinos....The political bosses decided who got in and who didn't. We were out."[52]

Rudy Lozano, Garcia and others established the 22nd Ward Independent Political Organization. The alderman of the 22nd ward that includes Little Village, was Frank Stemberk, a quiet, loyal machine member. Mexicans accused Stemberk of not even living in the ward, and of maintaining his main home in a western suburb. In 1983, Lozano challenged Stemberk for alderman. The political machine put three other Latino candidates on the ballot to split the Mexican vote. Lozano missed a runoff with Stemberk by seventeen votes, and Stemberk won the election. Lozano followers wondered if the political machine stole the election by purging Latino voters from poll sheets shortly before the election.[53] Mexicans highly respected Lozano. He was the first Latino to support U.S. Congressman Harold Washington in his 1983 bid to become the city's first African American mayor. Shortly after Washington won, Lozano was shot to death in his home in June of 1983. Police convicted a young, Mexican gang member of his murder. Yet police angered the Mexican community by stating that the young man acted alone. Police failed to establish a motive for the shooting. Lozano's family and supporters believed others were involved in the killing. They believed Lozano's labor and political activities were the motives for his killing.[54]

Thousands of people marched in the streets and attended Lozano's funeral. A Chicago Public Library branch, and a public elementary school, were named in Lozano's honor. A book about his life was published.[55] Lozano's campaign manager Jesus Garcia decided to continue Lozano's political work. Garcia and other Mexican community leaders supported Harold Washington in his bid for mayor. "We were very glad Harold Washington was running for mayor," says Garcia. "We had met and dealt with him in Springfield, Illinois in the mid-1970s. In Congress he had championed immigrant rights and bilingual education. It was natural to want to be for Washington. We became part of the movement to recruit Washington. We told him if he ran for mayor, he would have allies working for him in the Latino community." In 1983, Harold Washington, ran on a reform platform, and won election as the city's first African American mayor. In the general election, Washington defeated Republican Bernard Epton. The Latino vote for Washington helped him win the election. Washington won 79 percent of more than 95,000 Latino votes. Washington won 79 percent of Puerto Rican votes, 68 percent of Mexican votes, 75 percent of Central and South American votes, and 54 percent of Cuban votes.[56]

As the new mayor Washington immediately signed the Shakman Court Decree, which prevented city employees from being hired or fired for political reasons. Instead of having control of over 40,000 city jobs, like previous mayors, Washington only controlled about a thousand administrative jobs. Mayor Washington hired African Americans, whites, women, and a few Puerto Ricans to top city jobs. Mexican community leaders soon met privately with Mayor Washington. They expressed disappointment that he was hiring mostly Puerto Ricans, and not Mexicans. Mayor Washington quickly learned that Latino groups use the term "Latino" mainly as a show of force, and for political mobilization purposes. Yet each specific Latino group expected political spoils, and members of their own group in top city jobs. Mayor Washington subsequently appointed Jesus Garcia and Juan Velasquez to top, high-paying positions in the city's Water and Streets and Sanitation Departments.

Mayor Washington supported and endorsed Mexican candidates like Jesus Garcia and Juan Soliz for political office. With the combined strength of Mexican and black votes, Mexicans began to win political office. In 1984, about 71 percent of the 22nd Ward's black voters backed Jesus Garcia in his defeat of incumbent Frank Stemberk in the March 20 election for Democratic committeeman. Juan Soliz, a young Mexican attorney, was elected to the Illinois state legislature in 1984, from the 20th district, which encompasses the Pilsen-Little Village area. It was the black vote that helped elect Soliz, who won by only 57 votes.[57] "The significance of Washington's election is that he opened the doors of city hall to our community," says Garcia. "We're become a part of the permanent political equation in Chicago politics. He took steps that were unprecedented in city government, like setting up the Mayor's Advisory Commission on Latino Affairs. That entity could analyze and criticize his actions, and they did. In Washington we saw for the first time an opportunity to elect people that would put the needs of our community before the interests of the machine. That was the turning point for Latinos. That was the beginning of real political empowerment."

In 1982, the Mexican American Legal Defense and Educational Fund, along with Puerto Ricans and African American plaintiffs, joined together and sued the city of Chicago. Plaintiffs charged that the city's newly redrawn map of city wards deliberately diluted the voting strength of African Americans and Latinos. The U.S. Court of appeals ruled the map was discriminatory. Chicago's regular Democratic Organization appealed the case to the U.S. Supreme Court, which declined to hear the case. The Supreme Court let stand the lower court's decision. Seven city wards had to be redrawn to provide for African American and Latino "supermajorities" of 65 percent minority populations. Four wards—the 22nd, 25th, 26th, and 31st—were made majority Latino. In March 1986, the court ruled that a special election had to be held in the seven, newly redrawn wards. It was an historic year for Latinos. Mexicans won two aldermanic seats. Puerto Ricans, who already had a Puerto Rican alderman in the 31st ward, picked up another in the 26th. Mayor Washington backed Jesus Garcia for alderman of the newly redrawn 22nd ward. Frank Stemberk declined to seek reelection. Instead party regulars slated a couple of Latino candidates to run against Garcia. But Garcia won, and he won again in the 1987 aldermanic elections.

In the 25th ward, Vito Marzullo retired. State representative Juan Soliz, decided to run for alderman. Once a supporter of Mayor Washington, Soliz denounced the mayor for supposedly dragging his feet on Latino hiring. Once a crusading, independent reformer, Soliz was supported in the aldermanic race by alderman Edward Vrdolyak (10th) and other party regulars. Vrdolyak formed a majority-bloc of aldermen in the city council who opposed Washington at every turn. Soliz beat Washington-backed, Juan Velazquez. Soliz won again as alderman in 1987. In the city council he was a solid anti-Washington vote.[58] Soliz had ambitions of someday becoming Chicago's first Latino mayor. But his reputation of jumping from one political camp to another, won him few friends. He was eventually defeated as alderman, and disappeared from the political scene.

In redrawn 31st ward, Puerto Rican Miguel Santiago, won with support from the regular Democratic Party. And in the redrawn 26th ward, Washington-backed, Puerto Rican candidate, Luis Gutierrez won as alderman. Jesus Garcia was a rising political star in the Mexican community. He was articulate, liberal, and a mainstay of the Latino independent political movement. He ran for higher office and seemed unbeatable. "In 1984, I was elected committeeman of the 22nd ward. In 1986, I was elected alderman of the 22nd ward. I was reelected to the city council in 1991. As alderman, residents came to me complaining about basis city services like garbage pickup, bait for rodents, street cleaning, abandoned cars, and street lights. In 1992, I was elected to the Illinois state senate. We enacted legislation to improve health care and protect consumers from being ripped off by unscrupulous immigration practitioners called notarios, or notary publics, who pass themselves off as immigration specialists and lawyers. I was reelected to the state senate in 1996."

When Garcia was first elected to the state senate, he recommended that his chief of staff, Ricardo Munoz, become alderman of the 22nd ward. Munoz became alderman in 1993. Then in March 1996, Garcia and Munoz helped Sonia Silva get elected as an Illinois state representative. The three shared offices in Little Village. They prided themselves on being independent from regular Democrats.

However, other up-and-coming Mexican politicians aligned themselves with the regular Democratic Party. Shortly after Daley was elected mayor in 1989, a new group, called the Hispanic Democratic Organization (HDO), was formed with the mayor's blessings. HDO members donated funds, and actively worked in campaigns to reelect the mayor, and to elect Latino candidates who were loyal to Mayor Daley. HDO members saw their close ties to regular Democrats and Mayor Daley as an asset. Most HDO members were city employees. It appeared that over the years a good number of HDO members got good-paying city jobs and promotions simply because of their political campaign work. It was estimated that in their heyday, over 800 Latino city employees belonged to HDO. In 2006, the Federal Bureau of Investigation alleged that the city of Chicago repeatedly violated the Shakman Court Decree by hiring city employees based on their political clout, and not on qualifications. A few top assistants to Mayor Daley were sent to prison for political hiring. Furthermore, during 2006, the FBI was investigating whether political groups, including—the Hispanic Democratic Organization— were involved in getting its members city jobs, overtime, and promotions based solely on political clout.

In the March 1998, primaries, HDO channeled all its troops and funds to defeat Jesus Garcia. HDO backed Antonio "Tony" Munoz, 34, a Chicago cop. Munoz was a no-name opponent with no legislative or community experience. Yet, in a stunning defeat, Munoz beat Garcia, the six-year incumbent senator. Garcia picked up a majority of Latino votes, but failed to win necessary votes in several white precincts. Garcia lost the election by 960 votes out of nearly 13,000 cast.

"Mayor Daley's hit squad came after us big time," says Garcia shortly after his defeat. "His hit squad includes HDO, the Mexican American Chamber of Commerce, the United Neighborhood Organization, the Hispanic American Construction Industry Association, and alderman Danny Solis, of course. They came after us because we challenged the mayor on fairness, on empowerment versus bossism, on our right to speak. We dared to challenge the mayor's redevelopment plans for our community.... We were against the tax increment financing district for Pilsen. We were against low-income residents being displaced by high-income, white professionals. We sought to show how the mayor, developers, and Republicans wanted the University of Illinois expansion to happen despite its impact on Pilsen. We picked a fight with the big boys." Garcia admits he was partly to blame for his defeat. He ran a weak campaign concentrating instead on helping state representative Sonia Silva get reelected. "Our mistake was not recognizing that this fight was perhaps the most serious challenge I faced. We assumed people knew our record. We didn't mobilize all our volunteers. We lost it to the great number of patronage workers the mayor put out there. We were outspent. They were successful because we fell asleep."

New Political Players

Alderman Danny Solis of the 25th ward, believed Jesus Garcia was whining by claiming the machine beat him. "Instead of blaming that there is a conspiracy or political machine behind what is happening, Jesus Garcia and other liberal Latino politicians should hear what the Latino community is saying. It is saying, 'hey, we are of moderate political philosophy. We are about improving our quality of life. We are not about very left, liberal politics.'"[59] Solis, 57, was born in Monterrey, Mexico. His immigrant parents came to Chicago in 1956. Solis believed Garcia and other liberal Latino politicians were out of touch with the "new values" of neighborhood residents. "They are misguided because they play the victim card," says Solis. "They project to the broader community that Hispanics are a victim, a minority group. And as a victim, they are entitled to specific entitlements, like the African American community has asked for in the past.... Gentrification, police brutality, and bilingual education are not the top issues of the Latino community. I think employment, education, and jobs are the main issues. When an immigrant comes to this country, what they need to succeed is not a welfare check. It's not bilingual education. It's not protection from discrimination or racism. It's a job. Immigrants think, how am I going to get a job? Latino leaders should be pushing for jobs, homes, and naturalization. Those are the more important issues that have to be projected."

Mayor Daley appointed Solis as 25th ward alderman in 1996, after Ambrosio Medrano, the former Mexican alderman, was convicted in a federal Silver Shovel investigation of illegal payoffs to Chicago aldermen. Medrano served nearly two years in jail for taking $31,000 in bribes from an FBI undercover mole to allow illegal dumping in his ward in 1994. In a special election in 1997, Solis was elected as 25th ward alderman for a four-year term. "Yes I had my organization working against Jesus Garcia," says Soliz. "After two and a half years of him constantly blasting my positions, I'm certainly not going to be working for him. I worked hard for his defeat. I went door to door in the 25th ward campaigning for Tony Munoz, who I thought was the better candidate. Munoz is a third-generation Mexican American born here in the United States. He served in the U.S. Army. He is a paratrooper. He has strong positions on crime, which I support."

Once a community activist in Pilsen, Solis was now one of Mayor Daley's closest allies. He usually voted for the mayor's initiatives, and never disagreed with the mayor. The mayor rewarded Solis' loyalty by naming him the city council's president pro tempore over more senior alderman. Solis is close to members of the Hispanic Democratic Organization, and HDO has worked actively on his reelection campaigns. Some Mexican residents believed Solis joined the old boys' network of machine politicians he once fought against as an activist. Yet Solis strongly believed Mayor Daley is a good mayor who helps Latinos. "If you look at Mayor Daley's record, his Latino appointments to top city positions have been outstanding. His appointments are much better than any previous mayor, including his father. If you look at Latino neighborhoods, they are all improving in terms of better housing, education, and investment.... All the improvements I have done in Pilsen cannot be disconnected from the mayor and his supporting me. Even alderman Ricardo Munoz, who is not necessarily an ally of Mayor Daley, is getting a new high school in his ward. The mayor does not let politics get in the way of what has to be done in a community.... It certainly helps if you're an ally of the mayor. I can testify to that. But he helps everyone in the city. He wants to see this become one of the best cities."

Mexican women also made inroads in politics. In March 1996, Sonia Silva, 55, defeated Fernando Frias, to become the first Mexican woman elected to the Illinois State Legislature. She was from the first district, which included Little Village and the Back of The Yards. In the General Assembly she encountered a little sexism. "I think part of it concerns the fact that I am a woman. Some people would tell me, 'well, you don't look like other Latinos.' I think they meant that I am more fair-skinned. I would tell my colleagues, 'you know, we come in all shapes, colors, heights, and weights.' The other thing is they had heard of me before I got there, and they viewed me as aggressive. Some actually told me, 'I've heard you're aggressive.' Some men think women who are assertive are usually aggressive and radical. I am assertive and question things. I will not readily give my vote. I question things and I want to be clear about legislation and what the implications are." [60]

Silva's immigrant mother came to Chicago in 1950 from Mexico. Silva worked for Jesus Garcia for about 15 years when he was alderman and state senator. She lives in Little Village. She does not like to be called a politician. "The word "politician," conjures a negative image. I think of myself more as a legislator or a practitioner. But I'm not one of those "rich" legislators. That makes it more difficult for us as elected officials to get our message out. We don't have the money to get on radio and television.... It also makes it very difficult for us to raise funds. Legislators like me, do not get huge $30,000 donations from political action committees. We have to do a lot of work raising funds for reelection every two years. We have dances, receptions, and banquets. It's ongoing, all the time. I rely on a lot of volunteers" As a legislator Silva was concerned about protecting the rights of immigrants. She introduced legislation asking that Illinois restore some public aid and social security benefits that were cut from persons with "legal resident" status. She also passed a law prohibiting nursing homes from denying service to the elderly if they are not U.S. citizens.

Silva was hurt that Latinos in the Hispanic Democratic Organization helped defeat her mentor, Jesus Garcia. She, like others, believed HDO members got their marching orders from Mayor Daley. "Senator Garcia spoke out against the tax increment financing plan for the University of Illinois, and their expansion into Pilsen. He generated the kind of publicity the power brokers in the city did not want. Also, Garcia won consistently in this area for the last 15 years. Some people were saying he would be a good candidate for mayor.... The senator has been a thorn in Daley's side on the Southwest Side, and they don't want people who are independent voices. In my first year in the legislature, some of the mayor's lobbyists came to my office and said, 'we want you to vote on this and this.' I would listen. But if I did not think it was positive, I would not vote for it. They didn't like that. They want you to toe the party line, even if it goes against the interests of the community. I cannot do that."

Running for elected office in Chicago has not been for the faint of heart. Campaigns got nasty as candidates slung mud at one another, and accused each other of harassment and intimidation tactics. In March 1998, Silva ran against Susana Mendoza, a young Mexican woman. The HDO, along with the regular Democratic Organization supported Mendoza. "In the March 1998 election, I felt like I was in El Salvador. You had droves of city workers, many from the Hispanic Democratic Organization, who were physically and verbally abusing my campaign workers," says Siva. "Many of my campaign workers are housewives. HDO members were pushing them, and calling them bad names. HDO people, who were with city police officers, would surround me and say, 'bitch, you're going to go down.' There were people who wanted to put our campaign posters in their windows. And city employees, who are part of HDO, would come to their door and threaten them with city inspectors.... Someone hit my daughter's parked car with baseball bats, knocking out all the windows. My son's car tires were slashed three or four times. It's disheartening. Many people in this community have fought for years to have a voice. And in this district it seems like we have gone backwards."

Silva survived the March 1998 election by beating Susana Mendoza. But in the March 2000 primary, Susana Mendoza again challenged Silva. Each side accused the other of mudslinging and personal attacks. This time, however, of almost 5,000 votes cast, Mendoza beat Silva by about 850 votes. "I knew Mayor Daley, the regulars, and the HDO would come after me again," says Silva. "This time it was more of a concentrated effort to defeat me. They came with a lot of troops and money. They outspent us. I won most of the Latino votes, but I lost crucial white votes. The political climate now in Chicago is to upseat any candidate who is independent, whether that person is Latino, white or African American. They don't like independents because we raise questions that should not be raised. But there are enough people in our community who want their elected officials to be accountable to the community. So we are not going away."

Some Mexicans were disillusioned with the bickering and fighting among elected Mexican officials. They wished Mexican politicians could set aside their differences, and work more closely together. Some Mexican residents expressed embarrassment that some members of the Hispanic Democratic Organization were former gang members, and that the organization was being investigated by the FBI. Some residents believed the HDO was a detriment to the political empowerment of the Mexican community. Given their growing numbers in Chicago and Illinois, many expect that more Mexicans will be elected to the city council and General Assembly. The 2000 U. S. Census showed that the number of Latinos in the city increased by 210,000 during the last decade, while whites and blacks declined. A new city ward map was redrawn and approved by Chicago's city council. The new map increased the number of majority Latino wards from seven to 11. Thus, it's believed that the number of Mexican aldermen in the city council will grow in the near future.[61]

Moving to the Suburbs

The Mexican American Legal Defense and Educational Fund (MALDEF), carefully monitored how future city and state districts were redrawn. Like in the past, MALDEF will sue city and state officials if they feel Latino do not receive sufficient political representation given their growing population numbers. Moreover, Patricia Mendoza, 46, regional counsel for MALDEF, says the organization also monitored political developments in certain Illinois suburbs.[62] Some suburbs like Cicero, Berwyn, Aurora, Stone Park and Waukegan have seen their Mexican populations skyrocket in recent years. There are now over twenty Illinois suburbs with a population of between 13 to 74 percent Latino, mainly Mexican. Most suburbs with large numbers of Mexicans are working-class suburbs with plenty of manufacturing jobs in light industries. Some Mexican immigrants have come directly from Mexico to Cicero in search of jobs. Many suburban Mexicans are renters living in multi-unit apartments.

Some suburbs have not always welcomed Mexicans. During the 1980s Mexican homes were vandalized in predominately white suburbs like Cicero and Berwyn. When Mexicans moved in, whites usually left. By 2000, Cicero's population was 77 percent Latino and Berwyn was 38 percent.[63] Despite their large numbers, very few Mexicans were elected to political office in most suburbs. One major problem was that about half of adult Latinos in the metropolitan Chicago area were not United States citizens.[64] Thus, suburbs like Berwyn and Cicero usually elected white candidates over Mexican candidates. Lacking political power, Mexican residents in Cicero have complained about police harassment, exorbitant towing fees, overzealous antigang measures, restrictive housing ordinances, and intrusive housing inspections.[65] In 2002, the town president of Cicero, Betty Loren-Maltese, and four others were found guilty of taking part in a scheme to steal more than $12 million from the Town of Cicero. Loren-Maltese was sentenced to eight years in prison. The following year, Mexicans in Cicero made history when they elected Ramiro Gonzales as the town's first Mexican president. Community groups in Chicago and the suburbs were undertaking drives to increase the number of registered voters in the Mexican community. Some groups focused on naturalization and citizenship. They helped new citizens become registered voters. Groups like the Chicago-based United States Hispanic Leadership Institute were registering new Latino voters in Illinois and other Midwestern cities.

Chapter Three: Puerto Ricans

Early Jobs and Neighborhoods

Raul Cardona, 75, served in the U.S. Army in 1951. He was a member of the 65th U.S. infantry composed of young men from Puerto Rico. The 65th infantry distinguished itself for bravery on the battlefields of Korea. The infantry suffered heavy causalities. Cardona, who was only 18 years of age, fought in Korea and saw many fellow Puerto Rican soldiers wounded and killed. After the war, he was determined to make something out of his life. He would later become a well-known radio personality and businessman in Chicago's Puerto Rican community. "After the Army, I came to Chicago in 1954 from Ponce, Puerto Rico. I came looking for, what is it they say, the "American Dream." I came looking for work." says Cardona. "I came to Chicago and found work in a factory. There were small factories back then, but most of them are gone now. Most Puerto Ricans in Chicago at the time were working in small factories. We didn't have a lot of education. We were unskilled people and had regular jobs in factories. They were not high-paying jobs."[1]

Using his wits and determination, Cardona eventually landed better-paying jobs. "I was a mailman. Then in 1959, I bought an hour and later two hours of radio airtime. I started one of the first Spanish-language radio stations in Chicago, 'The Raul Cardona Show.' My program played traditional Puerto Rican music, and interviews with Puerto Rican artists. The show is still on after all these years.... In 1961, I joined the Chicago Police Department, along with four other Puerto Ricans. We were some of the first Latinos on the force. Those guys retired from the police department. I left the police department a year later to devote more time to my radio program. Later, I opened some music stores."

Like earlier waves of European immigrants to the city, Puerto Ricans came to Chicago searching for jobs and better economic opportunities. In 1950, there were only 255 Puerto Ricans in Chicago. By 1960, there were 32,371 Puerto Ricans. Thirty years later in 1990, Chicago's Puerto Rican population had more than tripled to 119,800. Puerto Rican migration to the city, however, has since slowed considerably. According to the 2000 U.S. census, the Puerto Rican population in Illinois rose 8 percent and stood at 157,851. Over seventy percent or 113,055 of these Puerto Ricans resided in Chicago.[2] Some Puerto Ricans, especially those who worked lifetimes in Chicago, returned to Puerto Rico upon retirement. Despite their shrinking numbers, Chicago's Puerto Rican community was second in size to New York. Nationally, the Puerto Rican population increased 25 percent from 1990 to 2000. There were over 3.4 million Puerto Ricans in the continental United States.

Puerto Ricans were the first ethnic group to come to America by airplane.

Their migration was dubbed the "airborne migration." Unlike other Latino im-
migrants, Puerto Ricans came as American citizens. The United States acquired
Puerto Rico in the Spanish-American War of 1898. In 1917, an act of the U.S.
Congress made Puerto Ricans American citizens. As American citizens, Puerto
Ricans easily traveled back and forth between Puerto Rico and the United
States. Because they were American citizens, some viewed Puerto Ricans more
as migrants than immigrants. However, like other immigrants, Puerto Ricans
came mainly as unskilled laborers escaping poverty in their homeland. Puerto
Ricans came with high expectations of finding a better life in the United States.
The first large wave of Puerto Ricans to major American cities came as con-
tracted workers shortly before and after World War II. Because of a labor short-
age during the war, American companies needed workers, so they looked to
Puerto Ricans from Puerto Rico to fill the void. Employers viewed Puerto Ricans workers as a source of cheap labor. Companies recruited thousands of
Puerto Ricans to work in major American cities on farms, foundries, steel mills,
canneries, and small industries [3] American employers liked the fact that Puerto
Ricans were American citizens. They were inexpensive to bring into the United
States. Besides, many were unemployed and desperately looking for work. They
were willing to work hard and cheaply.

Puerto Rican have a long history in Chicago. Beginning in the 1920s, a
handful of middle-class Puerto Ricans sent their daughters and sons to study at
prestigious universities in the city. Most received their educations and returned
to Puerto Rico. Yet some of the first Puerto Rican workers in Chicago came as
contract laborers. Castle, Barton and Associates, a private Chicago-based employment agency, set up an office in Puerto Rico to recruit men and women to
work in Chicago homes and factories. In 1946, the agency brought 329 Puerto
Rican women and 67 men to Chicago as contracted domestic and foundry workers. The employment agency offered a full-year of work, and paid the workers'
airplane costs, which they later deducted from their wages.[4] The contracted
Puerto Rican women were between 16 and 35 years of age, and most were un-
married. They were paid sixty-dollars a month. The domestics lived in the Chicago homes that employed them. The women were probably light-skinned as
Castle, Barton, and Associates had a Florida office that imported dark-skinned
Puerto Rican women to work as domestics in the Southern United States.[5]

The Puerto Rican domestic women in Chicago often worked 15 hours a day,
six days a week. Some became dissatisfied with their employment conditions,
and returned to Puerto Rico. Others stayed in Chicago and searched for better
work. The Puerto Rican men worked in unskilled occupations in the Chicago
Hardware Foundry company in North Chicago. They were paid thirty-five dollars a week. Few of the migrants knew English. The men lived in reconverted
railroad cars of the North Chicago Foundry. The foundry workers also became
dissatisfied with their jobs. They were promised thirty-five dollars a week, yet
their paychecks after deductions seldom were over a dollar a day. About half the
workers left and looked for work elsewhere. Others returned to Puerto Rico.

The foundry workers who stayed in Chicago met and married the Puerto Rican women who were working as domestics. They moved out of the railroad cars and searched for affordable apartments. The Mexican Civic Society helped Puerto Ricans find rented rooms in Mexican homes in neighborhoods like the Back of the Yards and South Chicago.[6]

In 1947, the United States Steel company bought several hundred Puerto Ricans to Lorain, Ohio for the National Tube Company, one of its subsidiaries. In 1948, U. S. Steel brought in over 500 Puerto Rican contract workers for its Gary, Indiana plant.[7] Hundreds of Puerto Ricans labored in the steel mills of South Chicago, Gary, and East Chicago, Indiana. Puerto Ricans worked largely in unskilled occupations in the blast furnaces, where the work was unbearably hot and dangerous. Other Puerto Ricans came voluntarily to the Chicago-Calumet area seeking steel mill jobs, and other manufacturing employment.

Cesareo Rivera, 75, was an early Puerto Rican migrant to Chicago. He came with plans of starting a new life in the United States. "I immigrated to New York in 1948 when I was 18. I came from Caguas, Puerto Rico. Like many Puerto Ricans in Puerto Rico, I was unemployed. I came looking for work. I found a job washing dishes in a restaurant.... In 1951 I landed a good-paying job in the steel mills, I worked at Inland Steel in Indiana. The work was hard and you were always sweating, but it paid a lot better than washing dishes. I visited Chicago and met my future wife Luz Maria Rivera. We married in 1952. That same year I left my steel mill job and moved to Chicago to be with my wife. I found a job in a factory. The job paid less that the steel mills, but I wanted to be with my wife. And Chicago was not as smelly and smoky as Indiana."[8]

A major factor that pushed Puerto Ricans to migrate from Puerto Rico to American cities was Operation Bootstrap, a 1950s effort to industrialize Puerto Rico. Through Operation Bootstrap Puerto Rico's government gave generous tax breaks, free land, and low-interest loans to American companies if they relocated their plants to Puerto Rico. Puerto Rico's government promised these companies a large pool of supposedly docile and cheap workers. Many companies took up the offer. However, the much-heralded Operation Bootstrap did not create enough jobs for the growing Puerto Rican population. As a partial solution to unemployment, Puerto Rico's government encouraged Puerto Ricans to leave the island and search for work in the mainland United States. The Department of Labor of Puerto Rico established a Migration Office in Chicago in 1949 to help recruit Puerto Ricans for work in the city and the Midwest. Thus, Puerto Ricans became displaced migrants.[9]

Throughout the 1950s and 60s, hundreds of thousands of unemployed Puerto Ricans left Puerto Rico, and ventured to the big cities of America looking for decent work. Many young men came first hoping to establish themselves before bringing over their families. Some came with dreams of making money, and then returning to the island to buy a little piece of land and their own home. Others came with intentions of staying. "My father came to Chicago in 1953 from Las Marias, Puerto Rico," says Wilfredo Ortiz, 58, principal of Gage Park

High School. "My dad came first to get a job and get settled. Two years later, he sent for my mother, two sisters, my brother and me. My mother was a traditional housewife and never worked. My dad was uneducated and basically a laborer. He spoke only Spanish. He worked all his life at U.S. Steel in South Chicago. I guess that was a good-paying job. The work was very hard and physical, but my dad was real strong. He never complained."[10]

"I started working at U.S. Steel in 1953, and I worked there for 30 years," recalls Wilfredo's father, Eduardo Ortiz, 84, a resident of South Deering. "During those 30 years I worked day and night shifts. I was a laborer for 16 years, and then I worked in a semiskilled position for another 14 years. The work was hard and dangerous. You had to be alert and have four eyes. There were overhead cranes and moving trucks inside the mill. Some men were killed because it was dark in the mill and the trucks would hit them.... There were a lot of Mexicans in the mill and about ten percent of the workers were Puerto Rican. When I started in the mill, I was earning $1.70 an hour, and when I retired in 1983, I was making $10.00 an hour. I retired with a pension.... After I retired, I lived in Puerto Rico for three years. But Puerto Rico is too hot. I came back to Chicago to be with my kids. I love Chicago."[11] "Four years ago my father was diagnosed with leukemia," says Wilfredo. "We think he got if from being exposed to fumes and gases at the steel mill during all those years. No one in our family has ever had that disease."

Other Puerto Ricans dreamed of landing steady, good-paying jobs in the steel mills. But by the mid-1950s, steel mills and other heavy industries, were significantly cutting back on their labor force. Puerto Ricans came at the wrong time to the wrong place. For years, Chicago's image as a blue-collar town, with plenty of manufacturing jobs, was unquestioned. Successive waves of immigrants to the city found decent, well-paying manufacturing jobs. However, like most major, older American industrial cities, Chicago was losing thousands of manufacturing jobs. Manufacturing companies were leaving the city for greener pastures in the suburbs and Third World countries. Manufacturing jobs had peaked in Chicago in 1947 at 668,000, and then declined to 508,797 in 1963 and to 295,992 in 1982.[12] The trend continued well into the 1990s. Manufacturing jobs in the city decreased by 39,442 jobs between 1991 and 1996, for a lost of more than 200,000 jobs since 1979.[13]

Chicago's economy shifted from manufacturing to service. Employment growth was taking place in banking, legal services, management, insurance, retailing, health care, and education. These highly-skilled, service jobs required college education.[14] Most Puerto Ricans came poor, uneducated, and without knowing English. By the mid-1990s, Puerto Ricans had the highest poverty rate—33.8 percent—among Latino groups in the city.[15] Early Puerto Ricans arrivals in Chicago found mainly low-paying, menial service jobs. They found employment on the factory assembly lines, as janitors, and as hotel and restaurant workers. They toiled in the hot foundries, and worked in suburban factories making things like pipelines. Puerto Rican women worked as assemblers, laundry and dry cleaning operatives, and packers and wrappers. Women also took in lodgers, and did childcare and piecework. Even by mid-1966, most Puerto Rican workers were still employed primarily as operatives and kindred workers.[16] Some large families were forced to go on public aid.

Cesareo recalls factory work as boring and low-paying. "The factory jobs that Puerto Ricans had did not pay well. Most of us that came were workers without much education. But we came in the fifties and we said, 'our kids will not suffer like we did.' And that's what happened. Many of our kids are doing much better than us. We have 11 children and four graduated from college. All the others have good jobs." Early Puerto Rican migrants to Chicago settled near Chicago's downtown area in the Near North Side and Near West Side communities. Many worked in fancy downtown hotels and restaurants as janitors, busboys, dishwashers, and cooks. "When I arrived in Chicago in 1954, I lived near the center of the city on Harrison and Ashland," says Raul Cardona. "There were a lot of multi-unit buildings in the area. Puerto Ricans were not making a lot of money so obviously the rents in the area were low. More Puerto Ricans began moving into that neighborhood and around Madison, Washington, and Jackson Streets." Some Puerto Rican families found affordable shelter in public housing projects living along side African Americans.

Some Puerto Ricans lived in Chicago's downtown Loop area in cheap, cramped apartment buildings, and old, transient hotels on Clark, LaSalle, and Madison Streets. To share expenses, two and three families often lived crowded together in one and two-room apartments. Some dingy hotels where Puerto Ricans lived were next to Chicago's old, Skid Row area. Puerto Ricans were surely disheartened upon seeing Skid Row's walking dead: thousands of unkempt, beaten-down, unemployed, alcoholic men and women. The area also had plenty of bars, crime, and prostitution. Some Puerto Ricans, like Raul Cordona, did well for himself. With only an eight-grade education, and no prior business skills, Cordona founded a chain of music stores that catered to Chicago's growing Puerto Rican community. "Around 1972, I bought a music store, Disco City Record Shop on Division Street in front of the San Juan theater. Over the years, I had nine, small stores specializing in Latin music, mostly Puerto Rican music. I sold most of the stores to other family members. Some sold their stores. Four stores still exist with different names." Cordona's son, Felix, 40, owns the Disco City record store in the Logan Square neighborhood. The store sells a large volume of Puerto Rican salsa music. The father and son are also co-owners of several dance halls, and apartment buildings in Logan Square.

Besides Chicago's downtown area, Puerto Ricans settled on the city's North Side in neighborhoods like Lincoln Park, Uptown, and Lakeview. Other Puerto Ricans settled in Chicago's South Side in neighborhoods like East Garfield Park, West Garfield Park, Woodlawn, and Englewood. Beginning in the 1950s, many South Side neighborhoods were undergoing dramatic racial change as African Americans moved in, and whites ethnics fled to the suburbs. Some white landlords of big apartment buildings often preferred renting to Puerto Ricans instead of African Americans. But Puerto Ricans were forced to pay higher rents.[17] "When we came to Chicago in 1952, we lived on 63rd Street in Woodlawn in a big, four-story courtyard building," recalls Wilfredo Ortiz. "About 95 percent of the families were Puerto Ricans. There was a small group of white people who still lived in that building.... Our apartment was real decent. My mother always walked us to school and back in the morning, at lunchtime, and when school was over. She never allowed us to walk by ourselves. As kids, we would play ball in front of the building. We would have fights with the black kids. They would come over and throw rocks and we would throw them back.... My father used to travel from Woodlawn to the steel mills in South Chicago."

Yet some landlords on the city's North Side often refused to rent to dark-skinned Puerto Ricans, who they viewed as blacks. While Puerto Ricans did not face the extreme housing segregation experienced by African Americans, they were not welcomed in certain neighborhoods. Even some light-skinned Puerto Ricans like Cesareo, encountered prejudice. "We tried to rent an apartment in Lincoln Park," recalls Cesareo. "The landlords would put 'For Rent' signs in the windows. When they saw you, they would say, 'we already rented it.' Later we would find out they did not rent the apartment. They didn't want to rent to Puerto Ricans.... Whites would always tell us, 'speak English.' We spoke broken English." Says Luz Maria, "Many landlords in Lincoln Park didn't rent to Puerto Ricans because they had large families. Those families had a hard time finding decent apartments. They would find a decent place, but when they raised rents, they had to move again." Puerto Rican families constantly moved around the city looking for affordable apartments. In the process, children usually attended six or seven different elementary schools.

Yet other Puerto Ricans faced no discrimination in housing or public places. "I didn't experience any discrimination," says Raul Cardona. "But you see, I'm taller and lighter than the average Puerto Rican, and whites would think I was Polish, Italian or some other European. But I knew about discrimination. I knew, for instance, that instead of writing traffic violations, police would extort money from Puerto Ricans. The police called Puerto Ricans 'pork chops' and blacks 'shines.' Before they reformed Chicago's police department in the 1960s, the police were very corrupt." Cardona lived in the middle-class, northern suburb of Lincolnwood for many years. He then moved back to the city. "I moved to the suburbs to raise my kids in a quiet, safe environment. I wanted them to have good schools. But now my kids are grown. The suburbs are too quiet so I moved back to Logan Square. I moved back to the city where there is more noise, people, and action. I like the city."

After several years in Chicago, Cesareo and Luz Maria purchased a small home in Lincoln Park. Other Puerto Ricans moved to this attractive neighborhood by the lake. A distinct Puerto Rican community took shape in Lincoln Park during the 1950s. Families saved their hard-earned money and bought small homes. Two families often pooled their money and bought a two-story, brownstone or greystone building. Small Puerto Rican mom-and-pop grocery stores emerged on Lincoln and Halsted Streets. The stores had a niche specializing in Puerto Rican food the major food chains did not carry. The stores offered credit to families struggling to make ends meet. Puerto Rican restaurants, barbershops, music stores, and liquor stores thrived around Armitage and Halsted Streets. On hot summer days, Puerto Ricans cooled off at the North Avenue Beach. Puerto Rican families, like the Riveras, attended mass at St. Michael's Roman Catholic parish on Cleveland and North Avenue. Puerto Rican men in Lincoln Park supplemented their factory income by cutting the hair of their friends and neighbors in their basement apartments. Women added to the family income by sewing clothes at home or by babysitting. Other women were traditional homemakers. "I didn't work much after I got married," says Luz Maria, "I stood home to raise our 11 children. I felt that was an important responsibility."

By 1956, the Riveras noticed a dramatic change in Lincoln Park. The change, which took place throughout the 1960s, was called gentrification. The neighborhood became desirable to young, white middle-class professionals. The area contained good housing, and was near downtown and the lakefront. Developers realized they could make big money. High apartment rents and rising property taxes forced Puerto Rican families to leave the area. Families sold their small homes. The homes were torn down and replaced with expensive townhouses, condominiums, and high-rise apartment buildings. "The Lincoln Park neighborhood began to change and grow quickly," recalls Cesareo. "They started building big homes, and knocking down the small ones. We saw ourselves being forced to move from there because our house was small. We didn't have the money to renovate it. We had four children then. We had to find a bigger house in better condition. Some real estate agents pressured Puerto Ricans to sell their homes. They sold them cheaply."

Over 5,000 Puerto Ricans moved from Lincoln Park and the Near North Side. Today, both neighborhoods have the most expensive housing in the city.[18] Most Puerto Ricans from Lincoln Park and the Near North Side moved west to Division Street and the West Town and Humboldt Park neighborhoods. They started from scratch in rebuilding a sense of community. The Riveras moved to the South Side and bought an impressive, three-story Victorian frame house in the Englewood neighborhood. "In 1966 we bought this house. This was a good neighborhood, and we lived here for 32 years. We raised our family here," says Cesareo. "When we moved here it was white. As Puerto Ricans and blacks moved in, the whites began to leave. Puerto Ricans and whites sometimes fought with each other. There were a lot of single Puerto Rican men and some were trouble makers. The Puerto Ricans and blacks used to fight each other. Puerto Ricans and blacks did get along better than Puerto Ricans and whites. But there were still conflicts. They would sometimes shoot at each other."

Throughout the 1960s and early 70s, Puerto Ricans left South Side neighborhoods and moved to West Town and Humboldt Park. Puerto Ricans moved from these neighborhoods because of the gangs and crime. Some probably left because of prejudice; like other Chicagoans, they did not want to live next to

Englewood (
Bad (
Violence.

African Americans. Neighborhoods like Woodlawn and Englewood rapidly deteriorated. Disinvestment occurred as banks, insurance companies, stores, and other businesses left. City services like garbage collection, street cleaning, and infrastructure repairs declined. Housing was lost through neglect, abandonment, and arson-for-profit. Poverty, gangs, and crime increased. Despite the racial change, Cesareo stayed in Englewood. "I started my own business, a grocery and liquor store. I had it for fourteen years. I got along well with my black customers. But once I was robbed and almost killed. This guy came in and jumped over the counter and shot me. He ran off with money from the cash register. The bullet went through my hand and into my stomach. I couldn't work for six months.... But I was not afraid. I returned to work in the store. I had to work. The store helped us put all our kids through Catholic schools."

Cesareo and Luz Maria are probably the last Puerto Rican family in Englewood. Their living room was filled with framed photos of their children and grandchildren. "Most of our children live in the suburbs," says Luz Maria. "One of our older sons, who is a mailman, still lives with us upstairs. Our children worry about us. They want us to sell our home and move to a safer neighborhood. But we like our home and our independence." Cesareo adds, "I stay here because this is my house, and no one bothers me. I don't pay a mortgage, and I am happy. We have very good neighbors who look out for us." The Riveras were hopeful about the future of Chicago's Puerto Rican community. "The community is growing and growing," says Cesareo. "A lot more people are getting educated and preparing themselves.... We have more politicians, doctors, and lawyers. There's a growing middle class."

The Humboldt Park Community

From the late 1940s through the late 1960s, large American agricultural companies recruited thousands of Puerto Ricans from Puerto Rico to work as contracted farm workers in cities like Massachusetts, Connecticut, New York, Philadelphia, California, and other Midwestern cities. Puerto Ricans had a reputation as hardworking farm workers skilled at planting and harvesting.[19] American companies wanted Puerto Rican contract workers solely for their labor, and not as permanent community members. It was hoped that after their contract work was completed, Puerto Ricans would return to Puerto Rico. Even though Puerto Ricans arrived in American cities as U.S. citizens, many people in the United States defined them as "colored" and as "foreigners." But many contract workers did not return to Puerto Rico.[20] Instead, these workers left low-paying farm work, and searched for higher factory wages in cities like Chicago. These Puerto Ricans came with strong backs, strong arms, and a willing to work hard to get ahead.

Eligio Quiñones, 79, came to the United States as a contracted farm worker. He lived in the Humboldt Park neighborhood. He recalls his early days of struggle. "I first came to New York in 1948 at the age 18. I came alone and was a contracted farm worker. I am from Penuelas, Puerto Rico. The Puerto Rican government paid our airfare to work in the United States. The large mainland farms that contracted the workers later deducted the airplane costs from our checks. We were like Mexican braceros. I worked on a farm near Buffalo, New York with about five thousand other Puerto Ricans.... The contracts lasted from four to six months. We were from the hills of Puerto Rico. We were all young men and we didn't have any education. We would plant and harvest tomatoes, strawberries, beans and asparagus. They didn't pay well, we got about sixty cents an hour.... I would go back and forth from Puerto Rico to New York under different work contracts. I wanted to make money to build a home in Puerto Rico."[21]

The contracted workers lived in barrack-style housing isolated from main cities. The barracks were old and overcrowded. Workers became terribly homesick. They missed friends, wives, families, and their warm island. To escape boredom, some ventured into nearby towns. "Once, my brother and I went outside the work camp to a restaurant in Buffalo, New York," recalls Quiñones. "The owner told us they didn't serve niggers. We didn't know English, just a few swear words. My brother said, 'You son of a bitch.' He wanted to slap the man. They called the police and almost threw us in jail. A second time we entered a white bar for some cold beer. Again, they told us to leave. They classified us as black. This time we walked out without a fight." In 1952, Quiñones came from Puerto Rico to California as a contracted farm worker. He labored in the hot California farm fields alongside Mexican braceros. "We picked oranges, grapes, lemons, and lettuce. The work was dirty, low-paying, and backbreaking. You had to pick miles and miles of fruit. Some days you could not stand up straight. I picked crops in California for 19 years. A disk in my back came out of place. My back still hurts from my days of picking crops."

Quiñones'oldest daughter married and visited Chicago. She returned to California to tell her father that factories in Chicago paid much better that farm work. "The day my daughter came it was cold and raining. My shoes were full of mud. I didn't want to do farm work anymore. I told the Mexican woman I was living with, let's go to Chicago. But she had her family in California, and she didn't want to leave them. So in 1967, I came with my daughter and son-in-law to Chicago." In Chicago, Quiñones found a job cleaning kitchens in a downtown hotel. Later he found a better job at O'Hare Airport working in the kitchen cleaning and preparing food for American Airlines. Quiñones married a Mexican woman, and has two sons and two stepsons.

In the 1930s, Humboldt Park was home to Germans and Norwegians. Later, in 1960, the community was 99 percent white, mostly Italians and Poles. By 1970, however, Puerto Ricans were two-thirds of the Latinos in the neighborhood. By 1990, the neighborhood was about 43 percent Latino, of which one half was Puerto Rican and about 39 percent were Mexican. Another 50 percent of residents were African American.[22] Quiñones owned a two-story, brownstone in Humboldt Park, and he recalls the racial tension. "I worked hard and saved my money," he says. "In 1976, I bought this house for $24,000. But I had a problem with the Italian family next door. They had a 20-year-old boy. I had two junky cars. One day the Italian boy tells me, 'hey why don't you park your junks in front of your house.' I told him, 'it's a public street.' That night someone broke the windows in both my cars. The next day, I told him and his father that since someone broke my windows, I was going to break some car windows. That night the father slept in one of their cars, and the son slept in the other. They later sold their house.... They tried to get back at me by selling the house to a black family. But the black family is real good." Quiñones was hopeful about staying in Humboldt Park. "I don't want to leave the neighborhood. My two brothers-in-law own similar brownstone houses right next to each other. For security, we installed, six-feet, wrought-iron fences in front of our homes. We look out for each other's families." Despite his years in the United States, Quiñones never learned English. "I didn't have any education in Puerto Rico. English is a hard language to learn as an adult. Yet I understand it. I admit my lack of English has hurt me. Once, my white boss at American Airlines wanted to promote me to a supervisory position. He liked the way I worked, but I couldn't pass the English test. They passed me over."

In July 2000, Quiñones experienced a personal tragedy. One evening his 36-year-old stepson drove through an intersection in Logan Square. Rival gangs members shot at each another. A stray bullet hit and instantly killed his stepson. Quiñones was heartbroken. Despite the tragedy, Quiñones believed his years in Chicago have been fruitful. He worked at American Airlines for twenty years and retired in 1992. While many Puerto Ricans worked lifetimes at jobs without pensions, Quiñones received a pension. "I receive a nice monthly pension from American Airlines. They also give me two, free travel tickets every year for a lifetime. My wife and I regularly visit Puerto Rico and California." During the summer months, Quiñones planted tomatoes, cucumbers, and green peppers in his back yard. He shared his vegetables with his neighbors. To earn extra cash, he cruised through alleys in his pickup truck searching for scrap metal.

The Other Generations

Noel Ruiz, 50, and his wife, Marcia, 49, are second-generation Puerto Ricans. They were born in Chicago and have lived all their lives in the Humboldt Park neighborhood. They reflected on the aspirations of their parents. "My parents came to Chicago in 1953," says Marcia. "They were from Arecibo, Puerto Rico. They were uneducated and came looking for work. My father worked in the farms in Puerto Rico. In Chicago, he worked for 15 years in a factory, painting furniture. Later he worked in a factory in Addison, Illinois. My father worked all his life in factories. He wanted to come here, make money, then go back, and buy a home in Puerto Rico, which is something he did fulfill. He retired and went back to Puerto Rico in 1978. My mother did not work. She was a housewife. She also returned to Puerto Rico."[23]

"My parents came in the late 1950s, from Yauco, Puerto Rico," adds Noel. "My mother and father were both factory workers. They didn't have much education. They never really talked about their dreams. I guess they just wanted to come here, work, and have a good life. My mother worked for many years at Zenith in Melrose Park. My father worked for years in a factory in Addison, Illinois.... Well, actually, my mother was more the supporter of the house. My dad really didn't work that much. My dad was a gambler. He was always in pool halls, and that was his way of making money because he was good at it. It used to make my mother angry." Noel and Marcia own a two-story, greystone building on the east side of the Humboldt Park neighborhood. They have fond memories of growing up in Humboldt Park. "My parents rented apartments in the Humboldt Park community, and I don't recall that they faced any prejudice. The Polish and German neighbors accepted my parents," says Noel.

In the middle of the neighborhood, sits the spacious 206-acre park named after Alexander von Humboldt, a German naturalist and author. The park has a large lagoon and a manmade beach for swimming. It has large, colorful flower beds, and a large field house, basketball courts, and baseball diamonds. "We have good memories of growing up in Humboldt Park," says Marcia. "Many of our family outings were at the park. We had many picnics there. We enjoyed going to the lagoon and the children's playground area. On hot summer days families used to sleep in the park. Every year they had a colorful Polish parade where people dressed in traditional Polish costumes. We participated in the Polish parade. Now, we love the Puerto Rican parade."

Unlike their parents, Noel and Marcia became educated. Both graduated from Roberto Clemente High School. With government loans and grants, Marcia earned her bachelor's degree. She was the first in her family to graduate from college. "At Clemente High School the teachers didn't really push you to accomplish things," says Marcia. "Being Latino, I guess they didn't expect that you would succeed. After high school, I worked as a waitress, a dietary aide in a hospital, and as a cashier. I decided to go back to school and finish my B.A. Later, while working full-time, I completed my master's degree.... I am now an elementary public school teacher at Jose de Diego Academy, here in Humboldt Park. My mother is so proud of me. She tells everyone in Puerto Rico that her daughter is an educated teacher in Chicago."

Instead of college, Noel opted for trade school. He graduated from the prestigious Washburne Trade School which trained carpenters, electricians, painters, welders, and other journeymen for the building trades. "I attended junior college for a while, but I didn't like the environment. I worked as a teacher's aide. Then I did janitorial work. I decided to go to trade school. I attended Washburne and became a journeyman carpenter in 1984. I specialize in finishing carpentry on homes and buildings. Sometimes trades people complain that construction work is not steady. But I've been lucky, my work through the years has been pretty steady." Noel makes good money as a carpenter. Yet becoming a carpenter was not easy. The building trade unions have a notorious history of excluding Latinos and African Americans from high-paying, journeymen jobs. Although Washburne was a public school of the Chicago Board of Education, the building trade unions operated it like a private school. For decades, civil right activists and lawsuits had little success in opening Washburne's highly acclaimed apprenticeship programs to Latinos, blacks and women.[24]

In 1983, when Harold Washington became mayor, city and school officials pressured Washburne's school officials to admit more minorities. The trade unions balked, and moved the school's eight apprenticeship programs to the suburbs. Washburne now stands empty. "I've been through a lot of prejudice," says Noel. "On my first job, my white coworkers started calling me 'hey taco and wetback.' I told them I don't appreciate being called that. They all started laughing, and even the foreman was laughing. They were trying to push me to quit the job.... Once, when I was going to lunch, I gave a black coworker a ride in my truck. When we got back, the white workers asked me why I would allow a nigger in my truck. I couldn't believe it. On another job, one guy called me a wetback. That was the last straw. I grabbed the wall we were putting up, about two stories high. I just started shaking the wall. He straddled the wall because I was going to knock it down. He was pleading and crying for me to stop. I grabbed my tools and left. He never bothered me again. On other jobs, some Latinos took the name calling. I wouldn't take it. I would tell Latinos not to allow it."

Says Marcia: "I couldn't believe all the prejudice Noel has had to put with on his job. It was just terrible. I was shocked that anyone would treat someone like that. I thought prejudice was over. It got so bad that I wanted Noel to quit his job as a carpenter even if it meant we were going to struggle economically. I didn't want him to go through that." However, Noel stuck with it. Eventually he won respect from his fellow workers on different jobs sites. "During the last seven years, I've actually run jobs. I've been the foreman on some jobs. Things have gotten better," says Noel. Noel and Marcia compared their lives to that of their parents. "I feel very happy about our lives compared with our parents," says Marcia. "We have education, which our parents did not. We have a bigger home. We have good jobs with pensions and health insurance. Our parents struggled for us to have better things. Now it's our turn to help our parents. Every two weeks we send our parents money in Puerto Rico. It's our turn to give back to them."

Yet Noel and Marcia worried about the future of Puerto Rican youth. "We're disappointed our oldest son stopped attending college full-time," says Noel. "He was a talented baseball player at St. Patrick's Catholic High School. He was double promoted in grammar school. He was very intelligent, but somewhere he got turned off by school. We dreamed that our three sons would get a college education. Some kids now don't have that drive.... We had to go out there and really work hard to get what we have. Today, some kids don't know what it's like to struggle or work hard. They don't know the value of responsibility or money. It's going be hard for them." Their 19-year-old son worked full-time and took an evening class at the local community college. They have two other boys, ages 11 and 14. With three growing boys, Noel and Marcia worried about gang activity in the neighborhood. "Once, some detectives mistook our son Noel Jr. for a gang member," says Noel. "The detectives tried to pull his car over. They were dressed in hooded jackets. My son thought they were gang members and kept driving. When Noel failed to pull his car over, the detectives became enraged. Four police square cars finally stopped him. They grabbed him and began punching and kicking him. Another cop arrived, a friend of ours. He told the other cops, 'this is a good kid, you got the wrong guy for sure.' He stopped them from beating him even more."

Noel and Marcia have known the temptations of the street. One of Marcia's brothers got involved with drugs and gangs, and another brother killed himself. They have thought of moving to another neighborhood. However, they decided to stay put. "Even my co-workers ask me, 'how can you live in Humboldt Park, isn't it crazy?'" says Marcia. "But we have lived here all our lives. We don't want to leave. My two sisters live here. I love this neighborhood." Noel jumped in. "This neighborhood is now changing. It's undergoing gentrification. Whites now want this neighborhood. Poor Puerto Rican families are moving out either because of high property taxes, or because they are making a little profit by selling their homes. Some Hispanic families are smart; they refuse to sell their homes. Others give in for the money and sell out. They forget their pride and the good times too. I want to stay here."

Gentrification

The forces of gentrification pushed Puerto Ricans from one neighborhood to another. Neighborhoods like West Town, Buck Town, and Wicker Park were once mainly Puerto Rican. However, during the last 20 years, these communities have undergone gentrification. Many Puerto Ricans left as young, white, middle-class, urban professionals moved in. Old, industrial factories were converted into expensive condominiums and lofts. Expensive town homes and single-family homes were rehabbed or built. Homes that once sold for about $60,000 sell for almost a million dollars. Trendy, upscale restaurants, chic bars, shops, coffee houses, clothing boutiques, and antique shops now dot the commercial strips of these neighborhoods. Gentrification has spilled over into the Humboldt Park neighborhood. Meanwhile, some local Puerto Rican leaders and politicians have attempted to stop gentrification. They want to maintain a section of Humboldt Park as the heart of Chicago's Puerto Rican community. They created a public space that celebrates the Puerto Rican presence in the city. In 1995, these leaders and politicians encouraged the city of Chicago to build two 59-foot, colorful, steel, Puerto Rican flags on Division Street. One of the flags arches across Division Street at Artesian Avenue near Roberto Clemente High School. The other flag stands five blocks east on Mozart Street near the entrance of Humboldt Park. The steel used to create the flags was in memory of the early Puerto Ricans in Chicago who labored in the steel mills and pipeline factories.

The area within the flags is a small commercial district known as 'Paseo Boricua.' Paseo is a public walk or mall. Borinquen is the name indigenous Indians of Puerto Rico, the Taínos, called Puerto Rico. The business strip was once decaying and almost deserted. But the city invested over two and a half million dollars to install the flags and beautify the business strip. Sixteen, small plazas complete with benches, domino tables, trees, and flower pots were installed. The project also included new streets, curbs, sidewalks, and 50 new street lights with Puerto Rican motifs. On the Paseo there were about ninety businesses and organizations, including an art gallery, Puerto Rican-owned bakeries, restaurants, barber shops, liquor stores, botanicas, and music stores.[25] A Puerto Rican Chamber of Commerce is located on the Paseo. The chamber has over 127 active members, most of them small, mom-and-pop establishments.[26] To generate more revenues in Paseo Boricua, local politicians and leaders hoped to attract new businesses to the area in the future.

It is uncertain if Paseo Boricua will deter the future displacement of Puerto Ricans from the Humboldt Park neighborhood. Longtime residents have been squeezed by rising property taxes and rents. Many Puerto Ricans sold their brick, two and three-flat brownstone and greystone homes, and moved to North Side neighborhoods like Logan Square, Hermosa, Avondale, Albany Park, Belmont Cragin, and Irving Park. Homes in these North Side neighborhoods, however, were the most expensive in the city. Puerto Rican families often pooled their money with another family to purchase a building on the North Side. Others became renters in older multi-family buildings. Puerto Rican paid a higher share of their income in rents and mortgages than whites or blacks.[27] Some Puerto Ricans moved to the suburbs surrounding Chicago. Puerto Ricans were drawn to blue-collar, satellite suburbs in search of affordable housing and manufacturing jobs. Suburbs like Waukegan, Aurora, and Elgin each have several thousand Puerto Ricans. But Puerto Rican and Latino increases in the suburbs have taken place in old suburbs of white flight, disinvestment, and deindustrialization.[28]

Puerto Rican Consciousness

The movement of Puerto Ricans from one neighborhood to another undoubtedly hindered their ability to establish a cohesive community. Also, early Puerto Rican arrivals were dealing with issues like finding jobs and surviving. They did not have the luxury to participate in creating community-based organizations. Mirta Ramirez, 78, remembers how many Puerto Ricans in the 1950s and 60s struggled with daily bread-and-butter issues. Ramirez lived in the West Town neighborhood for many years. She was an educator and community organizer during the 1960s. "A lot of them were migrant workers who came here to earn money. They told them all kinds of fairy stories about good-paying jobs. But when they got here, it didn't turn out that way. In the early 1950s, many Puerto Ricans worked in factories and did not make much money. They were living in poor housing. I saw kids sleeping in basement apartments on bare mattresses. They didn't have shoes.... There were a lot of poor families. They were cooking in cans because they didn't have money to buy cooking utensils. Families were dealing with issues like finding a job, making money, getting an apartment, getting a car, and doing the groceries."[29]

Like previous immigrants, Puerto Ricans relied heavily on informal networks of family and friends to help them find jobs, housing, English classes, and social services. Some Puerto Rican women worked hard, saved their money and managed to open up small businesses like beauty salons, bridal shops, and restaurants. Other women left the world of work to become homemakers and care for their families. But many women, like Mirta Ramirez, toiled in factories.[30] "I immigrated to the Bronx, New York in 1946, from Corozal, Puerto Rico," says Ramirez. "I was 18-years-old. My father had died when I was 12 from an acute kidney disease. My mother went to New York because she had brothers there who could help her. New York was a dreadful city. In 1948 when I was 20, I came to Chicago. I ran away from home because my mother wanted me to marry a young man. Oh, mothers do love to do that. I thought, no, that's not for me. So I came to Chicago to live with my brother at Ashland and Division.... I worked in various factories. I then worked as a cashier. I didn't know English well. But I took the GED. and passed it. I went back to Puerto Rico and I got married. But I married who I wanted. I returned to Chicago in 1957."

Early Puerto Rican arrivals lacked educated professionals who could act as community leaders. One priest who took a liking to Puerto Ricans was Rev. Leo T. Mahon, 79, an Irish priest, who spoke fluent Spanish. "I was assigned to the Woodlawn community to work with African Americans in the 1950s. Instead, I began working with the Puerto Ricans who were there," says Rev. Mahon. "They came asking for my help. During the 1950s and 60s, I was the director of the Cardinal's Committee for the Spanish Speaking."[31] Rev. Mahon recalls that Puerto Ricans complained about brutality and mistreatment by Chicago Police. "One of the most severe problems they had was with the police. In the 1950s, the police department was very corrupt and anti-foreigner," says Rev. Mahon. "There were payoffs and everything. A lot of verbal abuse. I don't think there was that much crime among Puerto Ricans. There's a gentility to most Puerto Ricans. They have manners and come from good families. Police talked to them harshly. Police didn't understand them. They always thought Puerto Ricans were using aliases because they used double last names. Police were suspicious and intolerant of Puerto Ricans. Puerto Ricans were afraid of police. We complained to city officials about police mistreatment."

Rev. Mahon, along with neighborhood residents, founded the Puerto Rican community's first large organization, Los Caballeros de San Juan (Knights of St.

John). The organization was founded in 1954 at Holy Cross Church at 65th and Maryland in Woodlawn. Backed by the Catholic Church, Los Caballeros established 12 affiliated councils throughout Chicago. The councils were formed in churches with growing numbers of Puerto Rican parishioners. The organization served the religious and social service needs of Puerto Ricans. "We named the organization after the patron saint of San Juan, Puerto Rico," says Rev. Mahon. "The organization helped the community.... Puerto Ricans were having a lot problems adjusting. They had credit problems. Sales people would take advantage of them by charging them high credit. They had police abuse problems, higher arrests, and brutality. They had social problems like not having a decent place to meet and dance, without spending your whole paycheck in a tavern."

Los Caballeros de San Juan catered mainly to men, and tried to keep them off the streets, and instead focused on religion and family. The organization was devoted to assimilating Puerto Ricans to American ways, and to adopting an American style of Catholicism. The group worked hard to convince white Chicagoans that Puerto Ricans were decent, religious, family-oriented people.[32] The organizations' letters to outside sources referred to Puerto Ricans as "good people." Los Caballeros sponsored dances, pool rooms, picnics, baseball teams, and an annual fancy banquet in an elegant downtown hotel. The group also helped Puerto Rican men prepare for the Chicago police test. In 1962, Luis Muñoz Marín, the first Puerto Rican governor of Puerto Rico, joined the group at Chicago's downtown Hilton Hotel to celebrate Puerto Ricans who were becoming Chicago police officers. From 1956 through 1965, Los Caballeros de San Juan sponsored an annual El Dia de San Juan that included a small parade, banquet, and dance. After 1965 this event became known as La Parada Puertorriqueña or the Puerto Rican Parade. Today, Los Caballeros de San Juan still exists, but solely as an independent credit union in Logan Square. It is one of the largest, fully Latino-owned financial institutions in the Midwest, with more than $10 million in assets.

Early Puerto Ricans in Chicago also organized social and athletic clubs for men. The clubs allowed men to socialize, play pool, play dominoes, and participate in baseball leagues. The clubs were not licensed to dispense liquor, but cold beer and Puerto Rican rum were usually available to members. The clubs were named after towns in Puerto Rico. By the 1960s and 70s, second-generation Puerto Ricans in West Town and Humboldt Park began to acquire political and ethnic consciousness. This was the era of black civil rights and social movements. A new generation of community leaders developed. Puerto Rican painters, muralists, poets, writers, and community activists began to emerge. They began to assert and express their ethnic identity, pride, nationalism, and militancy.

One event that awakened the political consciousness of Puerto Ricans was a riot that occurred in West Town and Humboldt Park on June 12, 1966. On that hot summer day, Puerto Ricans celebrated their first, large ethnic parade in downtown Chicago. Thousands of spectators enjoyed the festive parade, and symbols of Puerto Rican culture. But that same evening things got ugly. Police shot a 20-year-old Puerto Rican man in the leg. The young man was involved in a street fight near Division Street and Damen Avenue. Police claimed he was armed, witnesses claimed he was not. More police were called in, including police canine units. A large crowd refused to disperse. One police officer allowed his large German shepherd dog to bite a Puerto Rican man on the leg. For Puerto Ricans, the dogs symbolized all their hurts, real or imagined. The crowd of over 4,000, many teenagers, attacked the police. They pelted police with rocks, bottles, and cans. They smashed the windows of police cars, set two police cars on fire, and overturned another police car. About 58 police squad cars arrived on the scene. More than a hundred police using tear gas and swinging their night sticks tried to disperse the crowd. Six additional police canine units with dozens of dogs were brought in. The sight of the large dogs only further enraged the crowd.[33]

"They brought out the police dogs, and the whole community just united. They just turned against the police officers," says Victor Flores, 54, who lives in East Humboldt Park. "I was nine at the time but I still recall it. It was on the television news. They showed the busted heads. The police came in cracking heads, believe me. They were throwing Molotov cocktails at police. They had police dogs and were letting the dogs go. It just went on and on. They were putting four police officers to a squad car with riot gear. Everywhere they would go, the cops would get bricked. There were a lot of older Puerto Rican men involved."[34] Many believed Puerto Ricans rioted not only because of police brutality, but because they were angry about prejudice, poor housing, and their menial, low-paying jobs. "Puerto Ricans were angry about a lot of things, and discrimination was a big problem," says Flores. "My parents came to Chicago in 1956 from San German, Puerto Rico. My father worked at Midway Airport washing dishes and maintenance. My mother worked in a sewing factory. We came to Humboldt Park in 1961. It was mostly Polish and Italian. When we moved to Humboldt Park and you tried to rent an apartment the white landlords would tell you we don't rent to Puerto Ricans.... My father used to drink, but he could not go to certain bars on Division Street because they would not serve him because he was Puerto Rican."

Several Catholic priests tried to plead with the crowds to stop the rioting. Yet Puerto Ricans rioted the next day and a third day. The riot moved to Western and California Avenues in Humboldt Park. Large crowds attacked and looted white-owned stores. Mayor Richard J. Daley was tempted to call the Illinois National Guard for assistance. Finally, police restored peace. All told, 16 people were injured, 49 arrested, and about 50 buildings were destroyed. City leaders were shocked that Puerto Ricans rioted. This was the first time Puerto Ricans in any major city had rioted. Chicago's Human Relations Commission held two days of public hearings to determine the causes of the riot. Puerto Rican speakers complained about abusive police, lack of jobs, bad housing, poor education, union discrimination, and poor city services. Yet the Commission's final written report, and several newspaper editorials, blamed the problems of Puerto Ricans on their inability to speak English and rapidly adjust in a new city.[35] The riot underscored the political powerlessness of Puerto Ricans. Mayor Richard J. Daley ruled Chicago from 1955 until his death in 1976. Yet Daley's political machine refused to give patronage jobs, contracts, or political power to Puerto Ricans.

Some Puerto Ricans believed the riot was a bad thing that would forever taint Puerto Ricans as looters, troublemakers, and ungrateful Chicagoans. But others believed the riot created a new spirit of militancy among Puerto Ricans. New community organizations emerged as a result of the riot. For instance, Mirta Ramirez and community leaders formed a neighborhood group called the Spanish Action Committee of Chicago (SACC). Shortly after the riot, SACC marched to City Hall demanding that Mayor Richard J. Daley address the concerns of Puerto Ricans. "The mayor met with some people from our group who they thought were the leaders," says Ramirez. "They always do that, that's how they break up groups. The mayor co-opted some of those leaders. Some got city jobs. He also appointed a few Puerto Ricans to city commissions. Some appeared in the newspapers with the mayor. Some people got a little city money for their social programs. The city established this little outpost, an Urban Progress Center on Division Street to provide social services."

But Democratic machine politicians viewed the organizing efforts of Puerto Ricans as a threat. They embarked on a divide-and-conquer strategy. The Chicago Police Department's Intelligence Division, known as the infamous Red Squad, infiltrated community groups like the SACC. The Red Squad employed undercover operatives, smear campaigns, and contrived press releases to discredit SACC as a "communist" group. Police pitted Mirta Ramirez and her husband against other members. "They labeled members as communists," says Ramirez. "I left SACC and the organization was discredited as a communist group and fell apart. The Red Squad used me and I used them.... I was naive about what Communism was. I'm not anymore. Now I don't believe in this country and anything they have to say. This isn't even anybody's country. It's just a whole bunch of millionaires ripping off everybody else." In the 1970s, Chicago's American Civil Liberties Union, sued the Red Squad for violating the free speech of community groups. The city entered into a federal, court-ordered consent decree to stop the spying. Ramirez went on to earn her bachelor's degree. She and other Puerto Rican community leaders became concerned about the few Puerto Ricans attending college. In 1968, they established Aspira Inc. of Illinois. Aspira was a national, nonprofit educational organization with chapters in various cities. The organization helped thousands of Puerto Rican and Latino youth complete high school and enroll in college.

Victor Flores also wanted to do something positive for the community. In 1982, he and his brother established the Just Cruising Bicycle Club. The club consisted of Puerto Ricans from Humboldt Park who remodeled and rode old Schwinn bikes. The bikes were in mint condition with old-fashioned features like banana-seats, stick shifts, shocks, and saddle bags. For decades, the Schwinn Bicycle Company, located in Humboldt Park, produced first-rate bikes for America. But in 1993, the company emerged from bankruptcy and moved to Colorado. "Our bikes are Schwinn bikes with balloon tires," says Flores. "We have bikes from the 1940s and 50s. Our members buy them at garage sales and swop meets. We then buy the parts for them. Some bikes cost about $500.00 to $3,000. We have about 50 members. Some are little kids, some are guys in their mid-20s, up to their 50s. We even have women members. We ride throughout the neighborhood, to the beach, and in the Puerto Rican parade.... With our club, we're doing something positive and healthy." Victor Flores' wife, Migalia, 54, is an active member of the bike club. She also helps feed the homeless. "One big event I do every year is a cook out for the homeless," says Migalia. "The club helps me. The homeless come from the neighborhood. They eat in front of my house. We set up a table and feed them. We have about 50 homeless people. About 50 pounds of cabrito (goat meat) is cooked. We cook it outside and make a huge pot of rice. We make them salad and we give them pop. The homeless are my number one priority for that day."

Lacking political power, Puerto Ricans in the 1960s and 70s voiced their concerns through demonstrations and protests. In 1967, young second-generation Puerto Ricans, like Jose (Cha Cha) Jimenez, formed the Young Lords Organization. A former street gang, the Young Lords was similar to the radical Black Panthers. In 1969, the Young Lords occupied the administration building of McCormick Theological Seminary. They wanted the Seminary and the city to help poor people on the Near North Side where the Young Lords lived.[36] Later that year, the Lords took over the Armitage United Methodist Church. They opened a day-care center and a breakfast program in the church's basement. The Young Lords took over urban renewal land at Armitage and Halsted to make a People's Park. But over the years, the Chicago police came down hard on the Young Lords. They arrested many of its leaders for minor infractions. The Young Lords disappeared by the mid-1970s. Jose Jimenez later tried to work within the system. In 1975, he took on the city's Democratic political machine. He ran for alderman of the 46th ward against a strong machine candidate. He was badly defeated. Puerto Ricans did not yet have the political know-how to beat the machine.

A highly visible Puerto Rican protest group formed in 1976 was the West Town Concerned Citizens Coalition (WTCCC). Rev. Jorge Morales, 58, was president of the WTCCC during the 1970s and 80s. He led many of the group's protests. "The Coalition served the neighborhoods of West Town and Humboldt Park. We were a thorn in the side of Mayor Jane Bryne," says Rev. Morales. "We held several noisy demonstrations against the city and the Chicago post office over the lack of Latino employees. We pressured the city to fix schools, clean neighborhoods, and provide more city services. Those things were important to our community."[37] Not all of WTCCC's programs were successful, however. In the mid-1980s, WTCCC set up a housing program, called the

Community Housing Education Corporation (CHEC) in Humboldt Park. CHEC
bought seven buildings they hoped to renovate and sell to low-income residents.
But CHEC was severely mismanaged and only one building was renovated. The
program misspent over a million dollars of city and state monies.[38] The WTCCC
still exists today as a social service agency.

Morales, his mother and five siblings came from Quebradillas, Puerto Rico
to Chicago in 1957. In 1983, he and other Puerto Ricans helped mayoral candidate Harold Washington campaign in Puerto Rican neighborhoods. Morales was
the former pastor of the First Congregational Church of Chicago in Humboldt
Park. He lamented the current lack of Puerto Rican grassroots protest organizations. "When Jane Byrne was mayor, we had neighborhood institutions and people who could make some noise and trouble," says Morales. "Who's making
trouble now? Who's protesting at City Hall? Nobody is saying to this mayor,
look you're lacking here or there. That's not happening because we don't have
the grass-roots leaders or local institutions. This city would be a lot more exciting if some of us were still out in the trenches taking on the powers that be....
Latino politicians speak for us sometimes. But we are voiceless. We need
greater local control over institutions. We don't have local neighborhood empowerment like before."

Politics of Puerto Rican Independence

Rev. Jorge Morales believed the problems Puerto Ricans in Chicago faced
were the direct result of Puerto Rico being a colony of the United States. "You
got young Puerto Ricans who come from an island that is neither a state nor a
republic," says Morales. "They don't know if they're black or white. We have a
lot of black Puerto Ricans and they have a real identity crisis. In my youth, there
were dozens of times I wanted to join a gang, or form a group to protect myself
against racial bigotry and violence.... You can take serious problems like drugs,
gangs, and lack of education and you can track it to the colonial situation of
Puerto Rico. For example, how much power do Puerto Ricans have over the
smuggling of drugs in Puerto Rico? Or how much power do Puerto Ricans have
over immigration in Puerto Rico. Many people come to the island from other
countries and take the good jobs. Puerto Ricans are forced to migrate to places
like Chicago. People have a right to self determination."

The political future of Puerto Rico is a controversial issue in Puerto Rican
communities. In the mid-1970s, a small Puerto Rican group, called the Fuerzas
Armadas de Liberacion Nacional, FALN, or Armed Forces of National Liberation, was a leading clandestine organization advocating armed resistance to U.S.
rule in Puerto Rico. Most FALN members were young, second-generation
Puerto Ricans from Chicago. The group was responsible for killing five people
and injuring about 70 in dozens of bombings of banks and government buildings
in Chicago and New York. In April 1980, police captured about a dozen FALN

members in the suburb of Evanston near Chicago. They later apprehended five other members. All were charged with seditious conspiracy to oppose the U.S. government. They were given sentences ranging from 35 to 105 years in jail.[39]

Josefina Rodríguez, 85, and her husband, Bernardo, came to Chicago from Puerto Rico in 1951. They both worked in factories and lived in the West Town neighborhood. In 1980 they were making plans to permanently return to Puerto Rico. But in April 1980, they received a telephone call with bad news: their two young daughters, Ida Luz, and Alicia, were arrested in Evanston and charged with being FALN members. Ida Luz was sentenced to 75 years in prison, and Alicia was sentenced to over 30 years in prison. Josefina and Bernardo decided to remain in Chicago and support their two daughters. "The arrest of my daughters was very painful for my husband and me," recalls Josefina. "How do we deal with this? We can't begin to cry because we will get nowhere. No, right now they need our support. It seems sometimes the stronger the pain, the stronger one gets. . Our daughters were separated and put in a lot of different state and federal prisons in West Virginia, San Diego, and New York. They were very cruel to them in those prisons. They had them in segregated cells for 23 hours. They had one of my daughters in a dungeon, a behavioral modification program. They were constantly monitored. We had demonstrations, and telephone and write-in campaigns demanding that prison officials treat them fairly."[40]

In college Ida Luz and Alicia had acquired an awareness of the poverty of Puerto Ricans in Chicago. Trips to Puerto Rico exposed them to poverty on the island. In Chicago in the early 1970s, the two sisters became community activists. They organize the Pedro Albizu Campos High School in a Presbyterian church basement. At the time of their arrest, Alicia was a biology student, and Ida Luz had a three-year-old son. For being FALN members, they both served eighteen years in prison. Interestingly, very few Puerto Rican believe in Puerto Rican independence. For example, in a nonbinding plebiscite in Puerto Rico in 1996, about 40 percent of Puerto Rico's residents voted that Puerto Rico should become the 51st U. S. state, another 40 percent voted that it should remain a U.S. Commonwealth. Only about 15 percent voted for Puerto Rico's independence.

Although few Puerto Ricans have supported independence, Rodríquez is convinced the personal sacrifices her daughters made were the right thing to do. "Historically Puerto Rico has fought for its independence," says Rodríquez. "Puerto Rico was a colony of Spain for 400 years, and a colony of the United States for 100 years. Was the insurrection at Lares worth it? Was the 1950s Puerto Rican Nationalist attack on U.S. Congressmen worth it? Yes, it was worth it. The world knows that Puerto Rico has the right to keep struggling for its independence. I see this struggle of these Puerto Rican political prisoners as a continuation of that long, hard struggle. When you develop a consciousness, you realize that la patria (the nation), like Pedro Albizu Campos said, is valor and sacrifice.... My daughters did what they did for the glory of la patria. As a mother, it hurts. I love them. But yes, it was worth it."

Human-rights activists and religious and political leaders from Chicago, and other countries, engaged in a letter writing campaign to former President Bill Clinton asking for the release of the FALN members. Many felt the prisoners had already served long prison terms. Others, including some Puerto Ricans, were against the release, viewing the FALN members as terrorists. In September 1999, former President Clinton granted conditional clemency to 11 FALN prisoners. Another prisoner will be released in a few years. Two prisoners refused the clemency offer and remained in prison. No leniency was granted to Carlos Torres, described as the leader of the FALN. Under the clemency terms, the former prisoners renounced violence and accepted conditions that prevented them from associating with one another. Nine of the former prisoners— including Ida Luz and Alicia Rodríguez—returned to Puerto Rico, where they felt the public was more sympathetic. Two stayed in Chicago.

In cities like Chicago, New York, and Connecticut advocates of Puerto Rican independence were criticized—by Puerto Ricans and others—as being too leftist, dogmatic, and out of touch with the day-to-day issues of Puerto Ricans.[41] Yet, many leaders and politicians in Chicago's Puerto Rican community believe in independence for Puerto Rico, although they denounced the use of violence. "The independence movement has not hurt the community," says José López, 56, a leader of the independence movement in Chicago. "If you look at most of the leadership of the Puerto Rican community anywhere, that leadership ultimately believes in independence. It shows that people who are involved in a thoughtful process must come to the conclusion that there's something wrong with the relationship between Puerto Rico and the United States.... Racism and colonialism are pretty much two faces of the same cone. Living in San Juan, or living in Humboldt Park, does not change your relationship to the dominant power structure. We just changed from an external colony to an internal colony.... For us, the issue of independence is a very important issue in trying to adopt and create a holistic approach to the Puerto Rican problem. The movement has also made tremendous contributions to creating a Puerto Rican identity in the arts, music, literature, and the entire spectrum."[42]

López and others have been involved in promoting a positive Puerto Rican identity by creating alternative high schools and active cultural centers in the West Town and Humboldt Park neighborhoods. In the 1970s, the Puerto Rican Cultural Center, the Pedro Albizu Campos High School, and the Segundo Ruiz Belvis Cultural Center were established in West Town. In 1993, the Pedro Albizu Campos Museum was opened in Humboldt Park. These cultural centers featured artistic workshops, poetry, folkloric dances, performances, exhibits, and theater on Puerto Rican culture. While other educated, professional Puerto Ricans have moved away from Humboldt Park to more middle-class neighborhoods in the city and suburbs, López remains committed to living in Humboldt Park. "I came to Chicago with my mother and my sisters and brothers in 1959," says López. "We came from San Sebastián, Puerto Rico. My parents were laborers. My mother worked in a laundry cleaner. My father came to Chicago in the late 1940s. My father worked in various factories, then he worked in a pipeline factory in Franklin Park, Illinois.... I've always lived in West Humboldt Park. I've lived here for 40 years."

López teaches Puerto Rican history classes at various Chicago colleges. He is the brother of Oscar López, one FALN member who refused former President Clinton's clemency offer. Oscar López is still in prison, where he faces another 20 years. For decades, the FBI has tried to connect José López to the FALN. In June 1983, about 70 FBI agents and Chicago police raided the Pedro Albizu Campos High School, looking for FALN connections. The raiders came away empty-handed, although they did nearly $25,000 worth of damage to the school. "The FBI has been engaged in a campaign to destroy the Puerto Rican independence movement since 1960. I spent six months in jail for refusing to testify before a grand jury about the FALN, and where my brother was," says López.

Some wonder if pro-independence groups hindered the progress of Puerto Rican communities in the past, by telling Puerto Ricans to shun electoral politics.[43] These days more pro-independence groups participate in electoral politics. "In high school I wanted to be a politician," recounts López. "I started to do political work with the regular Democratic Organization when I was 14. Around 1971, the Democratic Organization was thinking about running someone for state representative, and they were encouraging me to do it. I probably would have been the first Puerto Rican elected official. But I believed that electoral politics was not the answer. There was a time, based on a nationalist position of non-recognition of the colonial system, that I believed in non-participation in electoral politics. There's been a lot of struggles about that in the independence movement. It's changing. I personally have a lot of problems with the idea that electoral politics can really make fundamental changes." Despite his reservations about electoral politics, López maintained a close relationship with U.S. Rep. Luis Gutierrez (D-Ill.) and Billy Ocasio, alderman of the 26th ward. Rep. Gutierrez played a leading role in the letter-writing campaign to free the FALN members. Ocasio was instrumental in bringing the two steel Puerto Rican flags to Humboldt Park, and in getting the business strip there refurbished.

Boricua Culture and Pride

One aspect of Puerto Rican life that has been well organized is its cultural expressions. Puerto Ricans acquire an important sense of self-affirmation and joy when they celebrate their culture and heritage. For years, the West Town Concerned Citizens Coalition organized the annual Fiesta Boricua. This free, popular, day-long event brought famous Puerto Rican salsa bands to town. Noted local Puerto Rican painter, Gamaliel Ramirez, painted commemorative posters for Fiesta Boricua. The colorful posters stressed themes of education, music, and culture. Fiesta Boricua now takes place in early September. The event is sponsored by 26th ward alderman Billy Ocasio. Fiesta Boricua is held on Division Street, between the large, steel Puerto Rican flags. The Fiesta was one of the best attended, most popular cultural events in the city. In 2003, over 120,000 people from throughout the city attended. On three stages, famous Puerto Rican singers from New York and Puerto Rico treated the crowd to the hot sounds of salsa. Numerous vendors sold Puerto Rican food. The large crowd was jovial and danced in the streets.

Puerto Ricans love their salsa music. The music, probably more than any other art form, expressed their urban experiences. Some second-generation Puerto Ricans who were born in Chicago do not speak fluent Spanish, yet they understand Spanish, and take a deep liking to salsa. Salsa lyrics speak about love, urban pain, poverty, heroism, love of country, and endless human emotions. Once confined to neighborhood night clubs, many fancy downtown clubs featured national and local salsa bands. On weekends the clubs were jam-packed. Puerto Ricans also regularly listened to salsa music on several local radio stations. A pioneer of Spanish-language radio in Chicago was Elias Diaz y Perez, an early Puerto Rican migrant to Chicago. In 1953, Diaz y Perez set up a Spanish-language radio program, the "Radio Club Familiar." His radio program played for almost 50 years and featured Puerto Rican music, sports, and news. Diaz y Perez passed away in 2002.[44] A large medallion honoring Perez was placed on the sidewalk on Paseo Boricua.

Puerto Ricans of all ages also enjoy traditional Puerto Rican music. A group of artists formed the Puerto Rican Arts Alliance, which promoted Puerto Rican culture. The group organized photography exhibits and performances. They sponsored an annual, popular, one-day festival on the Puerto Rican cuarto. Excellent cuarto players from New York and Puerto Rico played at the festivals. The cuarto is a popular, guitar-type, musical instrument native to Puerto Rico. The cuarto's music is associated with the Jibaro, or rural people of Puerto Rico. When listening to cuarto music, many Puerto Ricans reminisced about Christmas celebrations, and gatherings with friends and family. The highlight cultural event in Chicago's Puerto Rican community is Fiestas Puertorriqueñas. Every June 15th to 20th, the Puerto Rican Parade Committee sponsors Fiestas Puertor-riqueñas, a celebration of Puerto Rican culture. The celebration included the annual, festive Puerto Rican Parade on Dearborn and Wacker on June 15th. Thousands of onlookers enjoyed about 80 colorful floats, marching bands, bike clubs, motorcycle clubs, salsa music, and other symbols of Puerto Rican culture. The Puerto Rican Parade Committee was criticized for allowing the alcohol industry to partly fund the parade. It is believed Puerto Ricans already have a disproportionately high level of alcohol abuse, and some felt the alcohol industry was only interested in promoting more alcohol consumption, especially among youth. In addition to the downtown parade, Fiestas Puertorriqueñas sponsored a week of cultural activities in Humboldt Park. Thousands of Puerto Ricans enjoyed the week-long festivities. The park was filled with food booths, carnival rides for children, and vendors selling Puerto Rican arts and crafts. Famous national and local groups sang salsa, merengue, and musica Jibara in the park.

In 1977, the Fiestas Puertorriqueñas celebration in the park was marred by violence. Some Puerto Rican teenagers were drinking beer and driving their cars recklessly through the park. There were reports of several gang members fighting against each other. Police arrived and began making arrests. A crowd gathered and took offense to the heavy-handed methods of police. A few individuals began throwing rocks at police. One tall, white police officer took out his gun, aimed and fired two shots into the crowd. The bullets hit two Puerto Ricans, Julio Osorio, and Rafael Cruz in the back. The two young men, in their mid-20s, were both killed. Police claimed Osorio was armed, but a gun was never found. More than 100 arrests were made.[45] Years later, the city of Chicago settled with the Osorio and Cruz families. Each family received over $325,000. In future Fiesta Puertorriqueñas celebrations, police banned cars from entering the park, and the festivities have been peaceful. A caravan of cars now rides through the neighborhood with horns blaring, and riders cheerfully waving large Puerto Rican flags.

During summer weekends, families enjoyed outings in Humboldt Park. Families watched Puerto Rican teams play organized 12-inch softball. Older men drank beer and played dominos on makeshift tables and chairs. Teenagers played basketball. Children and adults swam in the man-made beach. In addition, groups of musicians put on impromptu, small salsa bashes. The smell of Puerto Rican food lingered in the air. The United Cooks of Humboldt Park, an organization of eleven members, sold Puerto Rican food from their mobile kitchen vans. The members sold favorite Puerto Rican dishes like pescaito frito (fried fish), pasteles (plantin tamales stuffed with pork), and pincho de lechon (pork shish kebab). Smaller Puerto Rican push cart vendors, or piragueros, sold homemade coconut ice cream or ice cones. Puerto Ricans shared the park with other ethnic groups like African Americans, Mexicans, and white, young professionals.

The annual election of the president of the Puerto Rican Parade Committee is a major event in Humboldt Park. Thousands of Puerto Ricans voted for their favorite candidate. Various candidates campaigned heavily promising to improve the finances of the Committee and better promote Puerto Rican culture. Some candidates hoped to use the position as a springboard for future political office. Daniel Ramos, 76, was president of the Puerto Rican Parade Committee in 1985. "I immigrated to Chicago in 1952 from Utado, Puerto Rico," says Ramos. "I drove a taxi for many years. Then I started my small moving company, called Ramos Movers and Daughters. I have five daughters and now that I'm older they help me run the company. In the 1950s, Puerto Rican families moved a lot around the city, and it was my company that moved them.... One thing we did when I was president of the Puerto Rican Parade Committee was to have an annual party in Puerto Rico. The party consisted of twenty-five people who lived most of their lives in Chicago. They retired and moved back to Puerto Rico. They asked us to bring them delicious food from Chicago. They grew up with this food, and they missed it. We would take them Chicago-style pizza, Mexican tacos, and hotdogs from Maxwell Street."[46]

Ramos planned to retire, and his lifelong dream was to return to Puerto Rico. "I love Chicago. But I love Puerto Rico more. I want to return to Puerto Rico. In fact, I bought a small house in Manati, Puerto Rico. That's where my wife is from. I hope to make a nice profit when I sell my house here in Chicago." Ramos will indeed make a nice profit on his single-family, frame house. He is one of the few Puerto Rican families still living in West Town. Almost every house on his block has been renovated. "The whites have now replaced Puerto Ricans in West Town," says Ramos. "Look around, all you see are young white professionals jogging, walking expensive dogs, and riding bikes. Some of them are okay, but some are not very friendly.... You see that three-story, brownstone building across the street. That building was selling for about $30,000 fifteen years ago. Now they made them into three condominiums, each selling for more than $200,000. In a way it's good the area is gentrified. The price of my house has gone up. But how come the police were never around, and no one cared about this place when it was Puerto Rican? Now that the Puerto Ricans have left, the whole neighborhood is being fixed up."

Street Poet

One individual who expressed Puerto Rican culture through his poetry is David Hernandez, 60. He is a recognized poet, performer, and teacher of poetry. Hernandez writes about the urban experiences of Puerto Ricans. He is credited with sparking Chicago's poetry renaissance. Where poetry was once frowned upon, many yuppie bars now feature poetry readings. "I graduated from high school and went to Wright City College because I didn't want to get drafted in the Vietnam War," says Hernandez. "I got a student deferment.... In 1971, I self-published my first book of poems, Despertando/Waking Up, and sold over 2,000 copies for 50 cents each. I started reading my poetry to street gangs on the North Side. I used some of the street language that was around them and they loved it. In 1971, I founded "Street Sounds," a music performance ensemble. I have been reading and performing poetry for over 30 years."[47]

While Hernandez recited his poetry, Street Sounds played Afro-Cuban rhythms, pop, classical, and jazz music to accompany the poetry. Hernandez's extroverted narrative style, and the music, engaged the audience. His poetry was very street and yet eloquent. His poems were sad, angry, and outrageously funny. "Puerto Rican and Latino youth love my poetry," says Hernandez. "I now give performances in public schools, colleges, bars, and festivals. I write about urban experiences. I write about drugs, gangs, bad schools, and hanging out on street corners. I personally experienced many of those things.... The young people like the honesty in my poetry. They like the images. A lot of my poetry is very image-oriented. When I founded Street Sounds, I wanted to make poetry more accessible to the public. I wanted to get away from the wine-and-cheese crowd. I can be a street poet or just a poet. I do write from the street experience.... There is really nothing original about me. I listen well and steal images. I write at home, and then I give it back and people say, 'Wow, that's great'. They don't know that it's theirs."

Hernandez and his parents immigrated to Chicago in 1955 from Cidras, Puerto Rico. He lives in Humboldt Park. Hernandez hung out on the streets, has been in gangs, and suffered from alcoholism and drugs. He is a self-defined street poet, who believed poetry belonged to the people. Hernandez enjoyed teaching poetry and writing classes to youngsters and college students. But Hernandez is no longer just a street poet. He has been discovered by mainstream publishers. He published four books of poetry with large publishers. His poems have been published in many anthologies. He won numerous grants and awards from arts councils and civic groups. Success, age, a new marriage, and a new baby daughter seem to have mellowed Hernandez and his poetry. "I'm called the unofficial poet laureate of Chicago, because I wrote poems for Harold Washington's second inauguration in 1987. I do write from the street experience, but the street has gotten bigger. The images might have mellowed, but the intensity of the heat is still the same. My poetry lately is to celebrate life. Some of my stuff is honestly raw and hard-hitting. But there are ways of presenting it. I use a lot of humor."

A Museum?

Puerto Ricans have longed to establish a cultural center on Chicago Park District property in the Humboldt Park neighborhood. Years ago, the Chicago Park District donated park field houses to establish the successful DuSable Museum of African American History, and the National Museum of Mexican Art. Puerto Ricans hoped to set up a similar museum to showcase artwork by local and national Puerto Rican artists. Puerto Ricans were involved in numerous meetings with park officials, but the Puerto Rican museum did not materialize. "For the last twelve years, Puerto Ricans have tried to put together a museum on Chicago Park District property. Our local group, the Latin American Museum of Art, has been meeting with park officials. We want to open an arts museum in a renovated Humboldt Park building that was a former horse stable," says Oscar Martinez, 54, president of the group. "The Chicago Park District agreed.... What has slowed us are changes at the Park District. You have had different superintendents of the Park District. And every time you have a new superintendent you have to go back and start all over again."[48]

Martinez is a well-known muralist and painter in Chicago's Puerto Rican community. In the mid-1970s and 80s, he painted seven murals with high school students on the outside walls of buildings and in church basements. The murals expressed themes of Puerto Rican and Latino gentrification. Chicago Park District officials initially agreed to the concept of a Puerto Rican museum in the century-old, horse stable building in Humboldt Park. The Park District allocated $1 million in 1991 to restore the building's exterior. But the stable was set ablaze by arsonists in July 1991. The interior was severely damaged. Park officials then invested $3.7 million to restore the building's exterior. A few exhibits of Puerto Rican photography have been held in the handsome building during summer months. Yet it will take another $4 million to completely renovate the building's interior.

Many believed the Chicago Park District did not want to give the renovated building to the Puerto Rican community. Instead, it's believed the Park District wanted to use the renovated building for its own administrative purposes.[49] Puerto Ricans longingly looked across town and saw all the exciting cultural events sponsored by the National Museum of Mexican Art. They wanted a similar museum to showcase the best of their culture. But after years of endless meetings and talks with Chicago Park officials, many Puerto Ricans believed the planned museum would never happen.

However, a group of Puerto Rican artists, community leaders, and professionals formed a new group called the Institute of Puerto Rican Arts and Culture. This new group met with Chicago Park officials, and park officials recently signed a 15-year lease granting the new group the right to use the building as a Puerto Rican museum. The new group has held several photographic and cultural events inside the renovated building. Millions of dollars, however, still have to be raised to renovate the building's interior before it can be fully used as a museum. Puerto Ricans are hopeful the money will be raised, and they will finally have their long desired museum.

Chapter Four: Puerto Ricans

Father, Where Is Our Church?

Martha Hernandez, 76, recalls the confusion she and her sister felt when they first walked into a Catholic church in Chicago. It was 1952, and the sisters had just arrived to Chicago from Juyuya, Puerto Rico. Martha was 22, her sister 18, and they were looking for a church they could attend regularly. Martha's younger sister was also looking for a church where she and her future husband could marry. The sisters stepped into the massive Holy Name Cathedral in downtown Chicago. "We lived near Chicago's downtown so we walked to Holy Name Cathedral," recalls Hernandez. "But nobody there understood us. We only spoke Spanish and everyone in the church spoke English. My sister and I were frustrated that no one could communicate with us. My sister started crying. The priests thought my sister was crying because she had committed some big sin and wanted to confess. We left.... My sister cried a lot that night because no one at the church understood us."[1]

Hernandez and her sister searched for a Catholic parish where they could feel comfortable. They wanted a parish that celebrated mass and the sacraments in their native Spanish. "We later learned they spoke Spanish at a church called St. Francis of Assisi on Roosevelt Road," recalls Hernandez. "We would travel across the city by bus to attend St. Francis. We also learned of a church in South Chicago where they spoke Spanish, Our Lady of Guadalupe. We were so happy that the priests there spoke Spanish.... My younger sister was married in Our Lady of Guadalupe Church in 1952. Later, in 1954, I married at St. Francis of Assisi."

Hernandez's husband, Gilberto, immigrated to Chicago in 1952 and worked in the steel mills of Indiana. He later drove his own taxi in Chicago. He dreamed of earning money, saving, and then returning to Puerto Rico. "We had intentions of returning to Puerto Rico," recalls Hernandez. "We even bought a little farm. Yet we realized that educating our kids in Puerto Rico would be difficult, because my husband did not have a professional job. I did not work because I had to take care of my small children. My husband learned English here by listening to how others spoke it. My husband drove his own taxi for more than ten years. He also worked in a factory as a meat packer for many years. He worked in the freezer of the factory, where it was very cold.... My husband died in 1982 of cancer of the pancreas. He was 51 years old. His death was very hard on my family and me."

Through the years, Hernandez has remained very close to the Catholic Church. All her seven children attended Catholic schools. Six of her children finished college. She regularly attended St. Sylvester parish in Logan Square.

"Religion is very important in my life. I am very religious. Religion helps you maintain your family in order. We have two Spanish-language masses every Sunday at St. Sylvester and the church gets full.... Every summer I have a large gathering here in my house in memory of my deceased husband, brother, father, and mother. We have a special mass at St. Sylvester Church, and then everyone comes here to my house. It is mostly family and close friends. This year my six sisters and my brother were here, some came from Puerto Rico. All my cousins, nephews, and nieces were here. My sisters and I cook Puerto Rican food and everyone has a good time."

Hernandez worked as a teacher's aide for 24 years with the Chicago Board of Education. She retired and has lived in Logan Square for twenty years. She wished more Puerto Rican youngsters would attend church, and lead more spiritual, religious lives. "Just this week some kids came into my garden and took all the tomatoes, green peppers, and cucumbers I was growing. They had a tomato fight in the alley. That hurt me a lot. I worked so hard growing them all summer. I got angry and called the police. The police talked to some 10-year-old kids from the other block.... What concerns me are the teenagers. Some teenagers from this generation are rebellious and involved in drug selling and gangs. I blame the welfare program, because some parents got accustomed to not working. Their kids also got accustomed to not working. We gave our children the example of working constantly."

Like Hernandez, the majority of Puerto Ricans are Roman Catholic. The Archdiocese of Chicago first reached out to Puerto Ricans under the leadership of Auxiliary Bishop Bernard Sheil, founder of the Catholic Youth Organization (CYO). The CYO maintained its club house at Congress and Wabash streets. The organization started a Puerto Rican project to deal with housing, employment, and health problems. It also provided recreational events, like a weekly dance. By 1947 a Sociedad Catolica Puertorriqueña had been founded in Chicago under the auspices of the CYO.[2] Moreover, in 1955, Chicago's Cardinal Samuel Stritch set up the Cardinal's Committee for the Spanish Speaking. Under the director of Rev. Gilbert Carroll, and Rev. Leo T. Mahon, this group worked closely with Chicago's Puerto Rican community. However, to the dismay of Puerto Ricans, the first decision of the Cardinal's Committee was to rule out any national parishes for Puerto Ricans.[3] The Cardinal's Committee believed national parishes would prevent the assimilation of Puerto Ricans. They wanted Puerto Ricans to quickly assimilate into American Catholicism and culture. Also, after World War II, church officials were following their flock to the suburbs. Church officials believed any newly constructed city parishes might quickly become white elephants.

The Cardinal's Committee was composed mainly of white priests and lay persons. Puerto Ricans found some of the white priests to be paternalistic. But Puerto Ricans respected priests like Rev. Mahon and Rev. Donald Headley. Yet even Rev. Mahon and Rev. Headley did not understand that many Puerto Ricans, like previous white ethnic immigrants, wanted their own national ethnic parish. The ethnic parish was an institution that provided a sense of community, and validated the lives of previous immigrants. It helped immigrants adjust to a new and often hostile society.[4] But the Catholic Church never developed a cadre of Puerto Rican priests in Puerto Rico. Thus, Puerto Ricans came to Chicago without their own priests who could push for the formation of national parishes. Chicago's Catholic Church did not offer Puerto Ricans— American citizens by birth—a single ethnic parish of their own.[5]

Instead, Puerto Ricans were encouraged to attend existing neighborhood parishes. But during the 1950s and 60s, some white pastors and parishioners refused to welcome Puerto Ricans. They viewed Puerto Ricans as foreigners, as poor, dark-skinned people who did not speak English or assimilate to American ways. "Some parishes didn't want Puerto Ricans," recalls Rev. Mahon. "They said Puerto Ricans didn't have money to give to the church. Or they would scare the whites away. The attitude of the church told Puerto Ricans they were not welcomed. Or they told Puerto Ricans, 'don't come here, go to your church, go to St. Francis of Assisi.'"[6] Rev. Mahon, as director of the Cardinal's Committee for the Spanish Speaking, pushed hard to get Puerto Ricans accepted at certain parishes. "I would go to churches and say, 'Now wait just a minute here. In the name of God, these are Catholic people.' Churches wouldn't have masses in Spanish. Or they would put Puerto Ricans in the basement.... I remember the pastor of St. Mark's on Augusta and Campbell. That was the worst. It was a Polish area. Many Puerto Ricans were moving into the area. The church was new. I asked for an appointment with the pastor. He wouldn't even let me in the rectory. He stood by the door and said, 'There are no Puerto Ricans in this neighborhood.' I said, 'come off it. I'm going to the Cardinal to complain you won't accept your own people.' Then we did get a basement there to meet. But it was bad."

Some Catholic parishes refused to baptize or marry Puerto Ricans. However, some white parishes did open their doors to Puerto Ricans. During the 1950s and 60s, Puerto Rican families in Lincoln Park attended St. Michael's Church on Cleveland St. near North Avenue. But even St. Michael's held their Spanish-language, Sunday mass in a hallway, away from white parishioners in the main church. This solidly built church, with its tall steeple, was constructed in the mid-1800s to serve German Catholics. Puerto Ricans fondly recall the sense of community they felt at St. Michael's parish. Some Puerto Rican families placed their children in St. Michael's grammar school. Couples were married there. Today, Puerto Ricans still come to St. Michael's parish.

The Cardinal's Committee eventually folded. As white ethnics moved to other neighborhoods or the suburbs, Puerto Ricans claimed the Catholic parishes they left behind in neighborhoods like Logan Square, Humboldt Park, Wicker Park, and Avondale. In a few instances, Puerto Ricans had developed such a strong attachment to their sacred space in the parish basement, they wanted to remain there. Priests pleaded with them to come out of the basement and into the main church. Even though they were Catholic, some Puerto Ricans practiced a popular Catholic religion. Families, for example, maintained home altars. The altars contained burning candles, photos of decreased relatives, religious statues, and images of Catholic saints.[7] Puerto Ricans also adopted the Mexican tradition of quinceañeras. For instance, St. Philomena parish in Humboldt Park held twenty-nine quinceañeras in 1999; Puerto Rican families arranged about half, and Mexicans arranged the others. Some were small inexpensive affairs, others were expensive and elaborate.

Saving Souls and Pentecostalism

Increasingly, Puerto Ricans drifted from a Catholic Church they claimed was cold and distance. They converted to Protestant denominations like Adventists, Jehovah Witnesses, and evangelical Pentecostalism. For decades, evangelical proselytizers swelled the membership of their churches in Puerto Rico and Latin America. The total population of Pentecostal and charismatic Christians was more than 150 million, with more than a third in Latin America. Pentecostalism was by far the fastest growing movement in worldwide Christianity.[8] It was difficult to estimate how many Puerto Ricans in Chicago were joining Pentecostal churches. Yet many small, storefront Pentecostal churches, and Christian nondenominational churches, were springing up in Puerto Rican neighborhoods. Of about 400 churches in West Town, Humboldt Park and Logan Square, about 200 were Pentecostal. Members attended these small churches as often as four times a week to pray, sing, chant in ecstatic rituals, and socialize. Pentecostals followed the bible to the letter, spoke in tongues, practiced faith healing, and sometimes predicted the coming end of the world.

Puerto Ricans liked the smallness and intimacy of evangelical and Pentecostal churches, in contrast to the bureaucratic feel of Catholic and certain mainstream Protestant churches.[9] The small, storefront churches gave Puerto Ricans a sense of belonging and solace. Some Puerto Ricans viewed Catholic worship as dull. They were attracted to Pentecostal worship that was emotionally charged with lots of music and singing. "I was born Catholic. I was once an altar boy at St. Boniface parish. But when I attended a Catholic church, I could not connect with my Puerto Rican culture. You didn't have Hispanic priests or anyone you could relate to," says Rev. Tomas V. Sanabria, 53, pastor of Emmanuel Fellowship Church, a storefront Pentecostal church in Humboldt Park. "I would go to a huge Catholic church with over 1,000 people. You could get lost in there. No one really saw you. The priest was up there on the altar and your're down below. Everything was in English.... I wanted to learn about my language, my culture, and my people. I wanted Christ to be real in my life. The Catholic Church was not providing that for me. I converted to Pentecostalism in the early 1980s."[10]

Rev. Sanabria's mother immigrated to Chicago from Manati, Puerto Rico in 1953. He is the third of eight children. He experienced poverty and hunger in his childhood. "We ended up living in public housing projects. My parents divorced while I was young. I saw my father for the first time at age 21.... My younger brother, who had a different father from mine, met his father later in life. His father was no longer living with our mother. But the man denied that he was his father. That ripped my brother's heart apart. He got into violence and drugs and he died from consuming drugs. He passed away in the streets of Chicago. He was only 21." The death of his brother deeply affected Rev. Sanabria. He became a preacher to help others. He walked around Humboldt Park, bible tucked under his arm, and talked to people. He no longer sported a beard, drank, or smoke. He no longer listened to salsa music, he listened to Christian music. He led a clean, humble life. Unlike most Pentecostal preachers, he wore a white collar and black shirt similar to a Catholic priest. "The collar is a way of letting people know that I'm a man of God," he says. "It's a way of opening doors."

Another major reason early Puerto Rican arrivals to the city—and those who came later—were attracted to Pentecostalism was because charismatic preachers, like Rev. Sanabria, usually headed the churches. The preachers delivered religious services in Spanish, and they came from the same cultural background as their parishioners. The training to become a Pentecostal reverend is not as long and rigorous as it is to become a Catholic priest. Therefore, while there were few Puerto Rican Catholic priests in Chicago, there were many Puerto Rican Pentecostal reverends. Most were married with families, and many were small businessmen, janitors, steelworkers or cooks.[11] Rev. Sanabria was born and raised in Chicago. He delivered lively, passionate sermons which touched on the real-life problems affecting his parishioners. "We are more like a family than a regular church," says Lucia Martinez, 70, Puerto Rican and a member of Emmanuel Fellowship Church. "Rev. Sanabria is always looking after the welfare of my three kids. I have been raising my oldest daughter's two children, Stephanie, 12 and Robert, 10, for about ten years. I also adopted Brandon who is four. I take my kids with me to church. They like it because there are other kids at the church that they meet. The church does a lot of wonderful things with my kids. Stephanie is going to preach in church next Sunday. We have big wonderful meals at church. I enjoy cooking for our pastor and other church members."[12]

Martinez is a longtime resident of Humboldt Park. She was born in San Lorenzo, Puerto Rico. Her mother and stepfather immigrated to Chicago in 1944. She converted from Catholicism to Pentecostalism. Pentecostalism has a reputation of attracting the poor, the uneducated, and those with troubled lives. Some former alcoholics, drug addicts, and common criminals wishing to lead clean lives, often find comfort in small Pentecostal churches.[13] Martinez lived a hard, troubled life. "My first marriage ended in divorce. My husband started drinking a lot and was physically abusive with me," says Martinez. "I divorced him. I was alone and started drinking heavy at 21 while trying to raise two daughters. I come from a family of alcoholics. I was a functional alcoholic drinking vodka. I would work and hide my bottle. I lost my job because of my drinking. I was drunk for about 20 years. My second marriage also ended in divorce." Pentecostalism helped Martinez pull her life back together again. She stopped drinking. However, her daughter's life hit rock bottom. Her daughter abused alcohol and drugs. She was evicted from apartments and was temporarily homeless. Her daughter endangered the lives of her two young children, Stephanie, and Robert, by abusing drugs. The Department of Children and Family Services threatened to place Martinez's grandchildren in foster homes. Martinez stepped in and decided to raise her daughter's children.

"I was going to Wright College. I wanted to do something positive with my life," says Martinez. "But I decided to leave college so I could raise the kids. It's hard raising these kids by myself, especially as I get older. It's hard because the kids have been emotionally and physically damaged by the life style of their mother.... I'm on public assistance. I get a subsidy for Brandon and social security for Robert, but it's still hard to make ends meet. Welfare wants me to go to work. I told them I have small children at home to care for. I'm concerned they might cut off my welfare and social security benefits. But I don't worry about anything happening to my kids. My church helps me." Martinez dreamed of moving to a better neighborhood, and owning a small house. "I would like to live in a place with a nice, little yard in front, and a big back yard where my kids can play. A place where I can put up the basketball hoop that Robert wants. A yard where I can put a little pool for the kids. I cannot do that here, I don't have a back yard, just the alley. I can't do anything here."

Pentecostal congregations are small and independent. Their members are poor and working-class, and many churches financially struggled to survive. Some shut down after several years because members could not afford to pay rent or utilities. Rev. Sanabria has only 20 members in his church. His church rented space out of a storefront. But the building was sold and the new owner did not renew the church's lease. "We are now floating around without a church," says Rev. Sanabria. "It's sad that investors are pushing poor people out of this neighborhood. We are temporarily using another church nearby, but we cannot acquire that lot. I'm praying to God for direction. I'm sure he will provide for us and we will soon find another church."

Rev. Sanabria has faced adversity before. He once held Sunday services in a vacant lot filled with rocks and broken bottles. His parishioners pitched in and cleaned up the lot. They held services there for three months and then moved into a renovated storefront. Parishioners helped pay the storefront rent by giving up ten percent of their annual income and holding carwashes and bake sales. Besides running his church, Rev. Sanabria directed the Ekklesia Ministry of Help, a social service agency in Humboldt Park that helped needy families. He operated the agency from his three-story building. His agency operated on a shoestring. Rev. Sanabria is also a community activist. He hoped to slow down gentrification in Humboldt Park. He and other community activists wanted the city to seize up to 159 vacant lots in Humboldt Park. The lots would be turned over to private builders to construct low-income, affordable housing. Critics called the plan racist, and saw it as an attempt to keep middle-class whites from buying homes in the neighborhood.[14]

Pentecostalism is not beyond criticism. Some view the neighborhood igelesias as conservative and controlled by mostly white, larger organizations such as Assemblies of God or Church of God. Some conservative Pentecostal preachers maintained strict control over their congregations. They wanted their members to be in church up to four days a week, and not to be involved in "worldly things" like community activism. Pentecostalism is also criticized for its strict rules; members cannot drink, smoke, gamble, or dance. Some members liked the rules. But others, particularly teenagers, had a hard time adjusting to a solemn Pentecostal lifestyle. Many teenagers leave the Pentecostal faith because of it rigid doctrines and rules.[15]

Jose Velgara, 59, was raised as a Pentecostal. His parents came from Santurce, Puerto Rico to Chicago in 1951. They lived in Humboldt Park. Velgara had a difficult time adjusting to the Pentecostal religion. "I was raised in the Pentecostal church. I never seemed to pick up on it because I guess I didn't like-it. My parents were hard-working people. My father and mother worked in factories. My dad became a well-known pastor in his own church on Ashland Avenue. My dad raised my two brothers, my sister, and me right, but he was very strict. I spent too much time with my parents because they were always into the church. I would go with them back and forth to church.... But as a kid, I never had real, honest family time. The Pentecostal religion was too strict. You couldn't smoke, you couldn't drink, and you couldn't dance. No parties or nothing. We used to go church Tuesday, Wednesday, Saturday, and Sunday. It was awful."[16]

Velgara broke away from the church. He dropped out of high school and searched for meaning in his life. In 1964, while the Vietnam War was raging, he voluntarily joined the United States Marine Corps. He was only 17-years-old yet he saw combat throughout his first year in Vietnam. "I wanted to do something in the world. I thought maybe the United States Marine Corps would help me.... I can't say I was afraid of death in Vietnam. I saw a lot of American boys killed and wounded in Vietnam. I was scared being in Vietnam, but I didn't mind it. I felt patriotic. I mean I'm American. I'll fight to my death for the United States." After a year in Vietnam, Velgara came back to the United States. But he could not readjust to civilian life and the strict rules of his Pentecostal family. He rejoined the Marines and saw another two years of combat. He was promoted to Sergeant and became a helicopter machine gunner. His religious upbringing taught him that killing human beings was wrong. But Velgara believed killing in war was different. "Killing in war is not something you're afraid to do. You need to do it to save yourself. I was in a banana helicopter. We had machine guns with 50-caliber, armor-piercing bullets on each open side of the helicopter. We would go into enemy territory and you see things exploding everywhere. You see the enemy coming at you and you're shooting down at them trying to keep them away. You go in and pick up the wounded American boys, the burned ones, the dead ones, and our reconnaissance guys." Miraculously, Velgara was never wounded in combat. He says God protected him. "There were times when the helicopter was shot up with holes in it. The bullets didn't even hit me. It was like God blessed me. On the front of my helmet I carried a little cross. God protected me. I'm not really religious, but my parents are very religious. They believed in the Lord and prayed for me."

The Pentecostal faith is also criticized for being male dominated. Women's roles within the church are secondary and limited. The church had strict rules telling women how they should behave in church, at home, and in public.[17] "Not all Pentecostal churches emphasize strict rules," says Rev. Sanabria. "Moderate Pentecostal churches say dress moderately. We do not put many rules and regulations. We say live your life in this world. We hope that with your faith, you can choose the right things. Our members don't complain about rules. In church they are happy, they are jumping for joy."

In Pentecostal churches some members indeed jump for joy, and work themselves into a highly excited, delirious state where they speak in "tongues," or unknown languages which are only familiar to other Pentecostal members. To outsiders, the practice of speaking in "tongues" is strange. Yet to Pentecostals, it is natural. "Sometimes people get moved with emotions and speak in tongues," explains Rev. Sanabria. "Those are true gifts. It is like an out-of-body experience. Suddenly your mouth starts babbling. You're speaking the word of God. While one person is speaking in tongues, another person should be interpreting what that person is saying. Or maybe that same person may have the interpretation. It used to blow me away whenever I heard someone speak tongues. I'm not one to speak in tongues, but some of my congregation speaks in tongues. In church, I have never seen anybody fool around. They speak in tongues because they feel the spirit."

The Catholic Church has tried to halt the exodus of Puerto Ricans to Pentecostalism. Catholics introduced the Cursillo Movement on a large scale after 1960. These "Little Courses in Christianity" used instruction by lay persons to transform Catholicism to a vital practice of faith. Personal testimony by laity and group dynamics, made the Cursillo into a Catholic version of a Protestant conversion experience.[18] Later, Catholics introduced the Charismatic Catholic Movement. It incorporated Pentecostal features within the Catholic Church. Some parishes in Puerto Rican neighborhoods regularly held charismatic masses. Yet during mass, the religious emotionalism of charismatic Catholics was subdued compared with Pentecostals. The singing, dancing, hand-clapping, and foot-stomping were not as loud or spontaneous as it was in Pentecostal churches.

Rough Start in School

Spotting Puerto Rican children in the primary grades of Chicago's public schools during the 1950s and 1960s was easy. They were usually taller, older, and sat quietly by themselves at a corner table. While other bright-eyed children busily read and practiced math, a good number of Puerto Rican children sat day-dreaming, doodling, or playing with toys. These Puerto Rican children were usually new arrivals from Puerto Rico to Chicago. They did not speak English, and teachers did not have the slightest clue of how to teach them English. Instead, first and second grade teachers put the Puerto Rican kids—some as old as ten or eleven—in a corner and hoped that by listening, they would learn English. At the time, elementary schools did not have Spanish-speaking teachers or bilingual education programs.[19] Because some Puerto Rican children did not know English, teachers often labeled them as "slow learners," tracked them into remedial classes, or forced them to repeat grades.

That is what happened to the Puerto Rican poet David Hernandez.. "I was nine-years-old when I came to Chicago in 1955. I was supposed to be in fourth grade. But the Chicago public schools put me in first grade because I couldn't speak English," says Hernandez. "The same thing happened to my cousins. It was very demeaning. I didn't understand things in English. In Puerto Rico the school bell rang twice, once to let you in and once to go home. In Chicago, my mother told me when the school bell rang, I should come home. Well, when the bell rang at recess or at lunch time, I would go home. Once I got busted by the truant officer who thought I was cutting classes. So then they put me in learning disabled classes. It took me about a year to learn English. Later, when you learned English, they put you in the grade in which you were supposed to be. But not always. My best friend Joe Perez quit school at eight grade because they held him back so much. He became frustrated and quit."[20]

Former Illinois state senator Miguel del Valle (D-Chicago), 55, had a similar experience. "My father came from Vega Baja, Puerto Rico to Chicago in 1952. He came looking for work," says del Valle "I arrived in Chicago in 1956 from Puerto Rico. I came with my mother and two younger brothers. We lived in the old Lincoln Park neighborhood. My parents worked for many years at Chicago Zenith television factory. My parents didn't speak English and I didn't speak English. I enrolled at age six at Immaculate Conception School. The nuns put me in the first grade. They put me in a corner with two other Latino kids who did not speak English. While other kids were learning, they gave us table games to play with. It was a terrible experience. At the end of the year they asked that my mother come to school. She brought someone to translate. The nun informed her that since I did not know how to speak English, I had to repeat first grade.... That was my first experience with failure."[21] Miguel del Valle did not let his first negative school experience dampen his quest for learning. "I transferred from Catholic school to a public school. I went to Wicker Park school for first grade and I did learn English. I had a great teacher in third grade who motivated me. I did so well I was double-promoted. I caught up."

The Division Street riot of June 1966, forced Chicago public school officials to pay attention to the needs of Puerto Rican children. School officials re-

ceived federal monies to provide daily, 35-minute lessons in English to students
who spoke only Spanish. Also, in 1968, four Chicago public school teachers
traveled to Puerto Rico to learn about Puerto Rican culture. Upon returning, they
published a report to help other teachers better understand Puerto Rican children. But the report stereotyped Puerto Ricans as simple, loud, somewhat culturally backward people, who did not understand important American values like
punctuality.[22] Latino parents came together realizing that Latino children were
doing poorly in school simply because they did not understand English. Puerto
Rican, Mexican, and Cuban parents pressured state politicians to pass a manda-
tory bilingual education program. In 1976, Illinois passed legislation requiring
that school systems with twenty or more children of limited English-speaking
ability provide transitional bilingual education. The Chicago public schools
eventually offered bilingual education in over 30 different foreign languages,
with Spanish being the biggest program.

School officials hired many bilingual Latino teachers. These teachers came
to the classroom with a heightened sensitivity toward Latino students. One such
teacher was Mirna Diaz Ortiz, 53, who has worked with the Chicago Board of
Education for over twenty-three years. She climbed up the ranks of the school
system. She was a teacher, bilingual coordinator, and assistant principal. She is
now principal of Alfred Nobel School in Humboldt Park. The public school is
half Mexican and a third Puerto Rican. "When I got here over eleven years ago,
this school was one of 100 lowest achieving schools," recalls Ortiz. "We
changed that pretty quickly. I changed over half my staff. We have teachers who
are Hispanic, African American, and white. You really need compassion as a
teacher. I tell my teachers to respect students. If you have an indifferent or defeatist attitude, then you really don't belong in teaching. There is a lot of respect
and pride among the teachers and students. Teachers are really encouraging students. The students are doing very well. Parents are involved in the school. It
proves that it's possible to implement a rigorous educational program if you
challenge students and work with parents."[23]

Before Ortiz arrived at Nobel, the school was dark and dirty. Very little
learning was taking place. Children walked the halls with no bounce in their
step. The school is now immaculately clean and bustling with learning. Children's artwork and school papers were prominently displayed in the hallways.
Colorful wall murals, painted by students, adorned the school. Preschoolers and
eighth graders unexpectedly dropped into the principal's office just to say hello
and hug "Mrs. Ortiz." Ortiz's parents came from Caguas, Puerto Rico to Chicago in 1949. Her parents, like many first-generation Puerto Ricans, had very
little formal education. But her parents dreamed that their children would become educated. Her parents worked hard in factories and sacrificed to put their
six children through Catholic elementary schools. Ortiz's first taste of schooling
was scary. "I attended kindergarten at St. Santa Maria de la Raza School. I was a
good student," recalls Ortiz. "But I only spoke Spanish. I was trying to find
someone in class to talk to. I was speaking Spanish and the nuns didn't like that.

So they put masking tape over my mouth. I would walk around all day with my mouth taped and they would put me to sleep. I told my mother all they did was tape my mouth all day and put me to sleep. I left kindergarten after two months. I told my mother I would rather stay home.... I learned English by watching television. Later, I returned to that school for first grade. By then I was an angel. They didn't tape my mouth anymore."

Ortiz's office is lined with awards she has earned for excellence in teaching and administration. In 1998, of nearly 500 principals, the Chicago public schools recognized Ortiz as one of 20 outstanding principals. Sadly, her parents never got the chance to see her become a principal. "My mother and father were my heroes," says Ortiz. "Picture yourself coming from Puerto Rico to America without speaking a word of English. Not really knowing what you're going to do. My parents really struggled. My mother not only helped her children, she brought over her mother, sisters, brothers, and cousins from Puerto Rico to Chicago. She took care of them and helped them find jobs. She was the center of the family. She got to see me graduate from college and become a teacher. She was so proud. She knew I was studying to be a principal when she died. My father and mother were 56 and died of liver cancer." Ortiz has identical twin daughters, and a stepdaughter. Her daughters were in college studying to become teachers.

In 1997, a new elementary school, Nobel West was built to relieve overcrowding at Nobel. The two schools are half a block away, but Noble was still overcrowded. Nevertheless, children at Nobel enjoy learning. "Our reading and math scores are up. Our student attendance rate is over 95 percent," says Ortiz . "We created a school band, a student choir, a sports program, a chess club, an art club, and a jazz band. We started everything from scratch. Our students want to come to school. We created a school with pride. Some of our kids don't make it. They end up in jail or in drugs. But many of our kids make it. I have a student who is at Harvard University. He's going to become a medical doctor. He started here in the bilingual program. One of my former students is now a public teacher."

Better Schools

Over the years, parents complained about the poor conditions of public schools in Puerto Rican neighborhoods. Many schools were overcrowded and falling apart. Kids were packed into old, mobile classrooms. Parents often had to protest to get basic improvements in their local schools. For instance, in 1989, Puerto Rican and Mexican parents at four elementary schools in Logan Square marched to Chicago Board of Education headquarters demanding expansions at their schools. In the mid-1990s, each school won a sizable addition with new classrooms. The parents also picketed the board for a new middle school. Their efforts paid off, and in 1998, the spacious, new Ames Middle School opened in Logan Square. Some Puerto Rican parents praised the efforts of Mayor Richard

M. Daley and his School Reform Board of Trustees in improving schools. But in the process of improving schools, some parents wondered if school administrators were trying to take away the decision making powers of Local School Councils (LSCs). Parents worried where the lines would be drawn between the reform board's authority, and that of their LSCs. The board has taken unprecedented actions such as hiring interim principals in troubled schools. The hiring and placement of principals seemed to step on the LSCs' turf.

Moreover, some LSCs were concerned that school officials repeatedly have tried to take away their authority to spend $261 million in Chapter One, anti-poverty funds that the state of Illinois allocates to Chicago schools each year.[24] "I think overall Mayor Richard M. Daley, and his school team have been good for the Latino community as to improving education," says former state senator Miguel del Valle. "I'm not giving them all the credit. The community made a lot of the improvements happen. But this School Reform Board came in with a mind set that is getting the job done. School improvements that were impossible before are now being done.... I don't think the school board is intentionally trying to weaken the role of local school councils and take away their authority. They just want to see things happen faster."

Former Chicago school board president Gery Chico insisted that school officials were not trying to weaken the authority of local school councils when he was board president from 1991 to 2001. "Critics criticize for political reasons," says Chico "They don't like Mayor Daley. They don't like me. Why? Because we're successful. Could you believe in your heart of hearts that some critics don't acknowledge that we're done anything good? We've accomplished labor peace with teachers, balanced budgets, done school construction, rising test scores. We have an excellent relationship with the vast majority of local school councils. We work great, I respect their authority and they respect ours. They have a quarter of a million dollars to spend as they see fit. But the local councils decide how to spend that anti-poverty money."[25]

The Dropout Problem

During the early 1970s, Puerto Rican parents were concerned about the high rate of students dropping out of high school. In 1971, one report found that 71.2 percent of Puerto Ricans dropped out of high school. Some left because of gang intimidation, some because of teenage pregnancy, and some found the school curriculum boring and unchallenging.[26] The dropout problem was particularly troublesome at Tuley High School in the Humboldt Park community. Tuley was once Polish, but during the 1970s, it changed over to Puerto Rican. Some Puerto Rican students complained that some teachers seemed to resent their presence. "Some Puerto Rican students and I organized student demonstrations at Tuley to protest the conduct of a white history teacher," recalls former state senator Miguel del Valle. "This teacher would call Latinas "Chiquita Banana" and he would pinch them. He was disrespectful to Latinas. That was my first experience in community organizing."

Puerto Rican students complained that Tuley's principal, Herbert J. Fink, was very hard on them. Many believed Fink was actually "pushing" Puerto Ricans out of high school by expelling them for breaking simple rules. "Fink was a very strict disciplinarian. He was anti-Semitic and anti-Latino. He didn't want students or teachers talking Spanish. Students would turn 16-years-old and their birthday gift was that he would kick them out of school for the slightest things. There was no second chance," recalls Aracelis Figueora, 70, a former counselor at Tuley. "Latina mothers came to school and dropped to their knees crying and begging Fink not to drop their kids. But he had no compassion, he was destroying lives. The dropout rate was scandalous. My anger was so intense, it's even hard for me to talk about it today."[27]

Figueora came to Chicago in 1951 from Humacao, Puerto Rico. She came alone as a 14-year-old to live with a sister in Chicago. "The reason my parents sent me to live with my sister in Chicago, is because they did not approve of my boyfriend," recalls Figueroa. "He was a dark-skinned Puerto Rican. My father, who had an English background, was highly prejudiced. He said he preferred if I dated a shoe shine boy, instead of a black Puerto Rican. So they sent me to Chicago so I would stop seeing my boyfriend." Figueroa was formerly a high ranking district superintendent for the Chicago public schools. She is now a teacher in an alternative high school. Figueroa recalls that students and teachers alike feared Fink. "Fink was crazy and had a dual personality. On one hand, he walked the halls with a measuring tape measuring the skirts of female students and teachers to see if they were so many inches above the knee. Yet, he was carrying on a shameless affair with a young teacher while he was a married man. He was hypocritical, he wanted to be a stern disciplinarian, but was setting a poor example. Students could not wear armbands to school to protest the Vietnam War. Fink stifled the self-expression of students.... He was also successful in dividing the Hispanics on his faculty. Some supported him and some of us did not."

Finally, Puerto Rican students demanded Fink's removal as principal of Tuley. They organized walkouts, demonstrations, and sit-ins. In February of 1973, students staged a demonstration in front of the school. Many police arrived on the scene. Scuffles between students supporting Fink, and those demanding his ouster, erupted. Police stepped in and began to rough up the protesters. Youths in the crowd began throwing rocks and bottles at the police. Six policemen were injured and 30 youths were arrested.[28] Shortly after the confrontation with police, Fink was removed as principal. He was promoted to a high administrative position at the board's downtown headquarters. Besides the removal of Fink, Puerto Rican students and parents demanded that a new high school be build to replace the old Tuley. In 1973, a new $15 million, nine-story high school was built on Division and Western to replace the old Tuley. The school was named in honor of the late Puerto Rican baseball star and humanitarian Roberto Clemente.

Figueroa was impressed with how Mayor Richard M. Daley, and school official were repairing and renovating public schools. She questioned, however,
whether the public school system was becoming politicized. "Many people with
experience and expertise are leaving the Chicago public schools," says Figueroa.
"And the people who are replacing them are coming without expertise straight
from City Hall. They are even moving the school headquarters back downtown,
so it becomes politicized. This mayor is having a tighter grip on the public
school system than his father did. Administrative positions at the Chicago board
of education are being used to pay political debts. So through the employment
and awarding of contracts, it's a very politicized system."

Despite the construction of Roberto Clemente High School, many Puerto
Rican students continued to drop out of school. In 1984, a group of about 700
parents, students, and community residents held a candlelight march in Logan
Square to underscore the dropout problem. The carrying of a coffin dramatized
the plight of Latino youth who drop out of school, and are victims of gangs and
street violence. The group was hoping that the march would create a citywide
coalition of parents, educators, and politicians to tackle the dropout problem.
But no citywide coalition was formed.

Some believed Chicago public schools needed more Latino counselors to
help Puerto Rican students finish high school. "You need mentors and counselors who can work closely with Latino students, guiding them and helping them
stay in school and plan for college," says Aida Sánchez, 54, former executive
director of Aspira Inc. of Illinois, an educational agency in the Puerto Rican
community. "You need to motivate them and show them they have the potential
and ability to make it. You also have to work closely with them on a road map
of how to get there. Most Puerto Rican students do not come from families with
professionals. They need close guidance. In most public high schools you have
maybe six counselors for over 2,000 students. Kids drop out of school because
of lack of supportive services inside and outside the school. You have to work
with kids from a very comprehensive perspective, doing whatever it takes to
motivate them."[29]

Sánchez's parents came to Chicago in 1953 from San Lorenzo, Puerto Rico.
They worked in factories. She was raised in Humboldt Park. She says community-based programs like Aspira are crucial in helping Puerto Rican students
remain in high school and proceed on to college. "I attended public elementary
schools and I graduated from Tuley High School in 1970," says Sánchez. "After high school, I was worked doing secretarial work. Then Aspira got a hold of
me and got me a scholarship to attend Rosary College. Had it not been for the
scholarship, I don't think I would have gone to college. Tuition at Rosary was
$6,000 a year. There was no way my parents could afford that. That is why fi-
nancial aid is so important for Latino students. I then graduated with a master's
degree." Sánchez is a director at the Chicago Community Trust, where she gives
grants to community agencies working with families.

Can I Go To College?

In the early 1970s, about a dozen Puerto Rican college students met with administrators of Northeastern Illinois University on the city's far North Side. This public, state university, with its sprawling lawns, was nestled in a middle-class, residential Jewish neighborhood. The students pointed out that of over 8,000 students at the university, only a handful were Latino. The students demanded that university officials give them a Puerto Rican counselor, and start a recruitment program to bring in more Latino students. University officials argued that a recruitment program for minority and black students already existed on campus. But Puerto Rican students insisted on having their own program. University officials conceded to the students' demands. In 1971, the recruitment program, Projecto Pa'lante or Project Forward, was born. Maximino DeJesus Torres, 74, was selected by the students to be the director of the program. The program's first group of about 80 Latino students entered the university in 1972. "Some students who founded Projecto Pa'lante had tried to come to Northeastern, and the university rejected them," recalls Torres. "They had to go to a junior college first. There were no academic support programs at the university for Latino students who graduated from public high schools ill-prepared do deal with college.... The students had political consciousness. They wanted a program to recruit about one hundred Latino students each year to the university, and student support services to ensure they graduated. The university administrators gave the students the recruitment program because it realized it was not meeting the needs of urban Latino students."[30]

Puerto Rican students greeted Torres on his first day of work. They walked excitedly to see his new office. But what they saw angered the students; the furniture, including the desk, chairs, typewriter, and filing cabinets were old and used. The small sofa had only three legs, a brick served as the fourth leg. "The used furniture symbolized things to the students. It symbolized distain for you and your director," says Torres. "It said that you came here by your pushing, advocacy, and activism. In higher education, you don't do that, people come here by their merits and degrees. The students decided to pick up the furniture and dump it in the president's office. I tried to stop them, I had to be a professional. They took the furniture, walked through the halls, and dumped it in the president's office. The president was not there that day, but the vice-president was amazed. Everybody was shocked. They contacted the president who was out of town at a conference. The next day they gave me all brand new furniture."

Torres had planned to become a Catholic priest. But he gave up the seminary and came to Chicago in 1952. He labored at odd laborer jobs like shipping clerk. Later he joined the United States Air Force. "When I got out of the Air Force, I decided to attend college. I graduated from Northeastern Illinois University in 1965," says Torres. "At that time, this was a teacher's college. When I attended here, there were three Hispanics. I was probably the first Puerto Rican to graduate from here. I worked as a teacher in public and Catholic elementary schools. I liked teaching but the pay was awful." Projecto Pa'lante recruited Latino students and helped them obtain financial aid. Besides Projecto Pa'lante, students started a student organization on campus called the Union for Puerto Rican Students, UPRS. Torres became faculty advisor to the UPRS. The organization held cultural events and dances. The UPRS used protests and sit-ins to pressure university administrators to implement student support programs in English, reading, and math. "Some faculty here labeled the students as activists and militants. They labeled me as an instigator," recalls Torres. "They did not want the students here and said they would lower the academic standards. Some faculty wanted students to attend a junior college. They did not realize that the Puerto Rican students would improve the university. But many white liberal faculty were very supportive of the program and the students.... Many support programs the UPRS pushed for, the university replicated for black and white students."

The UPRS pressured university administrators to hire more Latino faculty. One Puerto Rican professor the students brought to Northeastern was Samuel Betances, 65, who was educated at Harvard. Betances was born in New York and came to Chicago in 1958. He was a professor of sociology at Northeastern for 23 years. "The students at Northeastern had legitimate demands," recalls Betances. "They wanted studies that were relevant. They wanted badly needed support services and faculty members who understood them. They were very articulate in espousing their demands. The students brought in people who cared. The students recruited me, and I cared very much.... I think I helped generations of young Latinos. I helped a lot of people to appreciate race and ethnic relations, and to reduce prejudice and create teamwork. I think symbolically I served as a role model to Puerto Rican students."[31] During the late 1970s, the leadership of the UPRS changed and the group became more political. Student leaders increasingly espoused the politics of Puerto Rican independence from the United States. The political nature of the UPRS turned some students off. Some Puerto Rican students broke away from the UPRS, and started a less political student organization.

The split pitted students against each other. Puerto Rican students, who were once friends, stopped speaking to each other. Puerto Rican students began fist fighting with each in the halls of Northeastern. One student suffered a bloody lip, another a black eye. Leaders of the UPRS accused certain Puerto Rican faculty of being "sellouts," and abandoning the cause of Puerto Rican independence. Puerto Rican students marched outside the office of a high-ranking Puerto Rican vice-president the university had hired. The students accused him of being a "puppet of the university administration." The confused vice president resigned in disgust, and said the damn job was not worth a heart attack. Puerto Rican faculty on campus became divided. A few supported students in the UPRS. Others condemned the fist fights and personal attacks on Puerto Rican faculty as unprofessional, gang-like behavior. Students began boycotting the classes of Puerto Rican and Cuban faculty they perceived as "sell-outs." Students turned on Maximino Torres when he resigned as faculty advisor to the UPRS. They jeered him in the hallways of Northeastern. "Students had allowed themselves to get sidetracked by the politics of Puerto Rican independence," says Torres. "They were politicizing the UPRS, a student organization created for the betterment of students in the college. Some of those students were using violence against other students and I could not support that. During that time, I took a leave of absence for a year without pay."

Some students in the UPRS published a newspaper with disparaging articles about Torres and Samuel Betances. The students learned that Betances was providing race relations training to the U.S. Department of Defense. They then jumped to the wild conclusion that he was a CIA agent. Students taunted Betances inside the university, and heckled him at his outside speaking engagements. "It was a very painful time," recalls Betances. "These students were making false accusations. I came close to deciding that life was not worth living.... Puerto Rican students said to the university, 'give us professors.' Then they turn on us because the students and their sponsors wanted to control us, and have us say nasty things about the United States.... What they wanted everyone to believe is that you cannot make it in the United States, that there is nothing good in this country. So here I am, a person of color, a Puerto Rican who grew up on welfare. Then I make it from poverty, graduate from Harvard University, and now I am a professor of sociology. They see me and say, 'this guy must have sold out.' That drove them to want to destroy me.... We were interested in the independence of Puerto Rico. But we were also conscious that you can't build nationhood unless you are educated. They looked upon us as the enemy. That is one of the most tragic chapters in the history of the Puerto Rican community in Chicago: the day young people recruited to gain an education, behaved like scorpions spewing venom." Betances stayed at Northeastern and weathered the storm. "I stayed because I didn't want to be driven out. History has shown that I was not what they said. They said I was a CIA agent and I was not. They said I was betraying my people and I did not. I'm glad I'm still living three blocks away from Northeastern as professor emeritus. Those people have to swallow all those awful, nasty charges they made about me."

A couple of Puerto Rican students from the UPRS eventually got involved in the FALN, or Armed Forces of National Liberation, a clandestine group that advocated armed resistance to U.S. rule in Puerto Rico. One FALN member, a former student leader from the UPRS, turned state's witness and provided testimony against the others. The fights and heated disagreements between Puerto Rican students and faculty at Northeastern ceased after a couple of years. Yet the hurt lingered for a long time. "A lot of students got turned off by the politics and fighting," says Torres. "It created a bad reputation for the program, the students, and the university. Puerto Rican students got turned off being identified with Puerto Rico and Puerto Ricanness. Thank God, we overcame that, but at the expense of many people."

Many Puerto Ricans in prominent positions in Chicago got their start and graduated from Northeastern. The university has one of the largest Latino student populations in Illinois. Maximino Torres retired after 28 years at Northeastern. "Projecto Pa'lante has been successful. Not just because of me, but because of the students and others who work in the program," says Torres. "I would say about 27 percent of the Latino students graduate from the program each year. That is a high number considering that many students come with academic limitations. I wish it were higher, but sometimes our young people squander the opportunities offered to them. One great thing Projecto Pa'lante did was open the door wide open for Hispanic students. My fondest memory was seeing Latino students graduate from the university."

No More Drugs

Angela Rodriguez sat in the living room of her modern condominium, in the west side of the Humboldt Park neighborhood. She watched over her two, young grandchildren. Although she is only 43-years-old, she has lived a hard life. She was involved in abusive relationships, drugs, welfare, and prison. She dreamed of overcoming the hard times and adversity in her life. "I'm not married. I was married three times, and each lasted about two years," says Rodriguez. "From my marriages, I have a 16-year-old son and a 17-year-old daughter. The marriages didn't work because my husbands were emotionally and physically abusive with me. They liked to take hard drugs, or alcohol, and they refused to work. They wanted to punch and beat me and I wouldn't allow for it. After being abused all my life by my mom and various stepfathers, I just refused to go through that in a marriage. I wasn't brought into this world to be someone's punching bag,"[32]

Rodriguez's parents came from Puerto Rico to Chicago in the early 1950s. She was the oldest of eight siblings. She was born in Chicago. "My dad came to Chicago to work. We lived in Lincoln Park and then moved to Humboldt Park. My mother had me when she was 15. My parents divorced early and she gave up the twins for adoption. My mother married three or four times. She had a lot of problems. She started taking cocaine and shooting up heroin. My mother became very abusive with me. When I was little, she used to pick me up by the hair and throw me against the wall. She would beat me up a lot and I had broken bones. I would come to school with black eyes. When I was 16, one of her boyfriends tried to sexually molest me in the middle of the night. I couldn't take the abuse. I left home when I was 17."

Rodriguez's life became a downward spiral. She went from one abusive relationship to another. She had children early and lived for many years on public welfare. Like her mother, she took cocaine. She also sold cocaine and other hard drugs. "I tried marijuana, acid, and heroin, but cocaine became my drug of use. I was always strung out," recalls Rodriguez. "I would also sell the drugs in night clubs in Humboldt Park. I would sell it mostly to Puerto Ricans and some whites. I was making over $1,000 a day. I wanted to make sure my kids had what they needed.... Once, after we make a big drug sale, my boyfriend started beating me in a nightclub. He dislocated my jaw and shoulder. Other men had to stop him. I never found out why he beat me. I took a hit of drugs to ease the pain. That same night I went back to our apartment and he tried to hit me again. I pulled out my gun and I shot him in the head. I didn't kill him. But I blinded him in one eye and partially paralyzed him on the left side."

For shooting her boyfriend, police charged Rodriguez with attempted murder. At age 24 she was sentenced to six years in prison. She served three years at a downstate female prison and served another three years of parole. In prison, Rodriguez reflected on her life. She checked herself into a drug rehabilitation program and studied for her associate of arts degree. Rodriguez became a self-taught artist and auto mechanic. Prison officials invited her to paint a wall mural inside the prison. "The prison wall was huge. The wall was over twenty feet by twenty feet wide," says Rodriguez. "It took me over three weeks to paint it. Two other people helped me. We used acrylic and oil paints. The mural has two bookshelves on each end with cobblestone walls. The bookshelves represent knowledge. They have encyclopedias, the bible, and books all lined up. The fire place symbolizes warmth and family. I had a big picture window in the background. From the window, you can see the Chicago lake. The moon was shining off the lake and you can see the clouds, the Chicago skyline, and all the buildings of Chicago. That mural is still there." Once out of prison, Rodriguez ran into her old friends from Humboldt Park. Most were still using and selling drugs. She wanted no part of that lifestyle anymore. She checked herself into another drug rehabilitation program. But she got into another bad, abusive relationship, and has a five-year-old son. She ended the relationship and entered a program for women of domestic violence. Rodriguez was accepted into the Habitat for Humanity program, a group that renovates homes for low-income families. To purchase her current condominium, she put in 300 hours of work to help renovate it. She helped frame the walls, hung drywall, and painted. She paid $525 a month in mortgage for her six-and-a-half room condo. Single women and their children lived in the other eight, completely renovated apartments in her building.

Rodriguez did not like being on welfare. She dreamed of having a good job and hoped to become an educated, self-sufficient woman. She enrolled at DeVry Institute, a four-year technical college. She worked hard to make her dreams come true. In June 1998, she graduated from DeVry with honors, earning a bachelor's in computer information systems. Says Rodriguez, "During my graduation my favorite professor announced my name, "Angela Rodriguez, with honors." When I came on stage to receive my diploma, everyone was cheering. My legs got weak and I thought they were going to come out from underneath me. I started crying.... I have not used drugs since I've been out of prison. I got off public aid. I have been working full-time for the last four months at Lucent

Technologies. I'm a computer programmer. I am now making over $38,400 a year." Rodriguez does not have time anymore for a male companion, and that is just fine with her. Nor does she have any contact with her mother. She dedicated herself to her work, and to raising her children and grandchildren. "I'm so happy now. It's another world now. I realized I had a problem and there were things I had to deal with. Drugs were not the answer. If I hadn't had that awakening, I'll probably still be out there in the streets."

Leaving the Gangbanging

Ricky DeJesus, (not his real name), was born and raised in Humboldt Park. His parents divorced in Puerto Rico when he was young. He is the oldest of four siblings. His young mother moved to New York, and then in 1989 relocated to Chicago. DeJesus, 26, was born in Chicago. At age 13, he joined the Spanish Cobras, a street gang. He says he joined the gang for protection. He attended an elementary school in Humboldt Park and the older kids beat him up. His fellow gang members protected DeJesus, and in return, he started selling marijuana and other drugs for the gang. DeJesus' mother used heavy drugs, was in the streets and neglected her children. The Illinois Department of Children and Family Services, DCFS, removed DeJesus and his siblings from his mother. His three brothers, 16, 10, and three, were placed in foster homes. DeJesus went to live with a grandmother in Puerto Rico and forgot about the gangs.

But a year later, DeJesus came back to Chicago and lived in a foster home. He enrolled as a freshman at Roberto Clemente High School. He was a gifted athlete who played on the school's baseball team and basketball teams. But the drugs and gangs lured him away from school. "I had this girlfriend and I was trying to treat her right. But I didn't have a job. I had to make money so I started selling drugs for this gang," says DeJesus. "On an average day I was making $600 for myself. It's a damn shame that I was selling that stuff to my own people, but I didn't care. It was good money. At 15, I had my own ride, a Delta 88. I had my gang colors on. We would cut classes, smoke weed, and gangbang inside Clemente. I liked going up to someone and saying, 'what you be about?' I used to stick or punch people for no reason. We used to fight with other students inside the school. We would fight with fists, bottles, and bricks. I got beat up a couple of time in the washrooms by the Blackstones, a black gang. They kicked and punched me pretty good.... I used to go to baseball practice stoned on drugs. I got kicked off the team for using drugs. School, baseball, and my dreams all went down the drain."[33]

DeJesus dropped out of high school in his freshman year. He had conflict with his strict foster mother and moved out of her house. He got his 16-year-old girlfriend pregnant. Her parents insisted she have an abortion and prevented her from seeing DeJesus again. DeJesus and his gang buddies would skip school and looked for trouble. "We would stand on Division and Western bricking cars.

Some guys would drive by in a car watching you. We don't know who they are. They might be a neutral, not in a gang, or they might be Latin Kings, or whatever. So we would start throwing bricks and bottles at their car. We would break their car windows and try to hurt them. If they were innocent, you know, they messed up. They were in the wrong place at the wrong time. That's the way it happens. You can't do bricking now, because there are cops out there."

There are over a dozen major gangs in Humboldt Park. Some summers were peaceful with very few gang shootings or killings. But during other summers, the gangs were at war with each other. Gang members in cars drove by and shot at other suspected gang members. Sometimes innocent teenagers or children were killed. While only about ten percent of a neighborhood's youth were in gangs, they wreaked havoc on the community. "I used to shoot at people in drive-bys. It was in my "hood" or neighborhood; I had to go along with my gang. I can't tell you if I shot someone, you know, it happens so fast. You shoot and you see people drop to the floor. The summer of 95 was real bad around here, there were many shootings. My best friend who was 16 got shot. We were just chilling and this guy crept up in a ride and capped him. He got hit in the chest, the leg and the neck. He died. I was shot at once. It was a drive-by. I've been in some scary moments."

DeJesus tried to pull his life together. He left the gangs and lived by himself. The Department of Children and Family Services helped him pay the rent for a small apartment in Uptown. He enrolled in a program in Humboldt Park hoping to earn his GED. "You know, gangbanging ain't nothing. The guys in my gang let me get out without a violation, meaning they didn't beat me up. They said, 'hey, you're doing real good, good for you.' I want to be a role model to my brothers. I don't want them to say I was a lowlife who was selling drugs. I want to get my GED. I want to attend a vocational school and become an electrician. I want to move up and be somebody. My mom is going to need my help. I want to look out for my brothers and I want to take them out of foster homes. I've been in this program for two years. I didn't pass the GED test the first year. So I'm studying real hard to pass it this year."

Yet DeJesus' past gang life has caught up with him. Some gang members threatened him. "There are Latin Kings in Uptown and they started telling me, 'You folks, get out of our hood, we don't want you in our hood.' Damn, I can't live in peace," says DeJesus. "Although DCFS is paying my rent, I can't stay in that apartment. I'm now staying with a friend here in Humboldt Park. Why should I take out my nose ring so I don't look like a gangbanger? We can't wear earrings, nose rings, certain clothes, or colors because of the gangs. Forget that, I'm not going to live by their rules. I regret what I did when I was gangbanging. But now I just want to be left alone." But now DeJesus finds himself in the wrong place, at the wrong time. "I was coming home from working at a mall. It was around 10:30 p.m. and I was at a stoplight. These gang members bricked my car and busted a window. This kid, about 14, pulled out a gun and shot at me. He shot out the tire and I drove away for blocks on a flat tire. Another time gangs rammed my car. They hit my car on purpose with their car. They hit me in the side and I hit another car. I got away. You have to be alert and know how to react. I think God decided to punish me for the stuff I once did. But I think I've paid too much already. I can't go to many neighborhoods any more because of gangs."

DeJesus shared his thoughts as to why young teenagers join gangs. "It's got to do with the parents, but it's not all the parents' fault. Gangs start recruiting kids at 13, and the kids are under a lot of pressure. I used to recruit. You would tell kids, 'hey, what's up, come to the hood and kick it, lay back, get a couple of beers, probably meet some girls, and make some money. The next thing you know, they're joining a gang. You're 13 and you're getting brainwashed by other people. They're really bright kids with potential. But it comes down to you making the decision to join the gang." DeJesus hopes to steer his brothers away from gangs. "The other day I picked up my 10-year-old brother from his foster home and took him bowling. We went to Waveland Bowl in the morning. You can't go there at night, there are too many gangs. He is a smart kid.... Five years from now, I'll like to have a nice electrician job. I'll have my own woman and a little family. I'll probably be married with two kids. I want a little house for my family and to work hard and support them. When I do have my life straightened up, I want to be part of the community. I want to get involved in Humboldt Park and do something good. I grew up here."

Saving Gang Members

Kenny Ruiz, 55, walks the streets with a bible tucked in his gym bag. A former boxer with muscular arms, he worked out in the gym every morning. He enjoyed punching the heavy bag. He stopped and talked to young men gathered on street corners. He tried to get gang members to accept Christianity and leave the dark world of gangs. For over fifteen years he has been the director of a program called Street Intervention, which helped kids leave gangs. The program operated from a small space in the McCormick YMCA in Logan Square. "This program was designed in 1990 to impact the gang war situation that was going on in Humboldt Park and Logan Square area," says Ruiz. "We have seven staff in our program. Most are ex-gang members. Last year we touched the lives of over a thousand kids. These are the kids called the 'throwaway kids,' the ones no one wants do deal with. I not only want to deal with gangbangers, but with kids affected by gangs. We go inside the schools giving kids ideas about alternatives to gangs. What to do to avoid gangs if they recruit them. Helping parents identify the behavior of potential gang members."[34]

Most of the workers in Ruiz's program were in their early 20s and born-again Christians. A couple of the workers worked the South Side in Little Village and Back of the Yards. The program's staff combined religion and social services. They held bible studies, helped kids in court, and took gang members out of the city for weekend camps. They directed kids into GED programs and community colleges. Workers cruised the neighborhoods in a YMCA van and pleaded with gang members to cease shootings and gang wars. They brought gang members to the YMCA late at night to workout or play basketball, instead of looking for trouble on the streets. Ruiz's parents came from Puerto Rico to Chicago in 1950. He was raised in Humboldt Park and he was once in a gang. "I was in a gang that I joined for protection. In the mid-1970s, the Gaylords, a white gang was big in Logan Square," says Ruiz. "The Gaylords were against anybody who was not white. They were trying to keep Puerto Ricans out of this neighborhood. Puerto Ricans got in gangs to protect themselves from white gangs. I remember the Gaylords sliced my car tires and bricked my car. They didn't mess with me personally because I used to lift weights. I had my hair long and I used to wear a headband. Guys in our gang would hang out and drink. The older guys used drugs. But now the gangs are more organized and violent. Their focus is to gangbang. They live for that."

The area around the YMCA in Logan Square was known for gang activity. In broad daylight, gang members sold drugs and shot at each other. "This area is very hot. You have four different gangs around here," says Ruiz. "They are mostly Puerto Rican gangs. Black gangs are more organized than Latino gangs. The black gangs are interested in making money by selling drugs. Puerto Rican and Mexican gangs are out there just to gangbang. They like the excitement of the violence. We're seeing an influx of Mexicans in this area. Mexicans get recruited and join Puerto Rican gangs. Kids join gangs out of fascination. Hollywood movies glorify gangs. They join for protection, for recognition, for power, and for money. Some lack a father figure at home. They're looking for a role model.... Some parents are in denial and refuse to believe their son is in a gang. Sometimes the parents know and they just don't know how to control it. The young person has taken control of the house."

Ruiz has tried to save gang members for over 38 years. He worked for the city's Community Intervention Network, a citywide program. But the program was dismantled in 1990. Few social service agencies were willing to work with hard-core gang members. Some believed Ruiz's religious approach to gangs was soft and did not work. Jail, not religion, is what gang members needed, many argued. "Gang members are hard to like. They are selling poison, they are shooting people, they are hurting people," says Ruiz. "Their behavior is antisocial. But sometimes we need to look behind that hard wall that gang members put up. You look behind that and there is a kid. A lot of them are trying to get respect. When you give them respect, a lot of that stuff drops.... They respect my religious values. Usually I don't start preaching to them. As time goes on, I share little bits and pieces with them. Many of them come from backgrounds where their parents were involved in the church. Some have joined the church I attend. It's Day Spring Church, a born-again Christian church."

Ruiz wanted to me a role model to gang members and he believed God selected him to save kids from gangs "I don't think about how dangerous my job is. I just do it in wisdom," says Ruiz. "But one of my staff members almost got shot by gang members. He was going to get some gang members together for basketball. Then these other gang members in a car came by and shot the two guys he was with. One got shot in the shoulder, the other in the stomach. They're now OK, but they could have killed my staff member." It was difficult to measure what success Ruiz's program has had with gangs. Some gang members promised Ruiz they would leave gangs, and then they went right back to the life of gangs. "Yes, measuring our success is a problem," admitted Ruiz. "How do you quantify what we do? How do you capture when you're able to intervene in a situation where there is gang retaliation and a gang war might break out? How do you capture how many lives are saved because of that? People don't know what goes on behind closed doors as we negotiate a peace settlement between rival groups. If we brag about our results, they say, 'oh, they were not really working with hard-core kids. They were working with marginal guys.' It's a no-win situation."

Police and city officials have tried various approaches in dealing with gangs. In the early 1980s, police arrested hundreds of thousands of Latino and African American males on disorderly conduct charges simply to get them off the streets. Community groups complained about the practice.[35] The American Civil Liberties Union, ACLU, sued the city and charged that many innocent kids, who were not gang members, were arrested. The courts ruled the disorderly conduct sweep arrests were unconstitutional, and the city was forced to throw out thousands of arrest records and cease the practice. In 1992, the city passed an anti-loitering ordinance aimed at getting gangs off the street. More than 42,000 arrests of mostly minority males were made. The ordinance was struck down by the U.S. Supreme Court as unconstitutional.

Ruiz believed gang members needed social services, education, and job training to get their lives on the right track. Yet he argued that major foundations do not fund agencies that work with gangs. "We continue having difficulties raising funds,"says Ruiz. "People don't really want to give money for working with gang members. We get funded from the City of Chicago's department of Human Services. We had funds from another nonprofit source so we could work in Pilsen and Little Village. But we've exhausted all our dollars there. We may have to let go some staff. We're trying to do important work. But the funds we get are a drop in the bucket. We're really hurting."

Getting A Little Political Clout

For decades, Puerto Ricans lacked political power. They had no Puerto Ricans in the Chicago city council, none in the state legislature, and none in Congress. White politicians from the regular Democratic Organization—the political machine—maintained a strong hold on the Near North Side's heavily Puerto Rican 26th and 31st wards. As Democrats, Puerto Ricans regularly voted for

Mayor Richard J. Daley, Chicago's longtime mayor. They also voted for white machine candidates in aldermanic races. In return, Puerto Ricans hoped the mayor and white aldermen would offer them some of thousands of high-paying city jobs they controlled. Yet the mayor and machine politicians took Puerto Ricans for granted. The mayor paid symbolic attention to Puerto Ricans by donning a Puerto Rican hat at their ethnic parade celebrations. Yet few Puerto Ricans held city jobs and Puerto Ricans were not invited to sit at the table of political power.

Thomas E. Keane, Mayor Richard J. Daley's city council floor leader, was the longtime alderman of the 31st ward, which included Humboldt Park. Since the turn of the 19th century, the Keane family controlled the ward. Keane did not have a single Puerto Rican precinct captain among his huge political army. In 1974, Keane was convicted and sentenced to jail for illegally buying land and reselling it to government agencies at enormous profits. In 1975, his wife replaced him as alderman and Keane still ran the ward from his jail cell. In 1979, Chester Kuta, a Polish American was selected by Thomas Keane as alderman of the 31st ward.[36] And the needs of Puerto Ricans were still ignored. "I observed the people involved in the 31st ward when it was controlled by Ald. Thomas Keane. I just rejected what they were doing," says former state senator Miguel del Valle. "It was awful. There was no connection to the Latino community, expect for a couple of individuals who were politically connected. They really acted like they didn't need us. We were just there. They had their political organization."[37]

Puerto Ricans lacked the political muscle to force concessions from Chicago's political machine. They wrestled with the problem of how to flex their population gains into political power. Puerto Rican independents had little success against regular Democrats in elections. From 1963 to 1982, about 16 Latinos ran as independents for city and state offices. They all lost by wide margins. Puerto Rican candidates lost the elections because they lacked money, experience, workers, a strong organization, and because many eligible voters were not registered.[38] It was not until 1981 that Chicago's 112,000 Puerto Ricans gained political representation in city government. White machine bosses handpicked the first Puerto Rican officeholders. For instance, Chicago's Mayor Jane M. Bryne, working with Thomas E. Keane, convinced Chester Kuta to step down as 31st ward alderman. He was given a city job at double his aldermanic salary. Then in 1981, Mayor Bryne handpicked Joseph Martinez as alderman of the 31st ward. Martinez had firm roots in the regular Democratic Organization. He was a lawyer in the law firm of Edward M. Burke, powerful alderman of the 14th ward.

Mayor Bryne thought the Martinez appointment would please Puerto Ricans. She courted the Puerto Rican vote for an upcoming mayoral election in 1983. The appointment only enraged some Puerto Ricans, who claimed Martinez had no record of community involvement. They argued that Thomas E. Keane would continue to control the ward through Martinez.[39] "The very time I

voted, it was for Mayor Jane Bryne. Before that, I had not voted," says del
Valle. "But I quickly became disappointed with Bryne.... I though the Martinez
appointment was an insult. I declared it a joke. We had evolved from having
non-Latino representation that was totally disconnected. Then we had the same
politicians, who had all the power, now determine what Latino would represent
us." Edward Nedza, a machine loyalist, was state senator of the 5th district on
the Northwest Side. He was also the committeeman of the 31st ward. Nedza
convinced Martinez, who served two years, not to seek reelection as 31st ward
alderman. Instead, Martinez was given a job with the city. Nedza wanted a
Puerto Rican alderman he could control. In 1983, Nedza slated Miguel Santiago,
a Puerto Rican school teacher and precinct captain. Santiago won the 1983 election as alderman of the 31st ward. Chicago's 50 aldermen had a reputation for
doing and saying outrageous things. Santiago added to the reputation. He called
a press conference to say some Puerto Rican community activists had threatened
to set his feet on fire. The activists had only told Santiago he had to be accountable to the community, and 'we're going to hold your feet to the fire.'

White Democratic politicians stubbornly refused to give up power even
though their wards were becoming increasingly Puerto Rican. The Mexican
American Legal Defense and Educational Fund (MALDEF), along with Puerto
Rican groups, charged that redrawn state districts—much like redrawn city
wards in the early 1980s—discriminated against Latinos. A federal court panel
agreed and ordered that a new General Assembly map be redrawn. The new map
gave Latinos an edge in two Chicago legislative districts, the 9th that is mostly
Puerto Rican, and the 20th that is mostly Mexican. "I didn't even know what the
word reapportionment meant," says del Valle. "I had to look it up in a diction-
ary, along with the word gerrymander. I was a social worker and not yet involved in the political arena. But after learning how they diluted the wards to
keep Latinos powerless, I became very angry."

In 1983, the regular Democratic Organization helped Joseph Berrios, a
Puerto Rican loyal to the machine, become the first Latino state representative
from the 9th District. Puerto Rican leaders had hoped to run an independent,
community-oriented candidate against Berrios. "Leaders from the Puerto Rican
community held our first political convention at Roberto Clemente High
School," says del Valle. "For the first time we were going to have the opportunity to elect an independent, Latino state representative in the 9th District. We
got excited. The idea was to reach consensus on our candidate for that position.
We selected Jose Salgado as our candidate. The machine selected Joseph Berrios. But we botched Salgado's petitions. The Chicago Board of Election Com-
missioners disqualified him from the ballot because of an insufficient number of
valid signatures. We didn't know what we were doing. Berrios ran unopposed
and won."

Meanwhile in 1983, Harold Washington ran for mayor of Chicago against
Jane Byrne and Richard M. Daley. Miguel del Valle and other Puerto Rican activists supported Washington, and helped him campaign in Puerto Rican neigh-

borhoods. White ethnic voters split their votes between Bryne and Daley, and Washington won. But the city was very racially divided. Whites refused to vote for Washington in the general election and instead supported the Republican candidate. Nevertheless, Washington won the general election as mayor with over 495,000 votes. He won 90 percent of black votes, 17 percent of white votes, and 50 percent of 95,000 Latino registered voters.[40] Unlike past mayors, Washington encountered strong aldermanic opposition in the city council. Edward Vrdolyak, the 10th ward alderman, lead a majority bloc of predominately white aldermen in the city council who opposed Washington at every turn. In the special elections held in seven city wards in March 1986, Washington backed Luis Gutierrez, a Puerto Rican city worker for alderman of the 26th ward. Vrdolyak backed Manuel Torres, a Puerto Rican who came up through the regular Democratic Organization. Gutierrez appeared to be the winner by 25 votes, but Torres challenged the count, forcing another election. In a special election the following month, Gutierrez beat Torres by 1,000 votes. And Washington finally gained control over the city council.

In 1987, with Washington's backing, Miguel del Valle beat veteran Edward Nedza to become the first Latino state senator in Chicago. Del Valle was regarded as a progressive, independent-minded legislator. "One important piece of legislation I introduced is the bilingual pay supplement," says del Valle. "This is where the state pays a little more to employees who use a second language in their line of work. I also worked directly on creating the judicial subcircuits in Cook Country, which lead, for the first time, to the election of a number of Latinos to the bench. People like David Delgado and other Latinos have won positions as judges in the judicial circuit court system. When I started, there was only one Latino judge, David Cerda. Today, there must be ten." There were aspects of his job as state senator that del Valle did not like. "I hate having to raise funds for every election.... I dislike fundraising because people who give money to politicians want favors and their interests promoted. Politicians feel they have to vote the way their big funders want them to, instead of voting according to their conscious. This is one of the most serious, structural problems with American politics. Average Americans are cynical of politics because of all the big money that special interests give to politicians. Americans feel my vote does not make a difference, so why vote. I support limitations on how much money politicians can receive from corporations, special interests, and individuals. Something has to be done or more Americans will lose faith in the system."

On November 25, 1987, shortly into his second term, Mayor Harold Washington died in office of a heart attack. In a special mayoral election in 1989, Richard M. Daley ran against Timothy Evans, an African American alderman. Many believed the fragile coalition between African Americans and Latinos would elect Evans as mayor. However, the coalition splintered. In a surprise move, 26th ward alderman Luis Gutierrez endorsed Daley for mayor. Some Latinos and African Americans called Gutierrez a traitor. They reminded him that Harold Washington and black votes got him elected. They felt he should have supported Evans. Gutierrez defended himself by pointing to the polls, which showed that Daley was a sure winner with solid support from Puerto Ricans and whites.[41] Yet many wondered what Daley offered Gutierrez for his support. Daley won the election as mayor. Shortly afterwards, reapportionment created the state's first predominately Latino Congressional district in Illinois. In 1993, with Mayor Daley's backing, Luis Gutierrez, 46, was elected as U.S. Congressman of that 4th district. He was the first Latino U.S. Congressman from Chicago. Gutierrez's district was an oddly-shaped area linking the Mexican community on the Near Southwest Side, with the largely Puerto Rican community on the Near Northwest Side. Opponents of the district, including a few whites and Mexicans, filed a suit against the district saying it is an example of racial gerrymandering. They argued that the two Latino communities should not be lumped together because they are culturally different. But in 1998, the U.S. Supreme Court upheld the constitutionality of the district.

U.S. Rep. Luis Gutierrez (D-Ill.) maintains staff offices in both the Mexican and Puerto Rican communities. In Congress, he consistently sponsored legislation protecting the rights of undocumented workers, legal residents, and immigrants. He was well liked among Mexicans in Chicago. Gutierrez was involved in controversy in 1998 over failure to pay property taxes on his expensive home in the Bucktown neighborhood. While his neighbors were paying $5,000 in property taxes, Gutierrez paid just $275 on his property that was listed as a vacant lot by the Cook County assessor's office. After the story broke in the media, Gutierrez paid $7,500 in back taxes.[42] Despite the controversy, Gutierrez was elected to a six term. He has publicly stated that he someday wishes to become Chicago's first Latino mayor. Most political observers believed Mayor Richard M Daley, who has been mayor since 1989, will be reelected to another term as mayor despite negative media and court publicity about extensive illegal hiring and awarding of city contracts in his administration. Yet despite constant controversy in his administration, many Latinos and African Americans have voted for Daley, even against prominent African American challengers.

"Mayor Richard Daley had been very good for Latinos," says Billy Ocasio, 45, alderman of the 26th ward. "He has hired more Latinos than any other mayor. And he has given Latinos more city contracts than at any other time in the history of Chicago. Harold Washington started the process, but this mayor is doing a lot more. The information they have given me from city hall has shown that this mayor has done more Latino hiring, and more awarding of contracts to Latinos, than previous mayors. Many of us worked for Harold Washington, but it was hard getting city jobs. I know that with this mayor, Latinos have gotten a lot more."[43] Gutierrez asked Mayor Daley to place Ocasio as 26th ward alderman when he became a congressman. Ocasio has been alderman since January 1993. He has lived in the Humboldt Park neighborhood most of his life. He believed having Latino political representation is beneficial for Latinos. "Having people like Miguel del Valle win a senate seat, and Luis Gutierrez win a congressional seat, brings a sense of pride to Latinos," says Ocasio. "When you see pride in people you see positive changes in communities. You see organizations and businesses start to develop. Politicians bring in more money for housing and business development.... Some accomplishments in my ward include building the Humboldt Park Vocational Center and the Humboldt Park Library. We built a nice baseball field for Roberto Clemente High School and the $11 million Ames Middle School. We built Paseo Boricua and did a lot of infrastructure repairs on Division Street."

Ocasio's ward includes Humboldt Park, Logan Square, and the gentrifying areas of Wicker Park, and Bucktown. A steady stream of Puerto Ricans and Latinos visit Ocasio's office. "People come asking for jobs. We've gotten a few people jobs, but we're not about patronage anymore," says Ocasio. "Jobs are very hard to come by. Housing is a big issue. There are not enough low-income, affordable housing or apartments. Many people are against having low-income housing being built in the ward." White, middle-class professionals have also come to see the alderman to voice their concerns. "They complain mostly about the gangs, drug dealing, graffiti, and homeless people. I learned that we have to work with everyone here," say Ocasio. "Although this ward is 69 percent Latino, we have a 40 percent voting power. And of those 40 percent, probably only 50 percent come out and vote.... Gangs are a big problem. I don't know what to do with it really. Latinos also complain about the gangs. I am not into just locking people up. I try to bring resources for the children to keep them away from gangs. If you don't have the library, or vocational education, or a safe park, or employment, or business opportunities, people have no choice but to turn to gangs, and drug dealing, and doing bad things."

Rep. Gutierrez and Ocasio have publicly supported the independence of Puerto Rico. Puerto Rican politics and neighborhood politics have often divided Puerto Rican politicians. There was an ongoing feud between Puerto Rican Democratic politicians. One camp contained businessman and longtime, powerful alderman Richard F. Mell of the 33rd ward, and his allies former Illinois state representative Edgar López (D-Chicago), and former alderman Vilma Colom (35th ward), who is Puerto Rican. In the opposing camp were Congressman Gutierrez, Ocasio, and Miguel del Valle. Besides political differences, the two sides were fighting for control over local political power, city neighborhood grants, and who decided the destiny of local neighborhoods. Former State Representative Edgar López, 42, (D-Chicago), made no bones about his dislike for the politics of Gutierrez, Ocasio, or del Valle. "They don't agree to disagree. I can understand the whole Puerto Rican independence movement. I even agree with a lot of it. I even came out and publicly supported the release of what they call the political prisoners of war, which I claim they're not prisoners of war, they're terrorists," says López. "They committed a crime against this country. A lot of my friends are independents. A communist is even one of my best friends. I'm for statehood for Puerto Rico. I think it's time for Puerto Rico to get its fair share of what it is to truly be an American citizen."[44]

Edgar López is Puerto Rican and Ecuadorian. His dad came from Ecuador in 1959. His mother came from Arecibo, Puerto Rico in 1961. His parents were factory workers and they raised him as a Seventh-Day Adventist. Some Puerto Ricans viewed López as a captive of special interests and a loyal member of the old-line, regular Democratic Organization. "There is no difference between them and us," says López. "I don't take orders from anybody. Who put Luis Gutierrez there? Who keeps Billy Ocasio there? Mayor Richard M. Daley put them there. Gutierrez and Ocasio call themselves independent. They want to continue keeping our community down and stupid. I'm not into that protest stuff. I'm into getting our people educated, and getting people jobs so they become self-dependent. The only thing they did is put some Puerto Rican flags and some brick seats on Division Street. Nothing is going to change unless they get rid of the crime. People are afraid to go on Division Street. And then they bring Fiesta Boricua and throw a party on Division Street. Wow, that's good for the community, throwing a party? It's just public relations."

The bickering between the two sides often got downright dirty. An anonymous newspaper called EL Pito, or the Whistle, was widely circulated in Humboldt Park. The paper was vulgar and crude. It made wild accusations against Gutierrez, Oscasio, and del Valle. It poked fun at their politics and sexuality and accused them of being women, gay, and bisexual. Many believed López and his allies published the newspaper. "They think I'm the one doing El Pito," says López. "Well, I don't do El Pito. Don't blame me, I know who does it. And I told them, you're being a little too crude. But it's their business to publish what they want" López gained notoriety as chairman of a controversial, 1998 state investigation into the alleged misuse of $150,000 of state education funds for low-income students at Roberto Clemente High School. The investigation alleged that instead of buying books, pencils, and school supplies the local school council spent the money on a campaign to promote Puerto Rican independence, and to free Puerto Rican political prisoners. Others saw the investigation as an attempt to use the politics of Puerto Rican independence to paint Gutierrez, Ocasio, and del Valle as crazed, pro-independence fanatics to hurt their reelection chances.[45] Ultimately, the investigation proved fruitless, and no one was officially charged with wrongdoing.

López was elected to the Illinois House in 1993. He was a four-term, state representative and he envisioned a bright future for himself in politics. "I'm the senior member for Hispanics in the Illinois House of Representatives. I would one day like to be speaker of the house. Maybe someday become governor of the state," says López. But in the March 2000 primary, López faced a tough challenge from Cynthia Soto, 37, a Mexican. Both sides accused each other of personal attacks and mud-slinging. López received heavy support from Illinois's Republican governor and Mayor Richard M. Daley. Congressman Luis Gutierrez, Ocasio, del Valle, and other Puerto Rican politicians poured plenty of money and troops into Soto's campaign. Soto scored a huge upset and defeated López. Soto's campaign was the first time that Puerto Rican politicians pooled their resources and helped a Mexican win political office. After Soto's victory,

Puerto Rican politicians held a conference to announce a new, independent political coalition between Puerto Ricans and Mexicans. However, only about 80 people, mostly Puerto Rican, showed up to the conference. It appeared a lot of effort was still needed to bring Puerto Ricans and Mexicans into lasting, political coalitions.

Political Future

Over the years, Puerto Ricans and Latinos made significant political progress. In 1980, for instance, only two Latinos held elected office. The city now has over 22 Latino, elected officials.[46] But some Puerto Ricans politicians have wondered if future Latino politicians will become beholden to the regular Democratic Organization and ignore community needs? Former state senator Miguel del Valle, and other Puerto Rican politicians, insisted that Mayor Richard M. Daley, like his father, was creating a political machine that expected absolute loyalty from Latino politicians. "I was very disappointed when Mayor Daley's hit squad of Latino city employees, the Hispanic Democratic Organization, went after and defeated state senator Jesus Garcia," says del Valle. "The reason Daley's hit squad does not like us is because we stand up. We are critical when there is a need to be critical. I don't consider myself one of the boys. When I was first elected, I vowed that when I left this office, I would leave acting and thinking pretty much the same way as when elected."

Representative Luis Gutierrez was also at odds with Mayor Daley. He was upset because Daley's people tried to tell him what candidate to support in a presidential election. "I'm very disillusioned with Mayor Daley. He's acting like an old boss. Like his father," said Gutierrez. "Illinois Democrats elected to Congress are supposed to be able to think and speak for themselves, not be directed in their political thinking by a boss from Chicago."[47] Representative Gutierrez and Mayor Daley eventually made up and supported each other. They blamed their past disagreements on poor communication.[48] Gutierrez also mended fences with his longtime rival, alderman Richard F. Mell. Gutierrez supported Rod Blagojevich—Mell's son-in-law—for governor in the 2003 gubernatorial race.[49]

Former state senator Miguel del Valle was optimistic that more Latinos will be elected to city and state offices in the future. He only hoped future Latino politicians will be independent thinkers, and not beholden to special interests or to other politicians. "There are politicians who feel that if you're not part of their political operation, they can't trust you," says del Valle. "Therefore, they want to put someone in political office who is totally reliable. My definition of reliability is being true to the community. Their definition is doing what they tell you to do.... Mayor Daley is looking for uniformity in Latino elected officials. In a democracy, that is not healthy."

Interestingly, despite his longtime political differences with the mayor, del

Valle eventually developed a close working relationship with Mayor Daley. To the surprise of many, Mayor Daley named del Valle as the new city clerk of Chicago in 2006. Many believed that by picking del Valle, the Mayor was hoping to draw attention away from scandals that plagued his administration during the last two years; the mayor was also hoping to gather Latino support for his reelection bid.

Chapter Five: Guatemalans and Salvadorans

Seeking Economic Opportunities

Since the 1960s, Cubans were the third largest Latino group in Chicago, after Mexicans and Puerto Ricans. That distinction now belongs to Guatemalans. The 1990 U.S. Census Bureau counted 12,895 Guatemalans in the city.[1] The 2000 census counted 20,000 Guatemalans in Chicago, however many believed that count was low. Since a large number of Guatemalans were undocumented, it was difficult to say precisely how many lived in Chicago. However, the Chicago Guatemalan Consulate, and others, estimated that there were between 85,000 to 120,000 Guatemalans in the Chicago metropolitan area, and the vast majority lived in Chicago.[2] The number of Latinos from South and Central America countries who immigrated to Illinois increased about 80 percent from 116,495 in 1990 to 209,583 in 2000.[3] The majority of these new arrivals were Latinos from Guatemala, El Salvador, Ecuador, and Honduras. Illinois' Guatemalan community was the fourth largest in the United States after California, New York, and Florida.

Guatemalans immigrated to large American cities like Chicago for both economic and political reasons. Unlike Mexicans and Puerto Ricans, their immigration was more recent. Guatemalans first began trickling into Chicago during the mid-1960s. Some were educated professionals, trades people, or skilled workers unable to find work in their homelands. They entered the United States legally. They came looking for high paying, white-collar jobs. They came hoping to make money quickly and then return home.[4] But many never went back home. They found good economic opportunities in Chicago and decided to stay. During the mid-1970s and early 80s, many others came fleeing a prolonged, bloody, 36-year civil war in their country. They wanted to escape from violence, repression, and government-sponsored killings of civilians. Some were middle-class intellectuals, students, professors, church leaders, and trade union leaders. But the majority were poor immigrants, who were undocumented, and did not speak English. They were unskilled workers with very little education: a substantial amount were Mayan campesinos or small farmers. They were escaping political persecution, unemployment, and poverty back home. They flocked to large cities like Los Angeles, New York, and Chicago searching for peace, jobs and a better tomorrow.[5]

In addition to economic and political reasons, some believed that United States multinational companies practically pushed Guatemalans and other South and Central Americans out of their countries. Some argued that these immigrants were forced to leave their homelands because powerful United States and European, multinational corporations controlled the land and economies of various South and Central American countries. The economic polices of these large corporation resulted in modernization, loss of agricultural jobs, reductions in work force, exploitation of workers, and an exodus of workers to other countries.[6] Despite being forced to migrate, many immigrants from Guatemala held a positive view of America. These immigrants did not naively believe that America's streets were filled with gold. Yet the image of America as a land of freedom, a place with a high living standard, and a country with unlimited economic opportunity attracted them. They came with big dreams that their sons and daughters could enjoy better education and a more prosperous life in America.

Guillermo Mendizabal, 58, and his wife, Maria, 59, were a case in point. They immigrated to the United States from Guatemala City, the capital of Guatemala. They came looking for work. "I came in 1969. I was undocumented and I didn't speak any English. I had only thirty-three dollars in my pocket," says Guillermo. "I went to New York and stayed there for about a year. I lived with a friend, who later became my brother-in-law. I worked in a clothing factory as a receiving clerk but quickly lost that job because I didn't speak English. Then I worked in a restaurant washing dishes. A friend convinced me to come to Chicago to find work. I took the bus from New York and arrived in Chicago in 1970."[7] Maria says, "I came to the United States in 1964 because I needed to make a living for my daughters. I was a divorced and a single mom. I was only 19. I had no support from anybody. I left my daughters with my mother in Guatemala.... I worked in New York babysitting for a well-to-do family in a suburb. I lived with the family. The little boy I was taking care of was teaching me English. Every time he would say something, I would laugh because I couldn't understand him. I was making one-hundred dollars a week. I would send money home to my mother in Guatemala. For seven years I was going back and forth from the United States to Guatemala. I finally came to Chicago in 1971. I quickly became a permanent U.S. resident."

In Chicago, Guillermo and Maria married in 1972. Her two daughters from Guatemala joined them in Chicago. Over the years their family grew to include five daughters, ranging in ages from 17 to 37. They own a small, brick bungalow in Logan Square. A "Neighborhood Watch: We Call Police" poster was prominently displayed in their front window. "This block is really nice," says Guillermo. "We have Guatemalans, Mexicans, and whites living on the block, and everyone gets along fine. We don't have any trouble. People here take care of their homes. There were a lot of old people here before, but now it's changed. Young people have moved in. You might see kids running around the street now, but it wasn't like that before. But we don't have big problems. This is still a good neighborhood."

Guillermo was an undocumented worker in Chicago. "I worked briefly in a printing company in Chicago. In that company some Guatemalan workers got into a fist fight with Arab workers. One Arab guy punched me in the face and I punched him back. Then they fired me for fighting. I was unemployed for a while. I used to catch the bus all the way to the suburb of Melrose Park looking for a job. I then found a job at Sears in Chicago." Guillermo realized he would have limited opportunities in Chicago as an undocumented worker. So in 1976, he became a permanent legal resident. That year, Guillermo was reentering the United States from Guatemala. He proudly held his permanent residency papers in his hand. "I was so happy to be a permanent U.S. resident. In Miami we had to change flights to get to Chicago," says Guillermo. "The customs man at the airport, who was white, looked closely at my residency papers. Then he shouted, 'Great, here's another wetback coming to America to live off welfare.' I was shocked. I felt so bad. I just grabbed my papers, smiled, and left. But we have never been on welfare. We have always worked."

Maria worked in a social service agency as a financial counselor for low-income families. But during her early years in Chicago, she did her share of hard factory work. Like other immigrants with limited education, Maria often worked in dangerous jobs. Maria is missing half her middle finger on her right hand. She explains: "In Chicago I worked at the Playskool factory for five years. They used to make toys, but they closed down. That's where I lost my finger. I used to work on a cutting machine, cutting wood blocks. The guy who set up the machine that morning did not tie up the cutting blade. When I turned the machine on, the cutting blade got loose and cut my fingers. I lost half of this one, I lost a part of another finger, and I had stiches on my third finger. The company gave me only a thousand dollars."

Unlike Mexicans and Puerto Ricans, Guatemalans did not settled in specific neighborhoods in Chicago. Instead, they were dispersed in neighborhoods throughout the city. Friends and family members helped each other find affordable, decent housing. Many Guatemalans moved into North Side neighborhoods like Albany Park, Lincoln Square, Uptown, Edgewater, and Rogers Park. These neighborhoods had numerous, multi-unit buildings, and rents were usually lower than in other parts of the city. Families often lived together and shared monthly rental expenses. The Uptown neighborhood was traditionally a port of entry for Latino immigrants from Central and South America. Several small, social service agencies catered to the needs of poor Guatemalan immigrants. Popular small restaurants like Antojitos Guatemaltecos and El Tinajon, catered to the neighborhood's Guatemalan residents. The unpretentious storefront restaurants offered inexpensive Guatemalan dishes like black beans, tortillas, tamales, soups, and stews. Gentrification in Uptown, Lincoln Square, and North Center forced Guatemalans to move and seek affordable housing in areas like Logan Square, Albany Park, and Irving Park. Since over a third of Guatemalans did not speak English well, some preferred to live in already settled Latino neighborhoods like Pilsen and Little Village. In these neighborhoods they got around and survived solely by speaking Spanish. There was also a growing Guatemalan community in the blue-collar suburb of Elgin.

The inability to speak English made it difficult for Guatemalans to get ahead in Chicago. Some Guatemalans were determined to learn the language. After a hard day's work, they attended evening English classes at various community agencies. "We really wanted to better ourselves in Chicago," says Guillermo. "We took English classes in the evenings at city colleges and we learned

English. That has really helped us." Maria adds, "I understand, read, and speak English, but I speak it with a heavy accent. I wish I could speak it beautifully without an accent. That's what I would really like. I want to take more English classes so I can get rid of this heavy accent." In 1971, Guillermo found steady work with Chicago's Sears department store. He began working as a stocking clerk in the warehouse, but the work was dirty and boring. He did not come more than 800 miles from Guatemala to the United States to settle on just being a clerk. He steadily worked himself up into a better-paying, skilled technician position. He repaired large household appliances like refrigerators, stoves, and air conditioners. As part of his job he drove a new, blue Sears' repair truck. He parked the truck outside his home every day.

"I took courses at Sears on how to repair large household appliances. They required three courses, but I took 20 courses," recalls Guillermo. "I didn't want to stay working in the Sears warehouse. I wanted to be a service technician. I loved the uniform they wear. They wear white shirts. In the warehouse, I saw a lot of guys with 25 years of service. They were doing the same thing every year. I didn't want to see myself, like that. I took courses and learned my trade. It took me three years to prepare myself, but I did it. This is a good, secure job. Sears rarely fires its service people. I belong to profit sharing and I'm fully vested in my retirement plan." Guillermo was such a good service technician, he trained others. He was delighted that Sears was hiring more Latinos as technicians. "I'm training ten service technicians right now. I have Puerto Ricans, Mexicans, one white, and two Guatemalans. The job pays well."

The Menidizabals are devoted Roman Catholics who attended church regularly. Guillermo is a longtime deacon at Saint John Berchmans Catholic parish in Logan Square. "My Catholic religion is very important to me. I come from a Catholic family and was raised Catholic. I was an altar boy in Guatemala. In 1971, my wife and I were involved in forming the Spanish mass at Mount Carmel parish on Belmont and Halsted. They did not give us the church. They gave us the hall to conduct an early morning Spanish mass. The hall is part of the church but it's not in the church. I guess the church has its politics too. In the Spanish mass we started playing guitars, and the women took part in the liturgy reading and singing. Before, there was no way a woman was going to read at the altar. We made a lot of changes." Maria reminded Guillermo that he was not always actively involved in the church. He spent a number of years organizing soccer teams. On weekends, hundreds of Guatemalans, along with Mexicans, gathered at Lake Shore Drive and Montrose to play soccer and socialize. "That's true, I was not always close to the church," says Guillermo. "When I moved to Chicago, I was involved in organizing soccer games and teams with other Guatemalans. Some of the first Guatemalan organizations in the city were soccer teams. I was paying more attention to my soccer games on Sundays than church. I used to drop off my wife and the kids off at church and go to my soccer games. Now, as a deacon, I'm very involved in the church."

Guillermo and Maria only finished high school in Guatemala. But they wanted a good education for their children and they encouraged their children to do well in school. They struggled to pay yearly Catholic elementary and high school tuition for their daughters. They proudly pointed to the framed diplomas hanging in their living room. Two of their daughters graduated from college and another was in her third year of college. "One of my daughters is an accountant and one is a legal secretary. I like the values and discipline that Catholic schools provide," says Maria. "Two things I want my daughters to have when I'm gone is a good education and faith in God. Money is money, it comes and goes, but these two things are important for them. That is the treasure I've given them." The youngest daughter, Brenda, was a senior at a girls' Catholic high school on the city's North Side. She hoped to become a pediatrician. The Mendizabals were proud of the musical and cultural talents of their daughters. Brenda, a noted salsa dancer, danced in a Puerto Rican folkloric ballet, and played saxophone in a jazz band. She was also director of Marimba Oxib K'Ajau, Groupo Cultural Guatemalteco, the only group of Guatemalan girls in the United States that played the marimba, an instrument usually played by men in Guatemala. There were about 15 girls, from nine to twenty-years-old, in the group.

"Four indigenous Guatemalan families in Chicago formed the group over ten years ago. The Jewish community in Skokie helped them," says Maria. "The Guatemalan families came to the United States not knowing English. The culture here was so different. They wanted to preserve the Guatemalan culture. I became close with one of the families and I pushed Brenda to get into the group. She was born here and I wanted her to know the Guatemalan culture. The other families moved onto other things and Brenda became the director. She is now teaching others how to play the marimba. The marimba is the national Mayan instrument of Guatemala. About nine girls play the instrument at once." The marimba is similar to a wooden xylophone. Players softly and collectively tap the steel keys of the marimba with wooden mallets, creating melodic sounds. In Guatemala the soft, harmonic sounds of the marimba are heard at baptismals, weddings, and funerals. Marimba Oxib K'Ajau recorded their first CD in 1995.

"The girls love what they do," says Maria. "Our daughter loves to teach young girls how to play the marimba. This is how we promote our Guatemalan culture. We play all over Chicago. We play at museums, universities, churches, and cultural events. In 1996 we played for Guatemala's president, Alvaro Arzu Irigoyen when he visited Chicago. He loved the performance.... Our marimba was getting old, so president Arzu promised us a brand new one from Guatemala, and we received it. In 1998, we played for Chicago's Mayor Richard Daley to kick off Hispanic Heritage Month. With proceeds from the CD, our group toured Guatemala and performed two to three concerts a day. We performed in places where they do not hear the music because the people are so poor."

On summer vacations Guillermo drives his van throughout the Southwestern United States with his wife and daughters. "This country is so big and beautiful. There is so much to see. I love the outdoors," says Guillermo. The Menidizabals have kept in contact with their Guatemalan friends who immigrated to Chicago during the 1970s. They acknowledge that some Guatemalan families are poor, have low-paying jobs, and are struggling to make it. But others are progressing. "My friends who came to Chicago are doing well," says Guillermo. "Many have become legal residents or citizens. Just about everyone owns their house. They are not big houses, but they're nice. They have mostly factory jobs.... Gatemalans keep coming to Chicago because friends and relatives from Chicago write them letters telling them they are jobs here. Many come for the work and to be close to friends and family." The Mendizabals were upbeat about their life in Chicago. They say most of their hopes and dreams have been realized in Chicago. "My dream was not to become rich. What is money? We're not rich. We don't even have money in the bank," says Maria. "But to fulfill your life with your family, and to give them your children a good education and a better future, that's important. It's hard work, we struggled, but it pays off. The future for our children and for my husband and me is O.K."

Fleeing The Horror

Guatemala's bloody, civil conflict triggered a mass exodus of Guatemalans during the 1970s and 80s. Tens of thousands of Guatemalans made their way to Chicago. Some came here with temporary legal status. Many individuals or their family members had been physically tortured and persecuted in Guatemala. The military government there had labeled them as subversives and targeted them for persecution. They fled in terror and in fear for their lives. Adriana Portillo Bartow, 54, was one of those who came fleeing for her life. She was from Jutiapa, Guatemala. "I left Guatemala fearing for my life," she says. "I was afraid the Guatemalan government was going to kill me and other members of my family. I came to the United States to save the lives of my two remaining daughters, my husband, and myself. I came to Texas in 1985. Two years later I moved to Chicago's Chicago Lawn neighborhood.... I love this country. I love the people, the cultural diversity, and the freedom that people here have to express their political views."[8]

Bartow spoke with profound pain about the persecution of her family in Guatemala during the 1980s. She admits her family was actively involved in Guatemala's opposition movement, both armed and unarmed. In Guatemala, she worked as a teacher and community activist. "I took the unarmed route of activism in Guatemala. I tried to raise the consciousness of Guatemalan peasants through political education," says Bartow. "I inherited my sense of justice from my father. My father was a vendor who sold ambulatory medical equipment. I come from a family of activists. My father was a trade unionist who grew up in El Salvador. Because of his union activism, the military dictatorship expelled him from the country in the early 1950s. He had to seek exile in Guatemala." Her father's activism led him into conflict with Guatemalan authorities as well. "The Guatemalan military forces constantly intimidated us. They would throw dead bodies near our house. They once detained me for lack of identification. They detained my husband one night. They forced him to undress. They took him to a cliff and told him they were going to execute him if he didn't confess to being a subversive. They let him go in front of my house, still naked."

The Guatemalan military picked up Bartow's younger brother, Manuel, who was 17, and forced him to join the military in 1978. "By serving in the military, my brother saw the atrocities committed by Guatemalan soldiers. He saw the torture and the rapes," recalls Bartow. "He saw the kidnapings, what is called the "disappeared." He saw the clandestine jails where they torture those they arrest. He saw the execution of innocent activists, teachers, university professors, students, and all kinds of people. Manuel deserted the army in 1981 and fled to the United States in fear for his life." Many Guatemalans who fled violence in their country during the 1970s and 80s, tried desperately to obtain political refugee status in the United States. United States law defined refugees as people with a "well-founded fear of persecution in their homeland." The United States granted Cubans political refugee status in the 1960s. Yet the United States denied refugee status to most Guatemalans and Salvadorans. While Adriana Bartow expressed admiration for the freedom she enjoyed in Chicago, she was bitter that most Guatemalans were denied refugee status. She was also angry about the American government's direct involvement in the civil war of Guatemala.

"Refugee status would have given Guatemalans and Salvadorans access to social services, health care, and temporary economic assistance," says Bartow. "The United States has long denied their involvement in the civil wars of Guatemala or El Salvador. The United States has consistently denied Guatemalans and Salvadorans refugee status. Instead they call us economic refugees.... To grant political asylum to Guatemalans or Salvadorans would be to concede that the United States poured in military aid into those countries and trained many military officers, who were later implicated in atrocities. American participation in Guatemala dates to the CIA-engineered overthrown of President Jacobo Arbenz in 1954. Arbenz was trying to carry out land reform. The American United Fruit Company, Guatemala's largest landowner, opposed this. Since 1954, when Arbenz resigned, military dictators and presidents have repeatedly tortured, intimated, and exploited Guatemalans."

Since they were denied refugee status, many Guatemalans entered the United States illegally. Guatemalan families paid coyotes—those engaged in illegal smuggling of humans—thousands of dollars to help them cross into the United States illegally. Their undocumented status, lack of formal education, low literacy levels, and lack of English were obstacles to finding good-paying jobs, and getting ahead in major cities like Chicago. Another major obstacle was economic restructuring and the steady decline in mid-level manufacturing jobs in Chicago and other large cities.[9] Guatemalans used informal networks to find employment. They found jobs through friends and relatives who are already employed in certain workplaces. Many undocumented Guatemalans obtained low-paying, dead-ends jobs. They worked as gardeners for landscaping companies maintaining the large yards of middle-class, city and suburban residents. Others worked in cleaning services, garment factories, and as laborers on construction sites. Some worked in factories in Chicago, or in suburban factories of Melrose Park, North Lake, and Stone Park. Guatemalan women worked in small factories and as street pushcart vendors in Latino neighborhoods selling tamales and fruit. Other women worked as domestic workers as nannies and maids in middle-class homes.

In Chicago, a large number of Guatemalan men and women worked in the rapidly growing service sector in low-paying jobs like janitors and maids in the city's downtown restaurants, hotels, and large commercial buildings. In April 2000, thousands of African American, Polish, Mexican, and Guatemalan janitors in downtown Chicago marched off their jobs in a 24-hour strike. The janitors won a decent wage increase, and assurances that their pension and company-paid health care coverage would be continued. Later, about 4,500 African American, Polish, Mexican, and Guatemalan suburban janitors also went out on strike. The suburban janitors, who were earning only $6.65 an hour, demanded high wages, health-care coverage, and pensions. After a one-week strike, contractors and building owners conceded to most of their labor demands. The suburban janitors won an hourly salary increase of $1.35 and family medical insurance after three years.[10]

Undocumented Guatemalan men who did not find full-time jobs, worked as temporary day laborers. Dozens of day laborers stood on street corners in various city neighborhoods hoping that individuals and contractors drove by and offered them a job for the day. The day laborers performed lower-income services like construction, painting, cleaning, welding, or gardening. They got paid in cash and were making minimum wages or less. The low wages paid to day laborers kept them at the poverty rate. Undocumented workers were among the poorest in the nation. Some Guatemalans worked in hidden sweatshops. A study polled 800 immigrants in Chicago and found that almost 300 of the immigrants worked in sweatshops in Chicago and the suburbs. Most were undocumented Polish and Latinos, presumably illegal Guatemalans and Mexicans. Most were making less that $5.15 an hour.[11] Undocumented workers were about 5 percent of the Chicago metro labor market. They earned low wages, worked in unsafe conditions, and had low rates of health insurance.[12] They had little job security and were viewed as temporary workers who were the last hired and first fired.

Many employers preferred to hire undocumented workers like Guatemalans, because they worked hard and cheaply. Guatemalan workers seldom complained about work conditions because they desperately needed work and wages. Many regularly remitted money back home to Guatemala to help support families and relatives. Moreover, undocumented workers rarely complained because they lived in daily fear of being apprehended and deported by officials of the immigration and naturalization service (INS). In the summer of 1998, officials of Chicago's INS raided a suburban factory employing over 200 undocumented workers, mostly Guatemalans. When INS officials entered, the workers bolted for the factory's doors. Most were caught and deported. Some undocumented Guatemalans pretended to be Mexican. They entered the United States illegally through Mexico. If they were caught by immigration officials, they insisted they were Mexican. Thus, if they were deported, they were sent back to Mexico instead of thousands of additional miles into Guatemala. This made it easier for them to reenter the United States illegally.

Because of escalating violence in Guatemala, Adriana Bartow and members of her extended family in Guatemala dreamed of seeking safety and freedom in the United States. Unfortunately, some family members never escaped from Guatemala. Bartow's young brother, Carlos, met a tragic fate. In July 1981, government soldiers bombed a house in a residential neighborhood of Guatemala. Her brother, Carlos, was one of eight young men killed inside the house. However, it is the day of September 11, 1981 that is forever etched in Bartow's mind. She left her hometown of Jutiapa and arrived at her father's house in Guatemala City. Her two older daughters, Glenda and Rosura, ages nine and ten, had been staying with their grandfather for a couple of days. Upon arriving at the house, Bartow learned the horrible news: Guatemalan soldiers carted off her 70-year-old father, 70-year-old stepmother, 18-year-old sister-in-law, 18-month-year-old infant sister, and her two daughters. They "disappeared," a common term for torture and death in Central America. Bartow has never seen them again, despite years of searching. "We don't know what happened to them," says Bartow. "We assume that the soldiers probably killed the adults—my father, my stepmother, and my sister-in-law. Because in Guatemala, there are no survivors. All the ones who "disappeared," it's suspected that they assassinated them. We're hoping they didn't kill the girls. We're hoping maybe they gave them up for adoption, or sold them to foreign families, or even to someone in Guatemala."

Bartow was sure the Guatemala government would eventually try to kill her and the rest of her family. She and her remaining family members decided to leave Guatemala. "We came to the United States undocumented. We came through Mexico," says Bartow. "In January 1985, my husband, my two surviving daughters, Ingrid 7, and Sabrina, 10, and I, walked through the Arizona desert to enter the United States. It was a traumatic journey. We walked for three days and nights through the desert. We walked 16 hours a day. It got terribly cold in the desert at night. Our shoes and clothes would freeze. Immigration helicopters were flying overhead. We would hide in the bushes.... We came with the support of a religious social movement called the Sanctuary Movement." Bartow realized that life in the United States was harder than she expected. She only finished six years of elementary education in Guatemala. "I was frustrated because I was cleaning homes in Fort Worth, Texas. I had to clean the toilets of the rich white folks. They paid me thirty dollars a day for ten hours of work. It hurt me that these rich people told me I had to eat by myself in the kitchen. I had expected to sit at the table with the owners of the house. I'm sure they didn't want me to sit with them because I was Latina."

Guatemala's civil war officially ended with a peace accord in December of 1996. A 1999 United Nations report, blamed the Guatemalan army for atrocities during the 36-year civil war that left as many as 200,000 people—most of them Mayan Indians—dead or missing. Other reports blamed the Guatemalan military for destroying entire villages and torturing over 100,000 people. While the civil war ended, survivors like Bartow were still traumatized from the violence and loss of loved relatives. She suffered from bouts of depression. Once in the United States, Bartow tried to pull her shattered life together. But then she then faced a different type of horror: her husband became physically abusive with her. "The Guatemalan culture is a culture of respect, generosity, and human solidarity," says Bartow. "But the culture also teaches men and women about machismo. The men are the ones who are supposed to control. The woman is subservient and had to take care of her home, husband, and kids. I believe in equality between men and women. I could not tolerate the machismo of my first husband. He tried to control me. I had to ask for permission to do anything. He would tell me what to wear. That's how it started. It ended with emotional, physical, and sexual abuse. I divorced my first husband. My ex-husband suffered a mental breakdown and returned to Guatemala."

After her divorce, Bartow enjoyed her safety and peace of mind. "I attended evening classes and learned how to speak English. At evening school, I met and married Jeff Bartow, my current husband, who is American," says Bartow. "He is very supportive and respects who I am. In our house we both participate in decisions. We lived in Texas for two years. Then in 1987, a synagogue in Chicago's Hyde Park neighborhood sponsored my family and me to come to Chicago. They gave us food, shelter, medical care, and education for my daughters. They wanted me to concentrate on speaking out on human rights issues." Bartow is a member of Amnesty International. In Chicago she regularly speaks to diverse audiences about human rights violations, and the violence her family experienced in Guatemala. Bartow and her husband bought a two-flat, frame home in Chicago's Chicago Lawn neighborhood. This area was known as Marquette Park, after the 300-acre park in its southern half. The community was formerly Lithuanian. It had a reputation as a neighborhood that refused to accept Latinos or African Americans. In 1966, Dr. Martin Luther King—promoting open housing—led a march into Marquette Park. Some white residents reacted to the march by rioting. Someone in the crowd threw and hit Dr. King with a brick.

Because many Guatemalans were dark-skinned, and did not speak English, they experienced prejudice in public places like stores, public transportation, jobs, and neighborhoods.[13] "When we moved in, something interesting happened," says Barto. "We bought our house from an Italian family. Our neighbors were an older Italian couple, but they never said hello. They looked at us really aggressively. They put up a "for sale" sign a week after we moved in. A month later, they sold their house to a Mexican family. I think they moved out because we moved in." Bartow lived in a residential area with well maintained, brick bungalows. The quiet block was worlds away from the poverty and dirt of many neighborhoods in Guatemala.

In addition to becoming a home owner, Bartow has become an American citizen. "I did it because the U.S. Congress passed an antiterrorist law. It is a vague law and they can accuse anyone of terrorism," says Bartow. "I was worried that based on that law, and my human rights work, they might arrest me and deport me to Guatemala. If they send me back, the Guatemalan government will kill me. They have killed half my family. I did it also because there now seems to be much resentment against immigrants in the United States. They are even stripping away the rights of permanent U.S. residents." Bartow's two daughters who are in their mid-twenties, steadfastly refused to become American citizens. "My daughters are not activists, but they are very politically aware," says Bartow. "They don't hold resentment against the American people. But they have much resentment against the United States government because of what happened to our family, and because of American involvement in our country." While they shunned American citizenship, both daughters realized the importance of education for getting ahead. They both worked in prestigious medical laboratories while attending college. They hoped to graduate from college and become educated professionals.

Not a day passes that Bartow does not think about her other two daughters and family members who "disappeared." She was hoping to learn the whereabouts of her family members when the 1996 peace pact ended the civil war in Guatemala. She returned to Guatemala three separate times and asked a presidential commission for help in finding her family. But she returned to Chicago with no information about the fate of her loved ones. "Guatemalan President, Alvaro Arzu Irigoyen signed the peace pact. The Guatemalan Public Ministry was supposed to investigate what happened to the thousands of people who "disappeared" or were killed," says Bartow. "But the Ministry is stonewalling. The Ministry does not want to take up my case. They refuse to investigate because of the implications of the case. They were little girls who had absolutely nothing to do with the conflict that was going on."

Members of Chicago's Guatemalan community hold different, often opposing views about political issues in their home country. For instance, many Guatemalans cheered when Guatemala's former President Alvaro Arzu Irigoyen, came to Chicago in June 1998 to deliver the commencement address and receive an honorary degree at DePaul University. The college honored Arzu because of the role he played in the signing of the peace accord in Guatemala. Yet, other Guatemalans, including Bartow, objected that Arzu was being honored.[14] "It is not Arzul or the military that deserve credit for the peace accord," says Bartow. "For many years the Guatemalan military and government were against peaceful negotiations. It is we, the people of Guatemala who deserve credit. We sacrificed so much for the civil war to end. Credit should go to the people of Guatemala, and the opposition that began the process many years ago to bring the conflict to an end."

Despite the peace accord, Bartow was convinced the killings and kidnappings did not stop in Guatemala. In April 1998, Catholic Bishop Juan Gerardi Conedera was murdered two days after issuing an extensive report blaming the Guatemalan army for 80 percent of the 150,000 deaths during the civil war. After much foot-dragging, two years later Guatemalan officials arrested two former members of the Guatemalan army and charged them with the bishop's killing. "When the civil war ended, the Guatemalan military reduced its personnel nearly 33 percent," says Bartow. "Thousands of soldiers and police were left unemployed. There is no employment in Guatemala. But these people kept their arms. They organized into paramilitary groups. What they are doing is kidnapping people and demanding that families pay ransom for their return." Bartow wonders if the long struggle of Guatemalans for social change in their home country was in vain. "It was not worth it," she says. "All the personal sacrifices, and they all died in vain. The political situation in Guatemala had not changed. There is no freedom or justice. There are no jobs. People are still poor and suffering. If those things were there, it would have been worth it. Still, someone had to make the sacrifice. We had a dream for our country. Sadly, it did not come true." In 1999, former President Bill Clinton finally officially admitted that the United States did support the Guatemalan government and army during the country's 36 years of violence and civil war. Clinton said America was wrong for supporting a country that hurt so many of its own people.

Bartow worked as the director of the Greater Lawn Community Youth Network. The group is a nonprofit agency offering tutoring, after-school programs, and multicultural understanding for children. While Bartow and her family have done well, she believed other Guatemalans in Chicago were having a difficult time adjusting. "The majority of Guatemalans are poor. The majority do not know how to read and write," says Bartow. "They don't have any education. They don't have legal papers. I know many Guatemalans who work in small factories. Many women clean homes and take care of children. They are undocumented and are exploited the same way they exploit undocumented Mexican people." As a community activist, Bartow is aware of the different Latino groups in Chicago. Bartow says, "Progressive Guatemalans get along and are close with progressive-thinking Puerto Ricans. We have used the Ruiz Belvis Cultural Center in the Puerto Rican community for some speaking events.... But we have differences with some Cubans who are more politically conservative. We don't see eye to eye with some Cubans."

El Cristo Negro

Every January 15th, hundreds of Guatemalan families—dressed in their Sunday best—gather at Nuestra Señora De Lourdes (Our Lady of Lourdes) Roman Catholic parish, 4600 North Ashland. During one particular mass, some of the gathered families came from across town, a few came from the suburbs, and still others came from nearby states. They came to celebrate the annual special mass and procession in honor of El Cristo Negro de Esquipulas, a black Christ crucified on a wooden cross. The black Christ is very dear to Guatemalans. The church was filled with parishioners sitting in pews and many others standing in the back. "Señor Crucificado de Esquipulas, a black Christ, is indigenous to the Guatemalan people,"says Catalina de Garcia, 86. "In Guatemala we have been celebrating the image for hundreds of years. Christians took the black Christ to the town of Esquipulas, Guatemala. There is a beautiful church in Esquipulas built in honor of the black Christ. Hundreds of years ago, the natives of Guatemala did not like whites. For the Guatemalan Indians to like Christ, they made him black. It's a replica of Christ. About 90 percent of Guatemalans support the black Christ."[15]

Catalina de Garcia introduced the annual celebration at Our Lady of Lourdes twenty years ago. She and her son, Raúl, still organize the yearly event. During the mass her son slowly walked the image of the Señor Crucificado de Esquipulas through the church and up to the altar, where it was carefully placed. Rev. Curtis Lambert, the pastor, delivered a moving mass in Spanish. Some parishioners shed tears. After mass, parishioners gathered across the street in the parish hall for coffee, sweet rolls, and socializing. Old friends exchanged the latest news about their families, jobs, and current events in Guatemala. Garcia immigrated to Chicago in 1948 from Guatemala City. She came as a legal resident with her husband and daughter. She claimed she is the second Guatemalan family to settle in Chicago. She and her husband lived in the Uptown neighborhood, a couple of blocks from Our Lady of Lourdes parish. They are the owners of a two-flat, brownstone building. "I was an elementary school teacher in Guatemala," says Garcia. "Like most Guatemalans, we came to Chicago for better jobs and a better life for the children. I became a U.S. citizen in 1955. I worked with the Chicago Guatemalan Consul General's office for 22 years. I retired three years ago.... This is a great city with a lot of opportunities. But you have to work hard to make it in this city. You just can't sit back. We live comfortably and our children are doing well. My son is attending college to complete his master's degree. He is an executive in a bank. My daughter also completed college. And my second daughter is married and is a homemaker."

Garcia has been very involved in Chicago's Guatemalan community for many years. She and her husband operate a one-hour, Saturday afternoon radio program called "Chapinlandia." The popular, Spanish-language radio program has been on the air for over 20 years. The program featured typical Guatemalan music, interviews, and stories about Guatemalan culture and history. She was also the vice-president of the Sociedad Civica Guatemalteca. The group sponsored folkloric dances, plays, and musical performances on Guatemala culture throughout the city. Garcia agreed that many Guatemalan families in Chicago are still struggling to make it. "Yes a lot of Guatemalans have problems with immigration because they are undocumented," says Garcia. "We used to help them become American citizens. A community organization would come to the basement of Nuestra Señora De Lourdes to help people fill out the paperwork to become American citizens. But unfortunately, they stopped the program.... Another problem is lack of education. We have the reputation of being illiterate in Guatemala. I hate to say this, but some Guatemalans in Chicago are lazy. They don't try hard to learn English and get an education. Guatemalans need to learn English. We need to become better educated. Those that learn English and get some education are doing fine. They are owners of homes and have good jobs. Chicago's Guatemalan community is making progress.... This is a grand city, thank God."

An Invisible Community?

But others insist that the progress of Guatemalans has been very slow. They argued that efforts to establish a cohesive community among Guatemalans in Chicago have been difficult. "Chicago's Guatemalan community is invisible," says Julio Revolorio, 48. "Though we are the third largest Latino group in Chicago, we're invisible. Unlike other Latinos, we are not concentrated in one neighborhood. We are dispersed throughout the city. Another major problem is the lack of trust among Guatemalans. This is the product of a long history of violence and repression in our country. We do not trust other Latinos or even other Guatemalans. This dispersion and lack of trust does not allow us to organize into strong communities. It's even hard to organize Guatemalans into block clubs."[16]

Revolorio was the former executive director of Casa Guatemala, a community-based, social service group in Chicago's Ravenswood neighborhood. The agency was founded in 1983 by a small group of young, educated Guatemalans who had fled violence in their country. Many in the group were former high school and college students in Guatemala. The group wanted Americans to become aware of the war and killings in Guatemala. They regularly published a bulletin on human rights violations in Guatemala. They were looking for American solidarity with the struggle of Guatemala. The group also wanted to inform Chicago's growing Guatemalan community about the fate of their relatives in Guatemala. But others in the Guatemalan community distrusted Casa Guatemala, and founders of the group were branded as Marxist radicals. "In our first two years of existence, we helped over 16,000 Guatemalans in Chicago with services and referrals," says Revolorio. "We helped people with immigration, landlord abuses, problems with employers, and problems with police.... Yet the Chicago Guatemalan Consul General, and the Sociedad Civica Guatemalteca, would tell people we were a center for left-wing guerillas. They said we recruited people and send them to fight in Guatemala with the guerillas. That was not true. We had conflicts with those two groups over ideas. They are very politically conservative."

Casa Guatemala's first building on Wilson and Broadway was mysteriously burned down. The group later acquired another building. Casa Guatemala became one of the main organizations that served thousands of Guatemalans yearly. The organization provided literacy training for adults, legal counseling, and classes on immigration and naturalization. It sponsored cultural programs including art exhibits, performances, and dances celebrating the indigenous Mayan culture of Guatemala. One room in the offices of Casa Guatemala was filled with brightly-colored paintings of Guatemala's countryside, along with hand-woven purses, rugs, and sweaters. The group was preparing for an exhibition. Revolorio was a student organizer in Guatemala. "I lived in the capital of Guatemala. My school mates and I organized a literacy campaign in Guatemala, says Revolorio. "We went to areas away from the urban centers to start programs of literacy for adults. Many of my high school classmates were killed by the Guatemalan military in the 1970s. I received four death threats. I fled for my life. I immigrated to Los Angeles in 1980 and lived there for a while. I had some problems with some Mexican youths there. They wanted me to join a gang. I told them I'm not stupid. I come from a country where they are killing innocent people. I'm not going to kill people here for nothing. I had two fights with the gangs."

Revolorio tried to adjust to his new life in Los Angeles. "I learned English by driving and making deliveries for a bakery. I worked in a gas station and washed dishes in a restaurant. Later, I found a better-paying job in construction.... I came to Chicago in January 1985 to visit a Guatemalan friend. I didn't plan to stay here. My friend didn't like that I wore my hair long and in a ponytail. We wore it like that in Guatemala. I promised myself that I would not cut my hair until the day that I could return and live in peace in Guatemala. My friend said this is America and he insisted that I cut it immediately. I refused, got upset, and left. I caught the train but I wasn't sure where I was going."

Unlike his friend, Revolorio refused to assimilate into American culture. He wanted to retain his Guatemalan culture and identity. He preferred to speak Spanish instead of English. Upon leaving his friend's house, Revolorio jumped on a train. Yet he did not know his way around Chicago. "I ended up on the South Side," recalls Revolorio. "It was night. I walked around looking for a hotel. I ran into a group of black men. They robbed me. They took my identification, my airplane ticket back to Los Angeles, and about $1,300 in cash. The airlines refused to give me another ticket. I was stranded in Chicago. I was homeless for about two weeks. It was February and freezing. A black man saw me outside, huddled in a hallway. He said, 'you'll freeze to death out here tonight, if you don't find a warmer place.' He took me to lower Wacker Drive. We were still outside. But he let me sleep in his card board house, which was on a grate. He had warm blankets. He took me to a church where you could bathe and change clothes."

Revolorio pulled himself up from the mean streets. He decided to stay in Chicago. He landed a laborer job in construction. He also volunteered to teach English to Latino adults at Universdad Popular, a Latino, social service agency on Chicago's North Side. Since some Guatemalans are illiterate, learning English in their adult years was difficult. "Many Guatemalans do not speak English.I know people who have been here many years and still do not speak English. They use their children as translators. But in the last five years we see many Guatemalans taking English classes at community colleges," says Revolorio. Revolorio believed Guatemalans get along with other Latinos in Chicago. "There are some small conflicts. It's a question of nationalism. Some Guatemalans feel I speak better Spanish than Mexicans or Puerto Ricans. Puerto Ricans don't pronounce their r's, those types of things. But we have good relations with Centro Romero, which serves Salvadorans. We also have good relations with groups like the Puerto Rican Cultural Center, Ruiz Belvis, and Casa Aztlán. During the last ten years there is a lot of intermarriage between Guatemalans and Mexicans, and Puerto Ricans. Intermarriage helps Guatemalans. For instance, if they are married to Puerto Ricans, well Puerto Ricans know they have a right to health care. Guatemalans begin to learn their rights."

While many Guatemalans have made Chicago their home, Revolorio planned to return to Guatemala. He wants to take his American-born wife and family with him. While he liked Chicago, he yearned to live in his homeland. He hoped the killing ended in Guatemala and he and his family could live in peace. "After 18 years of living in the United States, I have not stopped dreaming of returning to Guatemala," says Revolorio. Other Latinos in Chicago have become aware of the city's growing Guatemalan presence. Guatemalans have established their Guatemalan Chamber of Commerce. The chamber has about 100 members, mostly owners of small businesses, like grocery and jewelry stores, and restaurants. Moreover, the Chicago Guatemalan Consul General is an important mediating institution for Guatemalans. It helped in areas of immigration and naturalization, and regularly sponsored cultural activities emphasizing Guatemalan culture.

Guatemalans annually participate in a festive Central American Independence Day Parade in downtown Chicago on September 15th to celebrate their independence day. Guatemala, El Salvador, Nicaragua, and Honduras all celebrate their independence day on September 15th. They all gained independence from Spain in 1821. The parade featured floats, music, and children and adults dressed in colorful, traditional costumes from their home countries. In 1996, Rigoberta Menchú, a Guatemalan indigenous leader and Nobel Peace Prize winner, visited Chicago and spoke at several universities. A couple of colleges awarded her honorary degrees. Her speeches and moving autobiography informed Chicagoans about the Guatemalan struggles and culture.[17]

Making Their Voices Heard

Some leaders in the Guatemalan community believed Guatemalans have progressed in Chicago, although they still faced numerous social and political problems. Guatemalans still lack high-profile organizations or leaders that can advocate for their community. Because they lived in fear and distrust in their country, many Guatemalans preferred safety rather than visibility and community involvement. Another major hurdle was that the overwhelming majority of Guatemalans were undocumented. Guatemalans shunned community participation out of fear of being discovered and deported by immigration officials.[18]

"The undocumented issue is a big problem in the Guatemalan community," says Maricela Garcia, 47, former executive director of the Illinois Coalition for Immigrant and Refugee Rights. "Other problems include finding good-paying jobs, finding decent housing, problems with education, and problems with police. I think we have a lot in common with the rest of the Latino community. The big difference is that there are a lot of undocumented Guatemalans in Chicago.... The mission of the Illinois Coalition for Immigrants is to advocate for the rights of immigrants and refugees to fully participate in the social, economic, and political activities of this society. We challenge policies that negatively affect refugees. We also provide technical assistance to organizations that work directly with immigrants and refugees. We train and disseminate information on immigration laws, policies, and procedures."[19]

Despite a growing community, many Guatemalans did not vote in local elections because they were undocumented. Their inability to vote in large numbers rendered them politically powerless. Unlike other Latino groups, they lacked elected, political leaders. Also, many Guatemala families were still dealing with daily survival issues. They did not have the free time for electoral politics or community involvement. Yet some Guatemalan leaders like Garcia understood the importance of becoming involved in electoral politics and community advocacy. Garcia was a student organizer in Guatemala. Her organizing activities got her in trouble with the Guatemalan military. "I was a student organizing around human rights and civil rights issues," says Garcia. "It was very dangerous to organize around these issues in Guatemala in the early 1980s. In college we started a newspaper protesting the policies of the government. We had marches and sit-ins whenever peasants were forced off their land. Those activities were considered subversive. As we increased our solidarity with peasants and workers, we were the targets of oppression by the military because we were not considered nice, college kids anymore. About 35 of my classmates were killed by the military or "disappeared." I was in my last year of social work at San Carlos University. I had to leave Guatemala to preserve my life. I left Guatemala and arrived in Chicago in January of 1982. When I first came to Chicago, I lived in the Ravenswood neighborhood. There were many Guatemalans living there. There still are."

Garcia found life in Chicago a little strange. She also faced prejudice in public places. "It was a cultural shock to see so many people living together in one building, but not communicating," recalls Garcia. "In Guatemala, you say good morning and hello to everyone in the neighborhood. People here were very cold, individualistic, and distant. On the trains when I spoke Spanish with another person, a few whites would say, 'this is America, everyone should speak English,' or 'these wetbacks, that's why they never succeed.' The weather was also a cultural shock. I came to Chicago when it was one of the coldest winters. I think it was 25 degrees below zero with the wind chill. I just couldn't believe that people could live here in that cold." Garcia entered the United States as a tourist and overstayed her welcome. "I was undocumented here for about nine months. That was very scary because I knew that if I were picked up and deported back to Guatemala, they would torture me. In Guatemala, they first torture you until you give the government the names of other people who are involved in organizing, then they kill you. They would have killed me. I applied and won my case for political asylum in the United States. About six years ago, I became an American citizen."

Garcia taught herself English by reading English-language newspapers. She finished her bachelor's degree and earned her master's. She and her husband, Michael McConnell, own a home in the Edgewater neighborhood on the city's far North Side. Garcia got involved in trying to help the Guatemala community in Chicago. "I was the co-founder of Casa Guatemala. And I founded an organization called Women for Guatemala, which for 11 years raised significant amounts of money in Chicago to support widows and orphans in Guatemala. The organization was made up primarily of white people in solidarity with Guatemala. When they signed the peace agreement in Guatemala, the group felt that was the end of the commitment, and the organization no longer existed." Compared to other Latino groups, Guatemalans were a relatively new community slowly maturing. "Guatemalans are politically sophisticated," argues Garcia. "The war in Guatemala has made us very analytical in political matters. But because of the war, Guatemalans are very suspicious of government institutions. Guatemalans are also a new community in Chicago. We don't have the institutions, infrastructure, and the leadership that other Latino communities have because those communities have been here many more years."

Garcia agreed that Guatemalans and other Latinos from Central and South America look to America as a promised land. They will undoubtedly continue to flock to major American cities like Chicago. Poverty and natural disasters have triggered the exodus. In 1998, Hurricane Mitch, devastated regions of Central American, including parts of Guatemala, Honduras, and Nicaragua. "Yes, I think Guatemalans are still coming to big cities like Chicago," says Garcia. "I couldn't venture to say how many are coming. I know there were more coming in the early 1980s because of a combination of the war and the bad economy in Guatemala.... But people immigrate because they are looking for opportunities to survive. There are so few jobs and opportunities in Guatemala for people to survive. I have also seen some people who have gone back to Guatemala when the peace agreement was signed. Not in large numbers, but some have gone back."

Some Guatemalan community organizations cannot keep up with the growing demand for social services and assistance from the city's growing Guatemalan community. Casa Guatemala, for instance, was running on a shoestring with mostly volunteers. The agency's telephones were disconnected due to lack of payment. Yet Garcia was optimistic and had high hopes about the future of Guatemala and Guatemalans in Chicago. "Our struggle in Guatemala was worth it. It was hard work, but the seeds were planted. It will take a couple of generations to see fundamental change in Guatemala, but it will happen. I miss Guatemala. I go back and forth to Guatemala. I still dream in Spanish. And I still speak Spanish.... But Chicago is home. I'm committed to changing laws and policies that are unfair to immigrants here. I'm confident Guatemalans will find a way of making their voices heard and their presence felt in Chicago. Guatemalans need to get involved in the electoral process. We came with a political sophistication. They must make alliances with other Latino groups. They should also reach out to the black community. You have to have a rainbow coalition."

Salvadorans—Rocky Road Ahead?

There were striking similarities between the immigration experiences of Guatemalans and Salvadorans. Like Guatemalans, Salvadorans came to Chicago and other major American cities during the 1970s and 80s. They came for both economic and political reasons. Both groups came fleeing deteriorating economic conditions in their homelands, the traumatic experience of civil war, repression, and violence in their countries. The onset of civil war in El Salvador in 1979, forced hundreds of thousands of Salvadorans to flee their country. Like Guatemalans, some of the first Salvadoran immigrants to leave their country were students, teachers, and professionals. But a large number were poor, uneducated, unskilled laborers. Many did not speak English and like Guatemalans, most were denied political refugee status in the United States. Strict U.S. immigration quotas limited the number who entered legally. Thus, like Guatemalans, many Salvadorans arrived as undocumented workers.[20]

Nationally, after Mexicans, Salvadorans represented the second largest number of illegal immigrants apprehended by the U.S. Immigration and Nationalization Service. The majority of Central Americans—up to a half million— lived in Los Angeles, with substantial numbers in San Francisco, Texas, Washington, New York, Chicago, New Orleans, and Miami.[21] The 1990 U.S. census counted 3,877 Salvadorans in Chicago.[22]

But since many Salvadorans were undocumented, it was difficult to know precisely how many lived in Chicago. It's believed the Salvadoran population significantly increased in the Chicago area during the last decade. There are probably about 50,000 Salvadorans in Illinois and most lived in Chicago. Some early Salvadoran immigrants to Chicago came with a mentality of temporary exile. Many hoped to return to El Salvador once the civil war and killings stopped. Some did return when the civil war officially ended in 1992, but most stayed. They realized that while life was a struggle in Chicago, the city still offered more jobs, higher wages, and a higher standard of living than in El Salvador.

And like Guatemalans, Salvadorans continue to immigrant to Chicago. Although entering the United States illegally is now more difficult due to increased surveillance and border patrols. Salvadorans were lured by the materialism and affluence of America that they saw on their television sets back home. They come escaping natural disasters, poor economies, and intolerable poverty in their country. Some came with dreams of working a few years, making money, and returning home to buy a small home or business. Recent arrivals were mostly poor, uneducated, and did not speak English. "We have a large Salvadoran community in Chicago that is undocumented. They are dispersed and live in many neighborhoods," says Daisy Funes, 42. Funes is Salvordoran and executive director of Centro Romero, a social service agency in the Edgewater neighborhood. "The big problem is adaptation. They come thinking they will be here for only two years and then they will return to El Salvador. They don't establish themselves. Many do not speak English. They want to learn English, but they struggle raising families. They work in hard jobs that pay little. The hours are odd. Many have emotional problems because of the civic war in El Salvador. Many saw the military kill their sons or entire families right in front of them."[23]

Since Salvadorans have not been in Chicago as long as other Latino groups, they have not craved out their own distinct neighborhoods. In a chain-like migration, many followed friends and relatives to neighborhoods with affordable housing. Most were renters as opposed to homeowners. They lived in large apartment buildings on Chicago's North Side in Uptown, Edgewater, Rogers Park, and Albany Park. Some lived in Mexican neighborhoods like South Chicago and Pilsen. Salvadorans, much like Guatemalans, immigrated to American cities like Chicago during a period of economic restructuring that involved a steady decline in traditional manufacturing industries. They encountered an economy with growth in high-technology industries and high and low-skilled services.[24] Many Salvadorans were employed in low-paying, unskilled jobs in the growing low-end, service sector. They worked as janitors, dishwashers, and waiters in restaurants and hotels in Chicago's downtown. Entire families often worked for years at temporary, daily-labor agencies that dot the North Side. Other Salvadorans worked in small factories in the city and in suburbs like Rolling Meadows, Des Plaines, and Waukegan.

Like other undocumented workers, Salvadorans were often taken advantage of by employers. Employers expected them to work long, odd hours and shifts. Workers were sometimes placed in unsafe working conditions. The jobs they held were menial and paid minimum wages or less. The jobs did not offer paid vacations, pensions, or family health insurance. Undocumented Salvadorans could not collect unemployment compensation if they lost their jobs. Some Salvadoran women also experienced sexual harassment on jobs. "When my husband and I came to Chicago, we worked in coffee shops washing dishes," says Funes. "They paid me a dollar an hour, though the minimum wage was $3.25. To survive we lived with three other families. We worked in various factories. The factory where my husband worked was very abusive. The workers could not go to the washroom or even have lunch breaks. I worked in a car-wax factory here in Chicago. The white boss would sexually abuse the women. Most of the women were Mexican. He offered you a permanent job in the factory if you had sexual relations with him. He sexually touched the women whenever he wanted. He offered me a permanent job. I turned it down. The women didn't do anything because they were undocumented. They needed the work. They didn't have any money. They had to survive in this country."

Founded in 1980, the agency, Centro Romero, helped many Salvadorans and other immigrant families from Central and South America. The agency was named after Arnulfo Oscar Romero, the Catholic Archbishop of El Salvador. Romero was assassinated in El Salvador in 1980, allegedly by right-wing, military death squads. He spoke out against the violence, human-rights abuses, and social injustices committed by El Salvador's government against its own people. His killers were never caught. Centro Romero made referrals to other public and private agencies that helped Salvadorans meet basic needs like shelter, clothing, and health care. But the agency concentrated on providing services to help immigrants in their long term adjustment. Centro Romero provided job referrals, English classes, literacy classes, GED, legal aid, and immigration and naturalization assistance.

Funes came to Chicago in 1980 from El Salvador. She feared that the Salvadoran military death squads planned to kill her and her husband. Her family was involved in union organizing of public school teachers. The military government in El Salvador saw the organizing as subversive. Funes' family members were labeled guerrillas. They accused her cousin of being a guerrilla. "Military soldiers killed my cousin in El Salvador. My cousin was only 18-years-old. They cut off his head," recalls Funes. "We found his body by a river, and we buried him. They killed him just because he had participated in some students protest marches. It is believed the government killed over 75,000 innocent people. And another 200,000 "disappeared." Many families lost loved ones during the civil war in El Salvador, which officially ended in 1992. Ask any Salvadoran and they will tell you they lost aunts, brothers, cousins, or parents in that war."

Like others from war-torn countries, Salvadorans who experienced horrible violence and death of family members, became distrustful of government and others. Many just wanted to be left alone to live anonymously and peacefully. Being largely undocumented, Salvadorans shied away from participation in politics. Their undocumented status prevented them from voting and rendered them politically powerless. "My husband and I entered the U.S. illegally," recalls Funes. "I was 17. We crossed over Guatemala and came though Mexico. We swam across the Rio Bravo river. It was dangerous and people sometimes died in the currents....Over half the Salvadoran community in Chicago are undocumented. We don't vote. We don't have any political representation. What counts in this country is a political voice."

Another hurdle many Salvadorans faced was their inability to speak English. Due to a lack of English, Salvadorans had a difficult time obtaining better-paying jobs or getting ahead. Obtaining basic services like quality health care was often a challenge. "When I came here, I didn't speak English," recalls Funes. "Once, I went to Cook County Hospital. I was pregnant. The white receptionist asked me my name. I told her I didn't speak English did she have a translator? She said, 'are you stupid. We don' have translators here. You're in America, learn English.' My husband and I both went to school to learn English. We still don't know it well, but we understand it.... Many Salvadorans want to learn English, but they cannot because they do not have a stable home. They are working in low-income jobs like washing dishes in restaurants, in hotels, and babysitting. The jobs do not pay well. They have to work and take care of their families. They cannot afford babysitters. They often don't have the time to take English classes."

Some Salvadorans faced a culture shock in Chicago. Their traditional, rural, Latino immigrant values often conflicted with those of the large, modern American city. Parents worried their children were asking for too much independence. Some children saw their parents as too strict and out of touch with big city living. Some marriages became strained. Some family members resorted to substance abuse or domestic violence. Centro Romero, for example, treated about 250 women annually who were victims of domestic violence. "The majority of men in El Salvador are accustomed to working, and women being in the house," says Funes. "They are the ones who provide. Coming here they have to deal with the fact that woman cannot stay home. Both have to work to survive. The woman learns new values outside the home. Some men cannot handle that. They get depressed and drink alcohol. Alcoholism is a big problem in the community. The men resort to domestic violence to control their wives. When domestic violence starts, we empower women to make decisions to stop it."

It also seemed like the physical health of immigrants from countries like El Salvador declined as they became Americanized. Since many immigrants worked odd hours and often two jobs, they had little time to prepare healthy meals or exercise. They adopted diets high in sugar and fat. Immigrants ate food at fast-food restaurants. Like other Americans they became overweight and obese, triggering problems like diabetes and heart problems. Funes is a home owner and lives in the Edgewater neighborhood. She and her husband have taken college classes. Her dream is to one day complete her bachelors' degree. Her other dream is to see Salvadorans progress. Funes says that Centro Romero works with other Latino groups in the city to help immigrants. "We have contacts with other Latino groups. It seems, however, that some Puerto Ricans think they are white, because they're American citizens. They think they're superior to Mexicans and Central Americans. We have closer relations with Mexican organizations like Caza Aztlán, El Progresso Latino, and Universidad Popular. These are professional groups that deal with issues like immigration and literacy."

Funes was concerned about the future of the Salvadoran community. "I think it will take a long time for Salvadorans to progress in Chicago," she says. "If you don't know English, it's hard to get ahead. If you don't have citizenship, then it's easy to think I'll just remain in this miserable, low-paying job where I'm being exploited. Workers think I don't have a union so I'll just keep quiet. I have to feed my kids." Some Salvadorans have made attempts to improve their lives in Chicago by becoming legal residents and American citizens. Others, however, became disappointed and frustrated when they realized that the immigration and naturalization process in Chicago was complicated, extremely time-consuming, and expensive. And even American citizenship without higher education, did not guarantee them a brighter future. Many Salvadorans did not have a high school or college education. Good-paying jobs required college education. And even many full-time, lower-level, service jobs did not pay a livable wage. Moreover, Chicago area companies were increasingly using part-time workers, who were poorly paid and lacked benefits.

Some Latino groups were doing well in Chicago, while others, like Salvadorans, were still struggling to make ends meet. For instance, in Chicago nearly

30 percent of blacks, 20 percent of Latinos, nearly 18 percent of Asians and 8.2 percent of whites lived in poverty in 1999. Median household income in the city was $49,222 for whites, $29,086 for blacks, $36,543 for Latinos, and $40, 519 for Asians.[25] Funes believed a good number of the Latinos living in poverty were probably Salvadoran. "It's true Salvadorans are living better in Chicago than in El Salvador," says Funes. "But how much better? We're seeing where three families get together to afford a two-bedroom apartment. Families are working all day, often at two jobs. While the parents are working, their kids often get involved in gangs, alcohol, and drugs."

Sanctuary and Help from Churches

About 75 percent of Salvadorans who came to American cities were Roman Catholic. Yet some were increasingly changing over to Protestant religions. Some embraced Protestantism because they were grateful that in the 1970s and 80s, Protestant churches spearheaded the Sanctuary Movement, and helped families flee from war-torn, counties in Central America. During the Sanctuary Movement, about 100 Protestant churches in the United States helped hundreds of Guatemalan and Salvadoran families enter the country illegally through an elaborate underground railroad. The first stop of the underground railroad was usually a church near the U.S. Mexican border. Refugees were given food, lodging, and transportation to the next stop. They were then transported to churches in Illinois, Wisconsin, California, New York, and other states.[26]

Churches in the Sanctuary Movement were angry that the American government did not grant political asylum to refugees from El Salvador and Guatemala. The churches gave shelter to families and allowed them to live in their church attics or basements. They provided food, clothing, and all the family's expenses.

Church officials were committing a federal crime by publicly announcing that they were harboring "illegal aliens." Yet the churches wanted to save the lives of undocumented families. They wanted to protect undocumented families from deportation to volatile, war-torn countries. They also wanted draw attention to the United States military aid to repressive Salvadoran and Guatemalan regimes.[27] "Our church was the first in the Midwest, and the second in the country to become a sanctuary and publicly announce it," says Rev. David Chevrier, 68, pastor of the Wellington Avenue United Church of Christ on Chicago's North Side. "We became a sanctuary in 1982. We knew the legal consequences of providing sanctuary. The government could fine you $5,000 and put you in jail for each undocumented person you helped. But our members decided it was the moral, just, and Christian thing to do. Our church has a long history of political involvement. In 1968, this church opened its doors to demonstrators from the National Democratic Convention. Our church members gained a greater sense of what their faith means because of their civil disobedience." [28]

Rev. Chevrier was the pastor of the Wellington church since 1970. In the

1980s, the Wellington Church provided sanctuary to a single man, and later to a family from El Salvador. They also gave sanctuary to a Guatemalan family. "They all did well with themselves," says Rev. Chevrier. "The family from El Salvador, the father, mother, four sons, and a daughter stayed in our church for a couple of years. The family settled in Chicago. We helped get them settled, get their children in good schools, and helped them find jobs so they could become self-sufficient. The family received American citizenship. The father got a good job. One son is working for IBM in Texas and is doing fine. The others are married with children." A few Catholic churches in the United States acted as sanctuaries. But Catholic churches were not as extensively involved as Protestant churches. "The Catholic church never publicly condoned the sanctuary movement. That's ironic because El Salvador and Guatemala are Catholic countries," says Rev. Chevrier.

In the 1980s, a few Catholic churches in Chicago's Uptown neighborhood helped Latinos from Central and South America. The churches supported an activist community group called Comite Latino. Comite Latino organized Salvadorans and other Latinos from Central and South America to demand better jobs, affordable housing, bilingual education, and improved immigration and naturalization services. Comite Latino used protests and demonstrations to present their grievances. The group used Catholic liberation theology as an organizing principle. Liberation theology was first used by some Catholic priests in the 1960s in the poor barrios of Latin America. The theology challenged people to apply the Christian gospel by helping the poor address the poverty and injustices they suffer. But after several years of organizing, Comite Latino fell apart.

A Catholic parish that is very popular among Salvadorans is Our Lady of Mercy in the Albany Park neighborhood. More than 1,000 Latino families, many from Central and South America countries, filled the pews of Our Lady of Mercy for Sunday mass. The parish lacked the ornate, interior architecture usually found in most Catholic parishes. Yet Latinos felt at home here. They listened attentively as Rev. Donald Headley delivered a Spanish-language sermon praising the virtues of community involvement. He challenged his congregation to become more active in the church and neighborhood. At noon, the parish was again jam-packed with Latino families coming for the second Spanish-language mass. "We have a lot of families from Central and South America in our parish," says Rev. Headley, 75, pastor of Our Lady of Mercy for almost twenty years. "We have families from El Salvador, Santo Domingo, Costa Rica, Argentina, Guatemala, and Puerto Rico. We also have many poor Mexican families. About 50 percent of the Catholics in this area are going to be Latinos within five years. Latinos are a very young community. I have 40 baptisms here a month."[29]

After Sunday mass, parishioners mingled around to converse with Rev. Headley. Rev. Headley has worked with Latinos in Chicago for over 45 years. He first began working with Puerto Ricans in 1958 as a newly ordained priest. He was the former director of the Archdiocese's Office for the Spanish Speaking, which replaced the Cardinal's Committee for the Spanish Speaking. Many Latinos appreciated Rev. Headley's efforts to combine religious conviction with community activism. "In the 1960s, we wanted to get Puerto Rican men more involved in the church," recalls Rev. Headley. "We were also trying to help the Mexican community get organized in unions. We were trying to help with the boycott of grapes and the things Cesar Chavez was doing. We were trying to get people involved in Alinsky-style groups like the Northwest Community Organization. Many things were going on. We tried to get people involved in their faith and the organization of their community. We are still trying to do that. It's an attempt to keep religion from becoming alienated from peoples' personal lives."

Rev. Headley explained that the major problem he saw among his parishioners was the lack of good-paying jobs. "Many parishioners from Central and South America are undocumented. Finding some kind of work that can sustain them and perhaps sustain somebody back home is a big problem. These people are really poor. They're poverty-stricken. The other problem is the high incidence of alcoholism among Latino men. Maybe it's discouragement as to why they drink. I think they are probably alcoholics and don't realize it. A lot come in and make a religious oath not do drink anymore. Sometimes they keep it. But many need help to stop drinking."

Many Salvadorans who attended Our Lady of Mercy parish lived in multi-apartment buildings in Albany Park. Two and three families often lived together to share expenses. Like previous immigrants, they looked to the church for help with their spiritual and material needs. Our Lady of Mercy provided an array of social services for immigrants. The need was often greater than what the parish could handle. "Many of our parishioners are recent immigrants. They are struggling economically and struggling to adjust to a new city," says Theresita Perez, 57, Puerto Rican and pastoral associate at Our Lady of Mercy. "Many are poor people. They use our food pantry. Our church also has four Spanish-speaking lawyers on Saturdays who provide free legal assistance. This is a very popular program. Latinos come seeking legal help regarding crime, jobs, divorce, accidents, and job-related issues. We have a social worker that gives counseling on family problems and domestic violence."[30]

Many Salvadoran female parishioners at Our Lady of Mercy have looked to Perez for guidance. They come to her for advice and help with family and marriage problems. Parishioners held a dance and raised funds to send Perez to Israel for three months of biblical studies. She completed her master's degree in pastoral studies. In the past, some Catholic parishes were criticized for their unwillingness to share decision making with laity. However, laity was very involved in Our Lady of Mercy. "Rev. Headley encourages people to take responsibility for lay leadership within the church and the community," says Perez. "Many parents are involved in our parish and in running our grammar school."

Hoping For a Good Life

One active member of Our Lady of Mercy parish is Judith Alvarado, 48.

She and her husband immigrated from El Salvador to Chicago in 1982. They came with high expectations of finding good-paying jobs and a better life. "We entered the country illegally through Mexico with the help of a coyote," says Alvarado. "I had a little education in El Salvador. I was a secretary, but the job didn't pay well. I wanted to improve my life. My first husband died in El Salvador. He died from drinking a lot of alcohol. He was only 24 when he died. My second husband and I came seeking better work in the United States. I didn't know how to speak English when I came here. I couldn't find a job as a secretary. For the first four years I cleaned the homes of white families in the suburbs. Later, my husband and I got better jobs in a plastics factory."[31]

Alvarado was confident things would improve for her and her family. She became active in her church. Though her involvement and activism at church, she gained self-confidence and independence. She took steps to improve her life. "Religious is very important in my life. I have been involved in the church for many years," says Alvardo. "At church I read the bible during Sunday masses. I was involved in the choir. I have been helping families and children preparing for the first communion. I enjoy my church. I wanted to better my life. I began taking English classes. I studied hard to become an American citizen, and I became an American citizen in 1990. I felt very happy. I didn't think it would ever happen. With government grants I began taking classes at San Augustine College on the North Side."

Unfortunately, however, Alvarado's husband became threatened by her education and newfound independence. He resented the time she devoted to church and school. She became trapped in the tyranny of an abusive relationship. Their dream of a better life together in America shattered. "My husband attended college for two years, but he did not want me to go to school," says Alvarado. "He did not support me while I attended college. In El Salvador men are socialized to be in control of the home. Women are subservient. He did not like that I began to question his decisions. His machismo came out. He began to drink a lot and use marijuana. He mistreated me mentally and physically. He pushed and slapped me. One day he hit me in the face with a shoe. He almost broke my cheek bone. I decided to leave him that day.... My husband and I divorced in 1997. I stayed in school and graduated from college with an associate of arts degree."

The divorce has been hard on Alvarado and her daughter. "It was a tough decision. I knew I had to work extra hard for my daughter and me to survive. My personal life has also changed. Now I feel awkward visiting my married girlfriends. I feel they are probably thinking that I'm trying to steal their husbands. I don't socialize much anymore. My daughter and I enjoy going to the movies to watch English-language films." Alvarado lived in a large apartment building in Albany Park with her twelve-year-old daughter. Her son joined the U.S. Marines for four years. Her father visited from El Salvador and has been staying with them for a few weeks. He says times are still very hard in El Salvador and people suffer from lack of employment Alvarado placed a court order of protection against her ex-husband. "He still argues and threatens me," she says.

"He is angry because the state is taking child custody payments from his check. He refuses to see his daughter.... I don't know that I will ever remarry. I've lost faith in men." As a religious woman, Alvarado does not like to pass judgment on others. However, she criticized the behavior of some of her neighbors. She lives on a block lined on both sides with large, multi-apartment buildings. "In one building down the street many Latino men sit outside drinking beer all day," she says. "That looks bad. In another building, people have their windows open with Latino music blasting away early in the morning. I think we need to be more considerate of others. If we want people to respect us as Latinos, we should learn to respect others."

Alvarado says her faith in God helped her cope with difficult times. She saw her life improving. She was rebuilding her life. "I work in an electronics factory in Skokie, Illinois. I solder electrical circuits. I'm making good money. I'm making over $14 dollars an hour. I've been working there four years. I work ten hours a day, sometimes six days a week. I come home tired from work. But I would like to someday buy a small house for my daughter and me. I just want to live in peace. I now dedicate myself to my job, my church, and raising my daughter."

Chapter Six: Cubans

Fleeing Communism

Elias Sánchez, 69, was willing to risk his life to come to America. He entered the United States in 1969 in dramatic fashion from Cuba. "I was imprisoned for one year and 45 days in a jail in Santiago, Cuba. They accused me of engaging in activities against Fidel Castro and the Cuban government.... I lost half my middle finger on my left hand when a dynamite detonator fuse exploded in my hand. I escaped from a Cuban jail and traveled three days without eating or drinking water. I walked through a big section of territory filled with landmines to reach Guantanamo Naval Base in Cuba. Many people have died trying to cross through that territory. I don't know how those landmines did not explode. The Cuban government would have shot me if they caught me. I climbed the fence and jumped onto the American side. I was so happy when I reached the American side. The Americans at Guantanamo Naval Base bought me to Miami in an airplane in 1969."[1] Sánchez was the former owner of Tania's restaurant in Chicago's Logan Square community. Tania's was a popular and fancy, Cuban restaurant, bar, and dance hall in Chicago. The restaurant closed in 1999.

Unlike other Latinos, Cubans were received into the United States as political refugees. Cubans came to the United States roughly in three major waves. During the first wave, 1959-1962, about 280,000 Cubans came fleeing Fidel Castro's revolution in 1959. Many had opposed the revolution, but others were Castro supporters who became disillusioned with the course the revolution ultimately took. The first wave ended with the Cuban missile crisis of October 1962.[2] Most Cubans, who came to the United States during the 1960s, and in later years, settled in Miami, Florida. Cubans preferred South Florida because it was close to Cuba, has a similar climate, and was home to the second largest Cuban community outside Cuba. Today, successful Cubans dominate Miami's economy, politics, and culture.

Sánchez did not want to settle in Miami. Instead, he preferred Chicago. "When I came to the United States in 1969, I stayed in Miami for only two days. I wanted to come to Chicago. I liked this city. I had read about Chicago in the Reader's Digest. They said this was a progressive city. They said this was a city where there was a lot of work and much money. But it also said you had to be willing to work hard to make a lot of money." Between 1959 and 1973, when Fidel Castro stopped emigration from Cuba, an estimated 20,000 refugees arrived in the Chicago area.[3] But those numbers steadily declined, as immigration slacked off, and Cubans resettled to other American cities. Many Cubans in Chicago eventually retired to Miami, Florida where they purchased and built retirement homes. The 1990 census counted only 18,204 Cubans in the six-county metropolitan Chicago area. A decade later, in 2000, the Cuban population in Illinois increased only 1.3 percent to 18, 438.[4] About two-thirds of these Cubans lived in Chicago.

Most Latino immigrants who came to the United States were viewed as subordinate workers and sources of cheap labor. This was not the case for Cubans. The first wave of Cubans were called the "Golden Exiles." They were members of the upper and middle classes in Cuba. They were mostly white, mature, and college educated. Many included professionals like doctors, lawyers, accountants, teachers, and engineers. Others included office and factory employees, artisans, and semiskilled laborers. Many first wave Cubans brought professional skills and investment capital.[5] These first refugees did not expect to stay long in America. They figured Castro's government would be quickly overthrown and they would soon be back in their Caribbean island. Now, after more than 40 years, many have resigned themselves to the fact that they might never return.

The second wave of Cubans, 1965-73, was more of an economic migration. Castro permitted Cubans with relatives in the United States to leave the island. It brought another 273,000 Cubans to the United States.[6] This group was not as prosperous as the first. In Cuba, they had been small businessmen, factory workers, and farmers. Many were women, children, and the elderly. America warmly welcomed Cubans from the first and second waves. They fit nicely with the anticommunist sentiment of the time. They were fleeing communism and embracing American democracy. Upon arriving in the United States some Cubans fell to their knees crying and emotionally kissing American soil. Many Americans were impressed by their displays of patriotism toward the United States. In 1961, the United States federal government established the Cuban Refugee Program, a generous program of aid that helped many first and second wave Cuban refugees. The government spent over one billion dollars between 1961 and 1976, helping these immigrants resettle in Miami, Florida, New York, and other states like Illinois. The program provided funds for resettlement, monthly relief checks, health services, job training, adult educational opportunities, college scholarships, bilingual education in public schools, and surplus food distribution.[7]

Some Latinos in Chicago were a little resentful that the American government bent over backwards to help Cubans, while most Latino groups did not receive any government assistance upon their arrival to American shores. Yet some Cubans believed other Latinos were jealous toward them because they rapidly climbed the ladder of success. Sánchez sat in his large, second-floor office of Tania's restaurant, shortly before it closed. Like many Cubans, Sánchez did not see himself as an immigrant, but as an exile forced out of his country. He felt betrayed by Castro and despised him and his communist ideas. "Many Cubans left Cuba when Fidel Castro betrayed the revolution and aligned himself with communism," says Sánchez. "There is no liberty in Cuba. There is a totalitarian dictatorship there. A dictatorship that has enslaved us for the last 40 years.

It had not given us any progress. It has taken the country backwards. Cuba used to be a progressive country. It was an internationally renowned country, second only to the United States. But when Fidel Castro took power, he said he was going to have free elections. He never did. What he did was to completely enslave the country."

Sánchez believed the situation in Cuba was worse than ever. "The situation in Cuba is bad and the people are suffering greatly. And they are not suffering because of the U.S. embargo. That stuff about the embargo is a lie. The problem is that there is no production. There is no money to buy things. The people do not want to work. Why should they work, for the government? You would not like to work for the government. I work for myself, not for the government. Fidel has carried out a political doctrine that does not work." In his early days in Chicago, Sánchez dreamed of someday returning to Cuba. Yet he decided to settle down and make a life for himself. Cuba was in the past and he tried hard to forget the past. He had to survive. He relied on his wits and determination to get ahead. He says he started with very little. "I come from a poor family in Cuba. I really didn't have anything in Cuba. We didn't have our own house in Cuba. We lived in a house we rented. My father and mother worked, and I also worked. I worked in the office of a toy company.... I had been married in Cuba, but then I divorced. I had two children from my first marriage. They stayed in Cuba. I only had a year of college in Cuba."

Like other immigrants, Sánchez used an informal network of friends and relatives for assistance. "A cousin in the Logan Square community helped me find my way around the city," recalls Sánchez. "My cousin helped me find my first job in Chicago. She and her husband let me stay at their house. She helped me a lot and was really good to me. She has always been a noble person. A tremendous person. I'm not just saying this because she is my cousin. I'm saying it because she's a compassionate person with a big heart." Sánchez was willing to take on any kind of work to get ahead. "My first job was in a Chicago factory loading and unloading large office supply trucks. My fellow white workers at the factory accepted me," says Sánchez. "The work was hard and didn't pay well. But I was always upbeat. I was always looking for ways to get ahead. In 1972, I met and married Martha DeJesus, my wife. I credit my wife for a lot of my success. I knew it was very important that I learn English if I wanted to get ahead. My wife helped me learn English. I learned by always having the radio and television on English channels."

In Chicago, Cubans were not concentrated in one neighborhood. Instead, they were scattered in various North Side neighborhoods. Cubans lived in Edgewater, Albany Park, and Irving Park. Some Cubans also lived in Logan Square alongside Puerto Ricans and Mexicans. Thousands of Cubans settled in Logan Square when they first arrived from Cuba. But Cuban families in Logan Square saved their money and eventually moved to the suburbs. About one third of Cubans in Illinois lived in Chicago's western suburbs like Melrose Park, Stone Park, and Oak Park, and northern suburbs like Skokie and Morton Grove. In the heart of Logan Square was an eight-block section of Milwaukee Avenue that was a bustling commercial shopping strip. Cubans owned many of the businesses dotting the strip. These businesses included taverns, clothing and jewelry stores, and music and furniture stores. There were floral shops, liquor stores, McDonalds, a small theater, and other food franchises all doing a steady business. Lately, other Latino groups opened small businesses on the strip.

The Cuban-owned stores on Milwaukee Avenue inspired Sánchez during his early days in Chicago. He was tired of working for others. He dreamed of opening his own store. "I started with ten dollars my father-in-law gave me as a loan. I worked and worked, saving my money. I wanted to open my own business. No, I never had any problems with prejudice.... I never had problems with Americans, with Poles, or with Greeks. On the contrary, America opened its doors to me and helped me. The Jewish owners at Albany Park Bank, where I have banked for the last 25 years, helped me a lot. They gave me the loans I needed to open my businesses." In 1974, Sánchez opened his small, grocery store on the commercial strip of Milwaukee Avenue. The quaint store was stocked with groceries appealing to the taste of Cubans and other Latinos. Inside the store Sánchez opened a tiny cafeteria which served delicious, inexpensive Cuban dishes, sandwiches, and strong Cuban coffee. The cafeteria became a favorite hangout. It was always crowded with Cubans and Latino customers eating and conversing in Spanish.

Two years later, the grocery store caught fire. "We were remodeling the store, when a carpenter mistakenly cut some electrical wires, and started a fire. It took firefighters 35 minutes to respond. The store and cafeteria were completely burned down," recalls Sánchez. A year later, Sánchez opened Tania's, a much larger and fancier restaurant on Milwaukee Avenue. He named the restaurant after his daughter, Tania. Sánchez, his wife, and their two children worked long hours to make the restaurant successful. Like most of the Cuban business owners on the Milwaukee Avenue strip, Sánchez lived in the suburbs. He and his family lived in the middle-class suburb of Morton Grove. "The reason Cubans are good businesspeople is because we believe in the idea of having our own businesses," says Sánchez. "Since we were very young, our parents taught us how to work hard. My parents taught me to how to struggle and work hard. My wife's parents taught her the same thing. I have almost 24 years of struggling in this restaurant and thank God we have been able to maintain it. Everything has gone well for us."

On weekends, Tania's was jam-packed. Latinos came for the food, drinks, the friends, and the live salsa music of local bands. Couples, dressed in their best evening clothes, danced late into the night to the fast-paced rhythms of Cuban and Puerto Rican salsa. Many assumed Sánchez was grooming his daughter Tania to take over his restaurant. But his children did not want to take over the business. Sánchez retired in the summer of 1999. Shortly afterwards, Tania's restaurant closed. Sánchez has not seen Cuba since he left in 1969. But he still had fond memories of his homeland. "No, I don't think I'll visit Cuba any time soon," says Sánchez. "I would like to because I have friends there. I just mailed some money to a friend of mine who is suffering there. But I don't want to spend my money over there while Castro's still in power. I would gladly give away the little that I have if Castro would leave Cuba. The Cuban people are suffering. Communism does not work."

Sánchez came out of his brief retirement and is now a successful real estate developer. He has built condominiums in a dilapidated section of Logan Square. When he finally does retires, Sánchez intends to travel and see the world. Unlike other Cubans, he does not plan to retire in Miami. "I like to visit Miami. But I love Chicago. Chicago's downtown is one of the beautiful that I have seen in all the United States. It has great shopping centers. This is a cosmopolitan city like no other." Sánchez beamed when he explained how his number one dream was realized in America. "My main dream of obtaining freedom in this country came true. Freedom is the most important dream a person can have. The greatest and happiest day of my life was when I crossed onto the American side at the Guantanamo Base. There will never be a greater day like that one."

Progress in Chicago

The Catholic Church helped many Cubans resettle from Miami, Florida to different cities across the United Stated during the 1960s. Chicago's Catholic Charities extended a generous helping hand, and assisted Cubans from the three waves to settle in Chicago and its suburbs. "The Catholic church spearheaded the resettlement of Cubans to Chicago from 1961 to 1968," says Jesus Zeferino Ochoa, the Mexican director of the Immigrant and Refugee department of Chicago's Catholic Charities. "Many Cuban professionals volunteered and helped us in our resettlement efforts. Groups like the Cuban Chamber of Commerce, and Cuban doctors and lawyers helped us. We resettled more than 10,000 Cubans throughout the Chicago area. Many were middle-class professionals. They needed assistance with relocation; they wanted to know where they could live in Chicago. ...We were totally responsible for those Cuban refugees that didn't have families. We provided food, housing, job leads, everything. We emphasized early employment. We were successful in placing many people in employment." [8]

Ann Alvarez, 60, was president of Casa Central, the oldest and largest Latino, social service agency in the city. She is Cuban and Puerto Rican. She believed many first wave Cubans prospered well in Chicago. "The first wave was middle and upper-class professionals," says Alvarez. "My husband had four sisters and one brother who came to Chicago. My four sisters-in-laws came with husbands and children. One sister-in-law is a doctor. The others were educators. These Cubans dreamed of going back to Cuba. But there was really no turning back. There was a very definite break, similar to European immigrants. They decided we're here to stay. My husband's nieces and nephews were very young children at the time, but they learned to speak English within a year. Their parents did not want them in bilingual education. They wanted full immersion. They and their kids are totally assimilated into the American value of achieving economic and financial success. They didn't identify as victims, but more as people who were taking advantage of an incredible opportunity.... Many in the first wave used to live in the Lake View and Ravenswood neighborhoods. The minute their jobs improved, they moved to the Northern suburbs. It was like the typical immigrant dream. You come here, make money, then you move to the suburbs."[9]

Casa Central and the Church World Service, an organization of fourteen Protestant denominations, helped resettle about 1,350 second wave Cuban families from Miami, Florida to Chicago. They helped Cubans find sponsoring families, housing, health services, jobs, and public aid. Many families were placed in apartment buildings in Logan Square and Uptown. The second wave also adjusted quite well in Chicago. Alvarez was born in the United States and came from New York to Chicago in 1965. Alvarez's parents immigrated to New York as religious missionaries in the 1920s. Her mother came from Puerto Rico and her father from Cuba. They worked in the sweatshops of New York. Ann is married to Daniel Alvarez, who is also Cuban and Puerto Rican.

As some second-generation Cubans assimilated into the American culture and moved to the suburbs, they struggled to retain their Cuban identity. Some lost their Spanish language and spoke only English. Others became fully bilingual and bicultural. "It was more assimilation in terms of taking on the American dream and striving for financial success," says Ann Alvarez. "I think many of our Cuban families have kept their Spanish, traditions, culture, and values intact. My two sons speak Spanish. They are not as fluent as I would like them to be. But it was a conscious effort on our part as parents that our children retained the Spanish language."

An important social service need among Cubans is care of the elderly. Cubans were generally older than other Latino groups. As Cubans aged, families grappled with how best to care for their elderly parents. A popular program at Casa Central is subsidized housing for Latino elderly. The agency has four new buildings where Latino elderly over age 60, lived in their own apartments with professional staff caring for them. Many of the residents were elderly Cubans. Some Cubans looked to Casa Central for other kinds of social service assistance. Yet, they are now the minority. "You do not have new or young Cuban families coming to Chicago anymore," says Alvarez. "But there is a constant flow of new people coming from Mexico, Puerto Rico, and Central America. We also have Puerto Rican and Mexican families that have been living here for many years and have not been able to make it into the mainstream. It's probably because of poor education or lack of employment opportunity. I really don't know why they're not making it. Most of our clients are Puerto Rican, Mexican, and Central American. We serve those in need."

In 1980, Fidel Castro allowed a third wave of Cubans to come to the United States from the Cuban port of Mariel. The exiles were dubbed the "marielitos." About 124,776 came and many were single men, black, and mulatto. They were mostly low-skilled and unskilled workers. Most did not speak English. Among the marielitos about 4 percent had been felons in Cuba. American public opinion quickly turned against these immigrants. Americans felt Castro had tricked the United States to rid Cuba of "undesirables." The marielitos were denied political refugee status. Upon arrival, many were placed in detention centers. The publicized criminal acts of some marielitos embarrassed Cubans already settled in the United States. They felt their golden reputation as model immigrants in America, was being tarnished.[10] An estimated 2,000 marielitos were resettled in Chicago.[11] In 1981, a respected Chicago Cuban businessman, Hermes Rey, 50, was stabbed and killed in his flower shop by a newly arrived marielito refugee. The refugee had been in prison in Cuba. Rey had sponsored more than 60 of the Cuban refugees in his store and Franklin Park home. Rey was well liked by Cubans and other Latinos. Puerto Ricans fondly recalled the many flowers he donated for the city's annual Puerto Rican Parade.[12]

The refugees from Mariel had a hard time adjusting in Chicago. They were not as successful as earlier waves of Cubans. A recession, lack of skills, the language barrier, and prejudice made it difficult for many to find jobs. Some found odd, temporary jobs. Other refugees found low-paying work as janitors, domestics, and dishwashers. Many had to apply for food stamps and public aid. Sponsoring agencies and churches had a difficult time finding jobs and affordable housing for refugees. Many of the refugees eventually left Chicago for other cities.[13] "Catholic Charities helped relocate several thousand Cubans from the third wave," says Jesus Zeferino Ochoa. "The marielitos required more intensive casework than the other waves. There were fewer families in this group. It was mostly men and women. Unfortunately, some had mental problems and some committed crimes. Delinquency is not exclusive to any ethnic group. Fortunately, most of the Cubans from the three groups did well in Chicago."[14]

Living Modestly

A persistent stereotype about Cubans was that they are all doing well in America. Since their arrival in America, popular magazines and newspapers have portrayed Cubans as a "model minority." It was pointed out that they worked hard and pulled themselves up by their own bootstraps. Cubans, unlike other Latinos, rarely protested or complained about their treatment in America. Instead, in a rags-to-riches kind of way, it was believed Cubans achieved the American dream. Some Cubans, to the chagrin of other Latinos, believed the model minority myth. They believed they were more industrious than other Latinos. A Cuban owner of a Shell gas station in Chicago's Humboldt Park community, offered his views on the work ethic of other Latinos. He was in his mid-fifties and came to Chicago in the second wave in the early 1970s. He did not want to be identified. He was a mechanic who made his living selling gas and fixing the cars of neighborhood residents. Yet he viewed Mexicans and Puerto Ricans as somewhat lazy. "We Cubans come to this country to work hard and to open businesses," he says. "We take advantage of opportunities offered. But I see a lot of Puerto Ricans and Mexicans around here who don't want to work.

They are lazy and prefer welfare to working. That's why they never get ahead." A split second later he qualifies his words. "I'm not saying they're all like that, but many are. Just look around this neighborhood and see for yourself."

But not all Cubans in Chicago were doing well. Maria Cardenas, 66, was struggling to make ends meet. She and her Cuban-born husband were once doing well in Chicago. They were married 21 years and had three children. But a divorce in 1980 set her back. Later, she remarried. Her second husband was from Ecuador. They rented a two-bedroom apartment in the Logan Square neighborhood. She worked for the Chicago Board of Education as an assistant teacher. Her husband worked in a factory making $8.50 an hour. He also held down another part-time job performing valet parking for two Chinese restaurants. "I came to the United States from Havana, Cuba in 1961," says Cardenas. "I had about two years of college in Havana. My husband and I were against both Batista and Fidel Castro. Castro turned to communism and we were anti-communist. The Cuban government under Castro considered us counter revolutionaries. The government of Cuba used to say that I planted bombs.... I came to the United Stated in an airplane after Cuban officials investigated me carefully. They took a lot of my things at the airport. My husband escaped from Cuba in 1961 in a boat with five other people. The water current carried them far north and away from their Florida destination. They were lost at sea. My husband's skin was sunburned and he became unconscious on the boat. He almost died. A Norwegian fishing boat saved them. When he got to the United States he was in a hospital for a month or two."[15]

Cardenas and her first husband stayed in Southern Florida for two years. But hundreds of thousands of Cubans were resettled to Southern Florida by the American government, and good jobs were hard to find. "When I came to the United States, I was traumatized. I did not talk to anyone for months because I thought they might call government officials on me," recalls Cardenas. "Then other Cubans told me you can talk. You can stand on any corner and say whatever you want about Fidel Castro. This is a country with liberty.... In Florida my husband was washing dishes, painting, and doing odds jobs. I couldn't work because I was expecting my second child.... The American government gave us money to find apartments. They gave use new and used clothes. The government gave churches food that they then gave to us. But we didn't want to depend upon the government. To us that was a stigma, because we both felt we had two hands and we could work."

By the early 1960s, United States federal authorities in Miami directed Cuban refugees away from Southern Florida and to other U.S. cities. Cardenas and her ex-husband tried their luck in Chicago. "We came to Chicago in September of 1963 because my husband did not have a permanent job in Florida," says Cardenas. "I began to work. My husband and I worked in the factory making telephones. My husband had only five years of elementary education in Cuba. Then my husband started working in another factory. He worked two jobs, sixteen hours a day. We saved our money and bought a new car with cash. We paid cash because we Cubans don't like to have credit debts.... We both learned English here in Chicago. And in 1971, my husband and I became American citizens."

Cardenas and her ex-husband bought a home in 1972 on the western edge of the Austin neighborhood, near the suburb of Oak Park. In the 1960s, Austin experienced dramatic racial change as Africans Americans moved in and white ethnics left. "After being in that neighborhood for two years some black boys hit my kids. They broke my daughter's glasses and pulled her earrings. Her ear was bleeding," recalls Cardenas. "It was not the good blacks who terrorized the neighborhood; it was the young kids in gangs. We were not prejudiced... In Cuba I had many black friends. But in Cuba parents wanted their light-skinned daughters to marry light-skinned Cubans. Some families would disown their children if they married dark-skinned Cubans. Parents would say to their children, 'we have to elevate the race.' We got scared of what happened to our kids in Austin. So after paying for the house for two years, we left it to the bank. We didn't want it anymore. We moved to Logan Square."

Cardenas and her ex-husband realized their dream of owning their own business. "The Small Business Administration gave us a loan to open our business. We were owners of a liquor and grocery store near California and Division Streets. We also owned the building housing the store. The business was good." However, maintaining the business required many long, grueling hours of work. Cardenas noticed her ex-husband becoming increasingly distant and abusive. "I divorced my husband because he would offend me in front of my kids," says Cardenas. "He would push and slap me. He hit me often. There was no communication. He was jealous. He did not have any right to be jealous because the only thing I did was go to church. He didn't attend church. He thought I was a religious fanatic. Once, we were in his car and he slapped me. I tried to get out of the car. He accelerated the gas pedal and I fell out. I fell and hit my head on the street. One foot stayed in the car and he dragged me about one hundred feet. I lost consciousness and was in a coma for five days. However, God is beautiful. He performed a miracle and let me live.The only thing affected was my ear. I don't hear completely in one ear."

Cardenas' ex-husband remarried and relocated to Miami, Florida. "We gave up the building and business after the divorce. I don't hate my ex-husband. I consider him an honest and good person," says Cardenas. "He came here and worked hard. But he was not a good husband like he should have been.... After the divorce I worked two jobs. I was working 16 hours a day. I've been with the Board of Education since 1966. I worked for many years in housekeeping at the Hyatt Hotel in downtown Chicago. I prepare the caddies the housekeeping staff use to clean the rooms. I left the hotel job two years ago." While Cardenas and her husband are still working hard these days, she seemed happy about life. Her husband was a teacher in Ecuador, and is now trying to become a bilingual teacher in Chicago. They hope to buy a house in Logan Square. Her three children are college educated, with families of their own.

"I am proud my three children speak Spanish and are bilingual. My grandchildren are also speaking Spanish. I have seven grandchildren, five boys and two girls. My youngest daughter will soon give me another grandchild. She is 29 and is married to a man from Ecuador." Cardenas and her husband are very religious. They are members of Primera Iglesia Hispana Unida De Cristo (First Spanish United Church of Christ), in Logan Square. This church is very dear to Cubans. The church helped second wave Cubans by providing living quarters, food, and job referrals. "My husband is now working in the church," says Cardenas. "We, the members, are fixing up the church. We want to raise more funds to fix the church. We love our church."

Reunited With Family

Angelica Garcia, 84, is another Cuban who lived modestly in Chicago. She lived in her daughter's house, a small, frame bungalow in the Logan Square neighborhood. Her daughter is a public elementary school teacher. Her son worked in a Chicago factory. Despite her age, Garcia still worked several hours a week as a teacher's aide in a nearby bilingual preschool. Like other older Cubans, Garcia was initially hesitant to talk to a stranger about her life in Cuba. But eventually, she told her story in Spanish. "I came to Chicago in 1971 from Matanzas, Cuba," says Garcia. "I came with my younger son. I came at a time when the Castro government was allowing Cubans to leave to be reunited with their families in the United States. I was happy to leave Cuba. Communism was not working. There was a lot of repression. There was no liberty. You cannot express your sentiments because immediately someone will denounce you and turn you into the government. You don't trust the people who live next to you.... I left Cuba with nothing. You cannot take anything. The government keeps your things and redistributes them. You cannot take money."[16]

Garcia had not seen her daughter in Chicago for four years. "When I came to the United States I arrived in Miami, Florida and stayed there for a couple of days. I liked Miami because there's a big, tremendous Cuban community there. However, I wanted to be with my daughter in Chicago. My daughter had immigrated to Chicago in 1967 with my sister. I came to be with my daughter." While many Cubans were allowed to leave Cuba during the second wave, families would still be split apart. The Cuban government made arbitrary decisions as to what family members could leave. Many Cubans in Chicago had relatives in Cuba whom they have not seen in years. To Garcia's dismay, the Cuban government refused to allow her husband to leave with her to the United States. Her husband, who is in his mid-80s, is still in Cuba. They have not seen each other since she left Cuba. Yet Garcia still dreamed that one day they might be reunited in Chicago. "Every year the Cuban government tells him he can't leave. My husband is a real good person," says Garcia. "We miss each other and we talk to each other on the telephone. He tells me he's waiting and hoping they will let him leave. We talk to each other about once a month, for a couple of minutes. Telephone calls to Cuba are very expensive. They're about $40 to 50 dollars for just a few minutes."

Garcia recalls the good times growing up in Cuba before Castro came to power. "In Cuba, we used to go to the dances. We would listen to music in the plazas. We would go the movies and the parks. In Cuba you always had music in the parks. We would sometimes last all day and night at the parks. Cuba is beautiful. Cuba has the most beautiful beaches in the world. But now Cubans can't swim on those beaches. They're reserved for tourists. Poor Cubans have no money." Yet Garcia also remembered how life changed once Castro took over. "They would send us to work in the fields. They worked you hard and paid you little. The people would suffer a lot. The government gave you a ration tablet. They would give you things and write it in the tablet. But it was very limited. There was a lack of food, a lack of medicine, a lack of everything. The people don't even have paint to paint their houses. The cars are old and falling apart.... Cubans who don't have family members in the United States suffer even more, because they do not have anyone to send them American dollars. Many families in the United States sent their relatives in Cuba a lot of money. Even today, the situation in Cuba is bad. Every day it gets worse."

Garcia smiled when she recalled her first impression of America and Chicago. "The people in America are really nice, real humanitarians. They helped Cubans," says Garcia. "They helped me. They gave us money and food stamps for the first couple of months. They helped a lot of Cubans find housing and apartments.... I remember the first time my daughter took me to a big department store here in Chicago. They were so many things we didn't have in Cuba. I was dizzy from looking at so many things. Chicago is very beautiful. It has so many attractions.... I was afraid the first time I went outside in Chicago during winter. It was snowing and very cold, and I didn't know how to place my feet on the snow to walk. However, now I'm accustomed to it. Even the snow is beautiful." Garcia says some of her older Cuban friends in Chicago faced economic problems due to failing health. "There are families in need. There is a Cuban family that my church is helping. The husband is very sick with cancer of the lungs. He's better now, but he can't talk. He writes everything. The wife is paying all the bills. She is about 50-years-old, and he's older. She's got some help because she's got social security. But she has a lot of expenses. He has been sick for a long time now. A nurse comes to the house so she can work. The nurse cost money. They have two kids, one's a doctor, and the other is a lawyer. They are good kids and they help their parents."

Despite her many years in Chicago, Garcia does not speak English. "I would like to learn English but how can I, I'm much older? I do not think we should lose our Latino roots. Many Latinos do not speak Spanish. They have taught them only English. They should learn English, that's fine, but you should also know Spanish. It's your own language. I like reading Chicago's Spanish-language newspapers. I like to know what is happening in the Latino community. I also like to watch Spanish-language novellas on Channel 44 and 66." Garcia has not slowed down despite her age. She enjoyed going to the movies, and visiting zoos. She enjoyed eating at Cuban-owned restaurants. "I ate a lot at Tania's. I know the owner, Elias. There's another nice, Cuban-owned restaurant called Cafe Bolero. I go there to eat. Some jewelry stores on Milwaukee are Cuban-owned. There is Armando's jewelry store. I buy jewelry there and I talk to the owners. We talk about Cuba."

In Chicago, Garcia found some of her old friends from Cuba. "I have friends who used to live in Cuba and now they are here. We have found each other. They don't live in this neighborhood. We talk about the old times. I have some friends that have also recently visited Cuba.... I've been told that young, Cuban women in Cuba are involved in prostitution. That's a way for them to get money from the tourists." Like other Cubans in Logan Square, Garcia was an active member of the Primera Iglesia Hispana Unida De Cristo. On a hot, summer, Sunday morning, the small congregation was engaged in spirited prayers and songs. "A lot of Cubans are Catholic, but I am Presbyterian. I don't know why Fidel Castro invited the Catholic Pope, John Paul, to Cuba. Castro didn't want the Catholic Church in Cuba. There is no religious freedom in Cuba. My religious faith is very important to me. I feel good in church. I sit there close to God. Our pastor is from Santo Domingo and his wife is Puerto Rican. But he gets along fine with Cubans." At church Garcia made friends with other Latinos. "Last Sunday we had an international dinner at the church," she says. "We had about two hundred people. Each family brought food from their country of origin. There was food from Puerto Rico, Mexico, Columbia, Hondurans, and Cuba. We have people there from everywhere. We had small flags from all the different countries. The people were eating and talking. It was beautiful."

Catholicism and Speaking to the Dead

Cubans were grateful to the Archdiocese of Chicago and the Protestant churches, for their assistance in helping many Cubans resettle in Chicago. Some of the first Cubans in Chicago settled in Chicago's Uptown area, on the city's far North Side. Uptown was known for its large apartment buildings and affordable rents. As newcomers, Cubans sought out a Catholic parish in the Uptown neighborhood where they could feel welcome. They gravitated to St. Ita Catholic Church, at 5500 North Broadway. St. Ita was formerly an Irish national parish. Today, it serves mostly Mexicans, Latinos from Central and South America, and Cubans. "St. Ita's parish has always been dear to Cubans. About 29 years ago, more than 80 Cubans who lived in Uptown attended St. Ita," says Candido Bouso, 85, a parishioner at St. Ita. "We asked for a Spanish mass at St. Ita because many of us didn't understand English. They gave us a Spanish mass in the basement. But we were not offended by being put in the basement. We understood that other activities were going on in the church. We were in the basement for about six years. Then we moved into the main church. We Cubans felt welcomed at this parish. Columbian and Mexican priests said the mass in Spanish. We never had a Cuban priest. I don't know that any exist. The pastor here, Rev. Laurence Maddock, now says the mass in Spanish."[17]

Bouso came from Havana, Cuba to Chicago in 1970, as part of the "freedom flights." "Cuba was not good, it was a repressive government," he says. He continued his education in Chicago and graduated from college with a degree in accounting. As Cubans found better-paying jobs they moved away from Uptown. "Many Cubans who lived in Uptown moved to the suburbs of Melrose Park and Skokie, Illinois," says Bouso. "They attend Catholic churches in the suburbs.... I worked for many years as a supervisor of sales for the Ekco Company on Armitage and Cicero Avenue. I am now retired. I also moved from Uptown. I live with my wife in the Portage Park neighborhood. My two children are both college educated and doing well for themselves. I have no complaints."

Cubans became so identified with St. Ita, that in the early 1960s, the church installed the shine of La Virgen De La Caridad De Cobre (Our Lady of Charity), the patron saint of Cuba. "Hundreds of years ago, Nuestra Senora de Caridad appeared to a fisherman in the town of El Cobre near Santiago, Cuba," says Bouso. "She is very dear to Cubans. I am the secretary of a group at St. Ita called the Virgin of Charity of Cobre Association. I believe the group was established in 1966. We celebrate La Virgen De La Caridad's birth on the 8th of September. At St. Ita, our association sponsors a yearly special mass and dinner on that day. Many Cuban restaurants in Chicago donate Cuban food to us. Over 200 Cubans attend our church that day. Many come from the suburbs. Many are professionals, including doctors, lawyers, and business owners. We invite a Spanish-speaking priest from another state to say the Spanish mass." While Bouso no longer lived near St. Ita, he still attended mass there every Sunday. Of about 200 Latinos who attended Sunday mass at St. Ita, about 20 were Cuban. Unlike other Latino parishioners at St. Ita, Cubans did not rely on the church for social services. They did not need them. They were mainly home owners and middle class.

Besides Catholicism, some Cubans in Chicago practiced Santeria and Palo. Cubans brought these two popular religions to the United States. These two Afro-Latino, folk religions included many symbols of Catholicism. But they were more a mixture of several African religions—mainly Yoruba, Fon, and Kongo—that came to the Spanish Antilles during the slave trade. Santeria, Spanish for "way of the saints," was widespread in Cuba. Other Caribbean countries, including Puerto Rico, the Dominican Republic, Haiti, and some segments of Brazil had parallel rituals. It was also strong in Miami and New York.[18] Cubans saw no conflict in practicing official Catholicism and Santeria. "I'm Catholic but I believe in Santeria, and in my religion which is Palo. There are similarities between Catholicism, Santeria and Palo," says Luis Carlos, 59, a dark-skinned Cuban. "The Catholic Church does not approve of Santeria and Palo. Maybe they see them as cults. But they do not try to understand them. All three religions use many of the same statues and saints. But we name the same saints different things. St. Francis of Assisi, for example, is the Yoruba god Orunla. Catholics only believe in one God. But in Santeria you have more than one. You have the Supreme God and then you have many others."[19]

In Santeria, the identities of saints and Gods were fused hundreds of years ago, when slaves adopted the saints of the Spanish Roman Catholics, sometimes with gender-bending results. In his home Carlos has a large statue of Saint Barbara, the God of thunder. In Santeria, the form was Chango, normally pictured as a powerful black man.[20] Carlos was from Havana, Cuba. He immigrated to Chicago in 1980 as a marielito. "I came seeking the American Dream. I do not believe in Communism," says Carlos. "I also profess a religion and in Cuba you cannot profess a religion. I came to America seeking a better life....The only difference in Santeria and Palo is that we work differently. In Palo we work with palos (sticks), with 21 or 77 different palos. We work with rocks we gather in the mountains. We work with a crucifix and blessed water. By concentrating on the palos, rocks and crucifix, together with God I can solve peoples' problems."

Carlos and his Puerto Rican wife, Wanda are also espiritististas, or spiritualists. They offered spiritual healing from their Logan Square apartment. Some rituals of espiritismo, Santeria, and Palo were often mixed together. Most of their clients were Puerto Rican, Mexican, Latinos from Central and South America, and some Cubans. In the Santeria faith, the babalawo was a high priest, a diviner, medicine man, and father confessor and his powers were limitless. Santeria does not allow women to be babalawos because the patron of the babalawos is a male orisha or god, and his priests are always men.[21] Carlos did not pretend to be a babalawo. He has very little formal religious training. But because he studied, practiced, and was devoted to Palo he felt he possessed many of the same powers of a babalawo. For instance, he says he solved the problems of many of his clients by speaking to the dead. "God has given me the power to communicate with the spirit of the dead," argues Carlos. "I concentrate peacefully and I have the power to tell you your problems and solve them. You die, but your spirit lives on. I talk to my guardian angel, or I talk to the dead relatives of others. People come to me asking how their dead loved ones are doing. They want to know how their dead ones are feeling spiritually. They want to know if their dead ones have any messages for them.... I often describe their dead relatives to them and how they looked while they were living. I tell them certain things their dead ones are saying. I give them messages. Then they say, 'that's amazing, you're telling me personal things that only a person with spiritual powers could know.'"

Some Cubans are attracted to religions like Santeria because a healer, like Carlos, spoke their language, shared their culture, and was able to describe and explain the problems they have.[22] "I heal people's problems. That's what I do best," says Carlos. "People come to me with sexual problems, impotency, or marriage problems. Maybe their son is a gang. Or sometimes families cannot communicate. I pray to God and the spirit of the dead. Then I give advice and yes it works. I have made marriages and families stronger. I have gotten kids out of gangs. I have gotten shorter prison sentences for some. I have helped alcoholics stop drinking. I've helped people get their lives together." While he helped others, Carlos himself encountered some personal problems. He was disabled due to a bad heart. He was also deeply saddened that he could not attend his mother's funeral. "I had a big lost. My mother died in Cuba in 1991 and I could not go see her. Fidel Castro did not let me enter Cuba to see her."

Carlos and his wife maintained two elaborate altars in their apartment. The altars held pictures and statues of saints from Catholicism and Santeria. They contained burning candles, flowers, rosaries, and incense. There was a glass of water representing purity. There were numerous talismans and charms. There were coconuts and cigars typical of gifts offered to saints as sustenance. A small kettle of wood with four coconut shells was prominent on Carlos' altar. "I throw the coconut shells. Then depending on how they fall and are arranged, I can interpret what the dead are saying to me whenever I ask them a question." Santeria is criticized because some rituals involved the slaughtering of animals like chickens, pigeons, or goats. The sacrifice of animals usually took place in someone's backyard. "The sacrifice of animals has existed in many religions," says Carlos. "In Miami, Florida Cubans won an important court case. The judge said because of their Santeria religion, Cubans can sacrifice animals. The killing of animals does not happen often in our faith. For instance, you might clean the bad spirits from a person's body by holding a pigeon in your hands and saying prayers. That animal is no longer good for eating because I am removing the evil spirit from the person that is now inside the animal. We destroy it properly. Sometimes we dig a hole, bury the animal, and say prayers. I don't like to kill animals, so I let the pigeon fly out the window. You're still getting rid of the bad spirit."

People come to Carlos seeking a "limpieza" or body cleansing. In the Santeria faith, it is believed that individuals did not have control over the bad things that were happening to them. Evil spirits possessed and controlled the person. The limpieza supposedly got rid of any evil spirits. Some individuals seeking a limpieza were suffering depression or emotional problems. Others had physical problems. Carlos recommended certain herbs, oils, or lotions to cleanse the body. The person usually applied the substances to the body and took a cold bath. "In a body cleansing you have to get rid of the bad spirit. Something inside that person is pushing them to do things they don't want to do," says Carlos. "You can use many things in a cleansing. It could be lotion, blessed water, an egg, or a coconut. There are many forms of cleaning. You can say a small mass where you elevate the spirit. In the mass you're telling the dead person to leave this living person alone. You're telling the dead to be a guardian angel to this person and not a spirit that comes to disturb."

Carlos also recommended substances for home cleansings. Or he came to a person's home and personally performed the cleansing to rid the home of bad luck, misfortunes, or evil spirits. Substances for body and house cleansings were usually purchased in a botanica, a small, neighborhood store specializing in folk medicine. Botanicas stocked herbs, teas, and plants to cure people who were sick. They did a brisk business selling oils, lotions, candles, soaps, and perfumes for almost every kind of problem. They sold such exotica like black cat spray to wash away evil in a home. They sold oils to make a person more sexually appealing. Certain portions promised to make your wife or husband a better lover in bed. There were even portions promising to help you win the state lottery and strike it rich. "A lot of things botanicas sell really work," says Carlos. "I've used them, but I don't believe in everything they sell. They're a business. When they sell things that don't work, they make people lose faith in religion. They sell a portion called "Money Grab" to help you win the lottery. Well, if that worked, then everyone would be rich. Whenever I visit Miami or Puerto Rico I go to the mountains to gather herbs and wood. I believe in what I do. I make my own herbs to cure people who are sick."

Carlos and his wife managed a newly opened, small botanica called Botanica 7 Rayos (rays) in Logan Square. The botanica belonged to Carlos' sister-in-law. The store advertised services for spiritual healing, card reading, body cleaning, and consultations on matters of love, health, and family unity. Santeria and Palo have traditionally been popular among poor, black Cubans. But that may change. "Some of my clients are middle class and white," says Carlos. "People are always looking for the occult. I never put out fliers advertising my business. But a lot of Americans are coming to see me." Yet Carlos admitted that most clients he sees are poor. "I cannot charge poor people what others charge. Some American psychologists charge people $50.00 for an hour of counseling. Some card readers charge $5.00 a minute on the telephone. I sometimes advise a person, or cleanse them or their homes, and only charge them $7.00. The dead tells me you cannot charge this person more than that. I cannot go over the voice of the dead.... I don't have the need to charge people a lot of money. I live very humble. I have a small apartment, but I have enough to eat. God looks out for me."

Cuban Influence

Cubans nationally, and in Chicago, have achieved a higher level of success than most other Latino groups. Cubans generally had a higher median family income, were better educated, had higher rates of home ownership, and a larger percentage lived in middle-class suburbs. Cubans were more successful for various reasons. First, the 1960s Cubans exiles were not typical, poor immigrants; they were from the upper and middle classes and they came with capital, skills, and education that aided in their socioeconomic mobility. Second, Cuban exiles from the 1970s and 80s while of lower-income, also came with some education, and worked for established Cuban businesses. Third, their status as political refugees and considerable government, church, and private sector funds and assistance helped Cubans in their settlement and upward mobility into American society.[23] Many Cubans used the generous financial packages offered by the American government to establish their own businesses. Many more Cubans, compared to other Latino groups, owned their own businesses.

Cubans also established organizations that helped other Cubans succeed in the competitive business world. For example, the Cuban American Chamber of Commerce, on the city's North Side, had over 200 members including retail stores, restaurants, insurance companies, and other businesses. About one-third of those businesses were found on Milwaukee Avenue in Logan Square. The others were in Latino business strips throughout the city. "Our Cuban Chamber of Commerce started in 1969. We helped many businesses obtain state and city licenses. We helped them obtain funds. We helped them run successful businesses," says José Garcia, 88, former president of the Cuban American Chamber of Commerce. "...I am from Matanzas, Cuba. I immigrated to Chicago in 1959 with my wife and two kids. I used to be a restaurant owner in Cuba. I came fleeing Castro's communism. For many years I operated a couple of restaurants in Chicago. I am now retired and live in the Lincoln Park neighborhood."[24]

Some members of the Chamber of Commerce were large businesses, but many were smaller enterprises. "We have some large businesses as members," says Garcia. "Los Cuarto Caminos is a very big, Cuban-owned business. It is a chain of three, big supermercados (grocery stores). Another big, Cuban-owned jewelry store is La Caridad. We have large insurance companies. But most of our members are small businesses. Luis Auto Parts, on North Avenue, is Cuban-owned. Some of our members are also Mexican, Puerto Rican, and Columbian.... We also have social events where we get together to socialize. Every year we sponsor a big, dinner dance for our members. It's usually in a fancy, downtown hotel."

Garcia offered his views on why Cubans were good at running their own businesses. "We're good businessmen. We work hard. We were not rich in Cuba. We didn't come with money. We work 14 to 18 hours a day. We don't live off the government. We're honest and we work hard to support our families. We went to school and we give our children education. That's why of all the Latino groups, Cubans dazzle. We know how to get ahead. We live off our work, not off the government. We have businesses throughout Chicago and in the suburbs." Like many older, first-generation Cubans, Garcia was vehemently against communism and Fidel Castro. Garcia was proud of the progress Cubans have made in Chicago and America. "The Cuban community is growing and prospering. The second and third generation of Cubans are rising to important positions of power and influence in the United States. You can see it in the political arena. Though we are one of the smallest Latino groups in the United States, we have three Cuban representatives in the U.S. Congress. One is from New Jersey and two are from Florida." Garcia has thought about retiring to Miami, Florida. Despite his advancing age, his dream was to one day return to his homeland. "We Cubans retire to Florida to be close to other Cubans and to be close to our country. We are still waiting for the communist system to fall in Cuba. And I think that government will fall. The wicked system of Cuba cannot stand. I have been in the United States over 40 years, but when Casto falls, I will return to Cuban. That is the dream of many Cubans."

Besides a high rate of self-employment, Cubans were influential in other major Chicago institutions. Alfredo S. Lanier, a Cuban, sat on the editorial board of the Chicago Tribune newspaper, one of Chicago's two major, daily newspapers. He was the only Latino on the editorial board. He wrote the newspaper's editorials on Latin America, the Latino community, and the gay community. The Chicago Tribune published a Spanish-weekly called Hoy, which is widely read among Latinos. Years ago, the Chicago Sun-Times published a Spanish-weekly called Los Vecinos, which they discontinued. In the past, both newspapers hired mostly politically conservative, Cuban reporters to cover the city's Latino beat. Over the years, however, both papers have hired more Mexican and Puerto Rican reporters.

A good number of Cubans are employed in various elementary, high school, and universities throughout Chicago. American government agencies and church groups helped Cuban women find teaching jobs in Chicago when they arrived in the 1960s. Many of the women had been teachers in Cuba.[25] Pastora San Juan Cafferty, a Cuban, was a longtime professor at the University of Chicago. She has written several books on the experiences of Latinos nationally. Some Cubans have been influential in city and state government. In 1989, Mayor Richard J. Daley selected Lourdes Monteagudo, a Cuban, as the city's first deputy mayor of education. Monteagudo's role was to champion public education. Yet her daughter attended a private school in the affluent suburb of Winnetka. A reporter asked her why and Monteagudo allegedly said, 'No Chicago public school is good enough for my daughter.' She later denied saying it. But the controversy pressured the mayor to remove her.[26]

The Rev. Daniel Alvarez, 81, who is Cuban and Puerto Rican, had a long involvement in social services and city and state politics. For many years he ran Casa Central. In the 1970s, he was assistant for Latino affairs to former Illinois Governor Daniel Walker. In 1975, Alvarez left state government. But he used his contacts with Governor Walker to obtain state funds to create the Hispanic Housing Development Corporation (HHDC). The group has developed over 1,900 units of new and rehabilitated affordable housing. Rev. Alvarez served as commissioner of the city's department of Human Services for ten years under Mayor Richard M. Daley. "In 1989, Richard Daley won election as mayor of Chicago," says Daniel Alvarez. "He knew me because he used to go to Casa Central in Humboldt Park often before becoming a candidate. We knew each other since 1969. He invited me to be commissioner of Human Services. I went back to my board at Casa Central and asked for a leave of absence. One board member suggested that my wife, who has a master's in social work, take over the agency."[27]

Rev. Alvarez was respected among Puerto Ricans for his many years of dedicated service to their community. Yet in 1993, he angered a small group of pro-independence Puerto Ricans in Chicago. The Chicago Park District had granted the group permission to erect a bronze statue in Humboldt Park of Pedro Albizu Campos, a Puerto Rican, pro-independence leader who died in 1965. Campos was the leader of the Nationalist Party in Puerto Rico during the 1950s. But Rev. Alvarez publicly spoke out against the installation of the statue. Park officials then denied the group permission to install the statue. "I received death threats. My house was under police protection for a month," says Alvarez. "Campos was violent. He declared war on this country. He ordered the shooting of our Congressmen in the 1950s. He ordered the assassination of President Harry Truman. We have famous Puerto Rican educators and political figures.

Why not a statue of one of them? We have enough violence in this country. We need people that will encourage us to live together in peace."

Other misunderstandings between Cubans and other Latinos have periodically flared up. In 1986, a Latino group invited Ernesto Cardenal, "poet of the Nicaraguan revolution," to Chicago to read his poetry. But some Cubans saw Cardenal as a communist and part of the Sandinista government in Nicaragua. Cubans loudly demonstrated outside the building where Cardenal was speaking. Pro-Cardenal Latinos also demonstrated. Police peacefully kept the two groups apart. In 1989, some Cubans protested that city officals invited Orquesta Aragon to the summer's "Viva Chicago" musical festival in downtown Chicago. Orquesta Aragon was a legendary, Cuba-based musical band. Yet older Cubans accused the group of being a propaganda tool for Fidel Castro's Cuba. Sponsors of the festival allegedly received death threats. The band did not play. Other differences have also stood in the way of better understanding between Cubans and other Latinos. The political values of many Cubans were similar to conservative American Republican Party members. Their Republican leanings often alienate other Latino groups, who are largely Democratic. And Cubans have not identified with the civil rights struggles of Mexicans and Puerto Ricans. They have viewed such struggles with a detached, even negative attitude.[28]

Solidarity With Other Latinos

Some younger, second-generation Cubans in Chicago have been more politically progressive, and have identified with the political struggles of other Latino groups. In a newspaper opinion piece, for example, two Cubans defended the right of Orquesta Aragon to play in Chicago.[29] Orquesta Aragon did play in Chicago in 1999. Over the years younger Cubans in Chicago supported First Amendment rights. Many are against the United States' economic blockade of Cuba. They supported negotiations or full normalization of diplomatic relations between the United States and Cuba. And Chicago does not have the extreme, right-wing, anti-Castro groups that are found in Miami. "Some older Cubans are conservative and even right-wing. That's because they were politically exiled from Cuba," says Achy Obejas, 50, a former reporter for the Chicago Tribune. "But in Chicago, the children of exiles have been quite progressive. For instance, María de los Angeles Torres, a Cuban, was the director of the Mayor's Advisory Commission on Latino Affairs when Harold Washington was mayor in 1983. Mayor Washington also appointed Natalia Delgado, a Cuban lawyer to the Chicago Transit Authority board. And Maria Bechily, a Cuban businesswoman, was on almost every board of every Latino organization in this city.... Cubans who live in Chicago have constant contact with other Latinos. So we are constantly challenged in our thinking in ways that we wouldn't be in Miami. In Miami the second generation of Cuban Americans continues to be very conservative."[30]

Some Cubans in Chicago were even embarrassed by the defiant, disorderly behavior of conservative Cubans in Miami during the highly publicized, six-month saga of 6-year-old Elian Gonzales. A small, Cuban group, the Chicago Cuba Coalition, demanded the return of Elian to his father in Cuba. The coalition of Cuban professors, pastors, psychologists, and professionals held a press conference in downtown Chicago stating that right-wing, Cuban organizations and leaders in Miami do not speak for everyone in the Cuban American community.

Obejas, her parents, and 44 others escaped from Havana, Cuba on a stolen boat in 1963. They fled because of Castro. They arrived in Miami, Florida. "My father got very depressed knowing we might never return to Cuba," recalls Obejas. "The U.S. government helped us. We received some assistance similar to public welfare. My dad was really proud and he hated taking the money. It lasted for about six months. My father worked as a waiter in a Chinese restaurant and he pumped gas. My parents worked for a while as migrant workers, picking tomatoes. What really shocked them was segregation in Florida. There were two trailers with cafeteria service for the field workers. One for coloreds, one for whites. My parents are light-skinned. They strolled over to the white line. The owners pointed to the Cubans and said, 'no, no, you guys get over there in the colored line.' Cubans were offended and horrified."

In 1965, the American government helped Obejas' educated parents find teaching jobs in the public schools of Michigan City, Indiana. Obejas grew up in Michigan City and came to Chicago in 1979. "When I first came to Chicago, I was always hanging around with the Puerto Ricans who believed in Puerto Rican independence," says Obejas. "I'm very grateful to these independentistas because they really raised my political consciousness. They made me rethink a lot of things about the Cuban revolution. They forced me to reconcile many issues. If it weren't for radical Puerto Ricans, I might not be as comfortably Cuban as I am today." As a longtime newspaper reporter, Obejas gained an appreciation of Chicago's diverse Latino groups. She wrote numerous stories on Latino arts, books, music, culture, and politics. Many Latinos considered her writings progressive. Obejas published two books of short stories. One book is titled, "You Came All the Way from Cuba So You Could Dress Like That." "That book is about immigrants in Chicago, lesbians, and gays," says Obejas. "They're not all Cuban, they're also Mexican and Puerto Rican. They are stories I collected in my head from my own experiences in the city. One interesting thing about working for newspapers, is that you meet people who live on the margins. And I'm fascinated by them."

Obejas, who is openly lesbian, did not believe Latinos are more homophobic than other ethnic groups. "I do not believe that for a minute," says Obejas. "Latino parents do not disown their children when they tell them they are gay or lesbian. A lot of white parents do. My parents have never been embarrassed or ashamed of me. My parents have never pretended I'm not gay. They might side-step, but they don't lie about me. My parents have never rejected anyone I've brought home. They are very proud of me. Admittedly, my experience is more among Cubans than among other Latinos. But when it comes to gay children, I think Latino parents are very accepting.... One thing that has always saddened my parents is the fact that I wouldn't have kids."

Over the years, other Latino groups acquired an appreciation for the contributions of Cubans to the life of Chicago. Noted Cuban artists, performers, professors, doctors, and businesspersons have been profiled in major newspapers and magazines.[31] Latinos and other Chicagoans enjoyed Cuban culture, especially Cuban music. Large audiences packed downtown nightclubs, theaters, and museums to dance and listen to island-based, Cuban bands play new and older Afro-Cuban music. Cuban bands like the salseros Los Van Van, rumba masters Munequitos de Matanzas, the dance troupe, Grupo AfroCuba de Matanzas, and the Afro-Cuban All Stars, and the Buena Vista Social Club have all played in Chicago. One popular, Saturday morning radio show in Chicago was "Mambo Express." For 13 years the show played older and newer Afro-Cuban music. The show's host was Victor Parra, a 63-year-old Mexican. Parra developed a lifelong, intense passion for pure Cuban music. But the radio station wanted Parra to change the station's format and include music from all over Latin America. Parra wanted to play only pure Cuban music. Thus, Mambo Express was canceled in 1995. Parra, however, formed his own live musical band called Mambo Express. The band played Cuban music at local clubs and city festivals.[32]

Cuban Professors

Angelina Pedroso endeared herself to generations of Latino college students. Pedroso is a professor of Spanish at Northeastern Illinois University. For over 40 years she patiently taught Mexican, Puerto Rican, and Cuban students how to speak, read, and write Spanish. Students were mesmerized with her dignified style, humor, eloquent Spanish, and her vast knowledge of Latino history and culture. "You don't need to know my age," laughs Pedroso. "What if I tell you I graduated from the University of Havana, Cuba as a lawyer in 1953. I am from Havana, Cuba. I came to the state of Maine in 1954 with my husband. He is a medical doctor and he came to do an internship. A year later, we came to Chicago and my husband worked at Cook Country Hospital. I was lucky to find a job with Standard Oil. At the same time, I was studying. Those were hard years."[33] Pedroso was from an educated, middle-class family in Cuba. Yet some of her relatives were slaves in Cuba. "I am the cousin of Juan Gualberto Gomez, one of the heroes of Cuban independence," says Pedroso. "There are two international airports in Cuba. One is Jose Marti, the other is Juan Gualberto Gomez. My great grandparents were slaves. They did not work in the fields. They got education and traveled to Europe with their owners. Their owners were French and Spanish. My father was a judge and my mother was a professor."

Pedroso was one of the first Latino professors hired at Northeastern Illinois University. Yet she recalls the raw prejudice she experienced. In addition to her law degree, Pedroso earned two advanced education degrees in Chicago. In 1965, she received a letter from the president of Northeastern Illinois University

saying she had been selected for a tenure-track position. At that time, Northeastern was a teachers' college affiliated with the Chicago Board of Education.
Pedroso went downtown to meet the Chicago Board of Education president.
"The president comes with my portfolio. He was a real tall, white man with blue
eyes," recalls Pedroso. "He said to me, 'You're crazy girl if you think, for a
minute, you're going to be a professor in an American university.' Then he
yelled, 'Give her a pencil and paper.' He screamed at me to stand up and take
dictation. He dictated the ABCs. He grabbed the paper from me and said,
'Someone taught this girl how to read and write.' Then he took my portfolio and
threw it up in the air. Then he said, 'Get on you knees and pick them up.' When
I was on my knees I just kept saying, 'God don't let me cry in front of this man.'
He was trying to provoke me to slap him.... I still got the job at Northeastern.
We were so happy, my family was celebrating in Cuba."

On campus, Pedroso was a strong advocate for Puerto Rican and Latino
students. She supported students in their demands for more Latino students,
courses, and faculty. But in the early 1970s, some pro-independence Puerto Rican students on campus had a falling out among themselves over political differences. A few Latino faculty, including Pedroso, were heckled by a small group
of students. "The majority of times I supported Latino students. They were justi-
fied in their demands," recalls Pedroso. "I didn't accept some of the methods the
students used and they knew it. There was one year when some Latino students
boycotted my classes. I try to honor the memory of Jose Marti, with my best and
honest conduct. And I suffered the consequences of my honestly. I didn't believe in some of the things the students were saying about other Latino students
and faculty. The price I paid was that students were telling other students don't
take Pedroso's classes. That hurt a lot. I went into my office and cried. But one
cannot buy respect, you have to earn it."

The boycott of Pedroso's classes did not work. Latino students eagerly registered for her popular, Spanish and literature classes. Many students saw her as
a role model. Over the years Pedroso helped numerous Cuban students enter the
university and graduate. In 1980, she helped 22 Cuban students enter Northeastern. The students were from the Mariel boatlift. "The university asked me to
direct and help these 22 students. They suffered the hurt of being all considered
criminals and escapees from Cuban jails. But they came here to study. They
came well prepared. They did not have any money. But as Cubans, they were
eligible for government grants. They finished in four years. Some have gone on
for their master's degrees. Others for their Ph.D.s." Pedroso lived in Skokie,
Illinois. Her ex-husband, Aldo Pedroso, is a highly respected pathologist in Chicago. Every semester Pedroso's classes were filled to capacity by Latino students. They left her classes with their heads held a little more erect. "I don't
think the Latino culture is being lost in the second and third generations," says
Pedroso. "It is still strong. It has gotten stronger to survive. We have realized
that we will always be Latinos. That forever our children will be Latino. When
the persecution comes, it touches all of us. I remember hearing a Cuban radio
station in California saying that Cubans respected the law but undocumented

Mexicans didn't. That insulted me. I didn't care that the station was Cuban."

A second-generation Cuban who has strongly identified with the political and civil rights struggles of Latinos in Chicago is María de los Angeles Torres, 51. Torres is a professor of Latin American Studies at the University of Illinois at Chicago. She wrote various articles and books on the Cuban experience in Chicago and nationally. Torres and other Cubans supported Harold Washington in his 1983 bid to become the city's first black mayor. In 1983 after Washington won, Torres became the first executive director of the Mayor's Advisory Commission on Latino Affairs (MACLA). The commission was composed of 15 members, mainly prominent Mexicans and Puerto Ricans who advised Mayor Washington on Latino issues. "No one opposed my appointment to head the commission," says Torres. "One reason I was the consensus candidate was because I didn't represent a particular city ward. I also didn't represent a community organization. I was perceived as more objective.... I belonged to a generation of Cuban Americans raised in the United States. Therefore I suffered discrimination, like many other Latinos. My father has blue eyes and white skin, yet he was called a spic and told to go back to Cuba. Who didn't call him that in Midland, Texas? People shot out the windows of his office and our home. Cubans raised in Miami had the cushion of the exile community to buffer the more brutal forms of racism.... Today, I and many Cubans are struggling to have a political perspective that is critical of both governments, Cuba and the United States. That has been difficult to have."[34]

Torres arrived in Miami, Florida from Havana, Cuba in 1961. She was a six-year-old who came without parents. She came as part of a secret, classified American government program known as the Peter Pan Operation. From 1960 to 1962, over 14,000 unaccompanied Cuban children were brought to the United States. The children were placed in foster families and with relatives in cities throughout the United States. Torres was quickly reunited with her parents. Her father was a medical doctor and her mother was a physicist. "My story is not that dramatic because it was four months later that my mother came to the United States," recalls Torres. "A month later my father came. As a medical doctor, my father couldn't leave Cuba. My father bribed his way out of Cuba with money. We were in Miami for a year, but my father could not find a job, although he was a professional. We ended up being relocated to Cleveland. I was raised in different parts of Texas like Dallas, San Antonio and Midland."

One controversial aspect of the Mayor's Advisory Commission on Latino Affairs was an annual report the commission published on city hiring. The report highlighted the lack of Latinos in city jobs, and challenged the mayor and department heads to hire more Latinos. The media had a field day with the report, sensing cracks in the fragile black, Latino, and white coalition that elected Washington. Many in the African American community felt Latinos were being ungrateful and pushy by publicly criticizing the mayor. Torres genuinely liked Harold Washington, but as head of the MACLA, Torres felt compelled to demand that the city hire more Latinos. "I think Harold Washington tried to be fair in bringing in whites, blacks, and Latinos into City Hall," says Torres. "He had a tremendous amount of pressure in terms of delivering to the African American community. I also think he had a lot less resources than his predecessors. As mayor, he signed the Shakman Decree that limited political hiring and firings.... Whenever I said something nice about the mayor I would get these pleasant phone calls from him. But whenever we went public with the Latino hiring reports, I couldn't walk into the mayor's office for three months. When the mayor was accused of not being fair, he did take it personally."

To complicate matters, Torres' husband, an attorney, worked for the city's law department. Yet Torres refused to pull back punches. The critical hiring reports kept coming. "City administrators would not threaten my husband's job. They would talk to him so he would try to cool me off," recalls Torres. "I remember him saying to me, 'You know, the mayor's really worried. He doesn't understand, bah, bah, bah.' That didn't cool me off.... But you know what the mayor told me about the perception that Latinos were being too pushy? That he would be doing the same thing." In September of 1987, Torres stepped down as the head of the MACLA. A month later, shortly into his second term, Washington died in his office of a major heart attack. "I don't know of any mayor who would allow us to do what we did with the MACLA," says Torres. "Mayor Jane Bryne sorts of opens the door of city government to Latinos. Yet Washington opened city government to Latinos, and developed a more respectful relationship with Latinos. He helped Latinos get elected to political office and develop an independent style of Latino political power."

Torres believed that unlike Washington, Mayor Richard M. Daley does not allow for an independent style of political power among Latino elected officials. She saw this as a step backwards for Latinos. "Mayor Daley hates to be criticized. He's very autocratic. He comes into office and places the Mayor's Advisory Commission on Latino Affairs under the city's Human Relations Commission, where it's basically a do-nothing commission. They don't criticize the mayor or publish reports on Latino hiring in city government. This mayor does not have a style that allows for independent politics. I don't know if in the future you will have more independent, progressive Latino politicians. It's too early to predict exactly what's going to happen."

Torres shared her impressions of Cuba. She has visited Cuba. "Few Cubans today would not agree that Fidel should leave. There's something wrong with someone being in power for 40 years, even if what he tried to do initially was a good thing. I think he did a lot of good things. There is something wrong with that much power that long, under the guise of an outdated ideology.... There are increasing differences between the rich and poor in Cuba. Remittances are the number one gross national product in Cuba today. These remittances come from the hated exiles in the United States. That's a major contradiction internally in Cuba because the government is supposed to be providing." As for the future of Chicago's Cuban community, Torres believed it will only get smaller over the years. "The Cuban community is getting smaller," argues Torres. "They're not moving to the suburbs, they're moving to Miami. It is a reverse migration to Miami. The testimony to the failure of relocation politics of the early 1960s, is that Cubans have moved back to Miami. Older people retire there. Younger people are searching for roots. And a lot of business people are moving there."

Epilogue

Latinos have had a long history and presence in Chicago. As early as 1916, a sizable number of Mexicans settled in Chicago. Like previous waves of European immigrants, Latinos were enticed by the prospect of a better life for themselves and their families. Like previous European immigrants, many of the first Latino arrivals to the city —specifically Mexicans and Puerto Ricans—came as contracted workers. They came to work on the railroads. They came to pick and harvest crops as migrant workers throughout the Midwest. They came as contracted domestics to work in the homes of middle-class families. They came as contracted workers to sweat and work in the foundries. But unlike European immigrants, Latino immigrants experienced much more prejudice and discrimination from employers and other Chicagoans. Some Chicagoans viewed Latino workers as dark-skinned foreigners, and they were not welcomed as permanent neighbors or accepted as American citizens. Large companies welcomed Latinos as cheap laborers, but these companies hoped that once the Latino laborers completed their contracts, and performed the necessary, hard work, that they would return to their homeland.

Some of the contracted workers did return home. But many decided to remain and settle down in the city. They left low-paying, agricultural work for better-paying, manufacturing jobs. During World War I and World War II, large, Midwestern companies recruited hundreds of Latino workers to toil in the steel mills, railroads, stockyards, foundries, and factories of the city and its surrounding suburbs. Over the intervening years, many more Mexicans and Puerto Ricans voluntarily immigrated to the city seeking work in industrial plants and factories. Marriages took place, families grew, and communities emerged. In subsequent decades, other Latino groups like Cubans, Guatemalans, and Salvadorans arrived and called Chicago their home. Many came because of political and economic reasons.

However, while European migration to the city has all but ended, Latino migration continues. The Latino presence in Chicago will undoubtedly grow in the coming decades. Already more than one in every four city residents, or 26 percent, is Latino, up from just under one in five a decade ago. Chicago, the city of immigrants, is no longer dominated by Poles, Irish, Italians, or Germans. Mexicans are now the dominant ethnic group in 25 of the city's 77 community areas.[1] Moreover, the Mexican population in the city and state will continue to grow steadily in the future as new arrivals are lured by the promise of better wages. Mexican immigration will continue because wages are seven times higher in the United States than in Mexico. Also, Mexicans have established a century-long history of immigration to the Chicago area.

Other immigrants from countries like Columbia continue to arrive in Chicago. Some of these were middle-class, educated professionals who were lured to cities like Chicago where jobs and advancement opportunities are supposedly better. Others were unskilled workers fleeing political violence and economic hardship in their homeland. It is estimated that there were about 35,000 Colombians in the Chicago area.[2] Additionally, immigrants from South and Central American countries like Ecuador, Hondurans, Venezuela, Nicaragua, Guatemala, and El Salvador trickled into Chicago and its neighboring suburbs. Civil strife, bad economies, poverty, and natural disasters in their homelands triggered a sizable exodus of immigrants from these South and Central American countries. Many applied for "temporary legal status" which would allow them to live and work legally in the United States for up to 18 months. Others hope the United States will soon implement an amnesty program for undocumented workers. However, as Chicagoans and Americans experience a lingering recession, high unemployment, and growing anti-immigrant sentiments few politicians were willing to push for "temporary status" or amnesty for immigrants.

Thus, many new immigrants from South and Central Americans countries come to Chicago as unskilled, undocumented workers. They are usually poor, uneducated, and do not speak English. Nevertheless, by coming to places like Chicago, these immigrants believe they have nothing to lose and everything to gain. They prefer to try their luck in Chicago rather than return and face civil strife, poverty, and unemployment in their homelands. Like earlier Latino immigrants, these newcomers come with high expectations and dreams. They come seeking steady jobs and decent wages. But these newcomers join an already large and growing pool of undocumented Latino workers in Chicago, who lack the requisite skills to compete in a 21st century economy. Surely these newcomers, and other unskilled Latino workers, will encounter obstacles and hardships. Chicago is a vastly different city from what it was fifty to seventy-five years ago. Well-paying manufacturing jobs that previous immigrants used to get a foothold into middle-class respectability, continue to leave the city. Manufacturing jobs that once paid well and required little education, are increasingly moving to Third World countries. Small factories in the city now sit empty or are being converted to high-priced condominiums. Chicago's economy is steadily being transformed into a service economy. Occupations at the higher end of the growing service industries require a college education and specialized, skilled workers. And many immigrants simply cannot afford the spiraling cost of a college education.

Only time will tell how newer Latino immigrants—and those already here who are unskilled and undocumented—adapt and adjust in Chicago. Will their dreams turn into some kind of nightmare? Will they eventually form a permanent underclass? Will they add to the unemployment, public aid, homeless, and poverty rolls? Will they be struck in low-paid, menial, dead-end jobs for years and years? Will they and their families find affordable housing in the city? Will they, like other immigrants, slowly climb the ladder up into the middle class? And how long will it take for these immigrants to achieve some level of economic, social, and political success? Their story is yet to be told.

Despite the hurdles and hardships some Latino immigrants may face, they can take some comfort in the optimism of Latinos who have been in this city for years. On the one hand, the vast majority of people interviewed for this book, including those from different generations, believed their lives have significantly improved in Chicago. Many said most of their dreams have been fulfilled. Among the dreams they mentioned was the pride of home ownership, and living in a safe, decent neighborhood. Some expressed joy being self-employed and owning small, thriving businesses. Some expressed happiness at working their adult lives in Chicago, and then being able to retire to their country of origin. Individuals were happy to have found good-paying, secure jobs. Others expressed satisfaction at being able to secure legal resident status—or even better—obtaining their American citizenship. A few mentioned the joy of finding liberty, freedom, and peace in America and Chicago. Others were appreciative of being able to learn English, or earning their high school diploma or a couple years of college. Many expressed pride in the fact that their children have earned college education, and work in highly-paid, professional occupations. They were indeed happy that all their hard work, sacrifices, and efforts paid off and that their children were living richer and fuller lives. Overall, a good number of Latinos believed the city still provides opportunities for betterment if one was willing to work hard, sacrifice, and preserve.

Yet, on the other hand, some of those interviewed have yet to achieve their dreams. Some were still dealing with bread-and-butter issues like trying to find a well-paying, secure job. Individuals wished they had steady jobs with benefits like sick days, health insurance, life insurance, and pensions. Instead, many worked in unskilled, dead-end jobs that paid minimum wages or less. Some worked as day and temporary laborers. Many worked long hours in small restaurants as waiters, busboys, washing dishes, sweeping floors, or as low-paid cooks. Some worked double shifts or two jobs to make ends meet. Some lived in bad neighborhoods and dreamed of moving to a better place in a clean, nice apartment. Some wished to work hard, save their money, and someday own their own homes. Others dreamed of one day owning a small business. Some worried about their illegal status and being deported to their home countries.

While some of those interviewed experienced setbacks and disappointments, and while they still struggled to make ends meet, they nevertheless maintained a positive outlook. While life in Chicago was harder than they anticipated, they did not have a defeatist attitude. They wanted to improve their human capital skills. They believed that if they just worked harder, learned English, acquired their GED or some type of training, or became an American citizen that their lives would improve. Ironically, long, irregular work hours, double shifts, and minimum wage jobs often left workers with very little energy to pursue English, GED or job training classes. But even if their lives were difficult, and they had to endure hardships, they were hopeful their children would achieve the American dream of good homes and quality education. They were optimistic that with hard work and dedication, combined with college education, the doors of opportunities would open wide for their children and future generations of Latinos.

Most of those interviewed—the ones doing well, and those still strug-gling—did not find paradise in Chicago. They were not Pollyanna. They ex-pressed concern about various social problems they viewed among Latinos. Some mentioned the high rate of poverty among Latino families. In 1999, for instance, 20 percent of Latinos reported incomes below the poverty line, com-pared with 30 percent for blacks, nearly 18 percent for Asians and 8.2 percent for whites. And the income gap between whites and blacks, as well as between whites and Latinos widened during the economic boom of the 1990s. In 1999, median household income in the city was $49,222 for whites, $29,086 for blacks, $36,542 for Latinos and $40,519 for Asians.[3] Other Latinos pointed to young gangs, drug dealing, and violent crime as serious neighborhood problems. They worried that fewer jobs today pay well, have unions, are secure, and offer important benefits like health insurance and pensions. They wondered if un-skilled, undocumented immigrants who speak little English, will achieve signifi-cant economic and social mobility. They were concerned by the high rates of high school dropouts among Latino youth. And they were troubled by the politi-cal bickering among Latino politicians. Some lamented the fact that different Latino groups did not interact more closely with each other. They hoped that in the future, different Latinos groups would help each other more and engage in coalitions around social issues affecting most Latinos.

Despite their concerns, the majority of those interviewed still saw Chicago as a good city to live in, work, and raise a family. They pointed to the achieve-ments and contributions of Latinos as obvious signs of progress. For example, where once Latinos were not welcomed in certain neighborhoods, they now lived in all areas of the city. A growing percentage of Latinos owned their homes. Where once Chicago had few Latino restaurants, it now had thousands. Latino-owned businesses were growing. Increasing numbers of Latinos were becoming college educated and middle class. There were many more Latino professionals in education, the arts, criminal justice, health, and social services.

Many also pointed to the increase of elected Latino officials as another sure sign of progress. About two decades ago, there were few Latino elected offi-cials. There were now more that 25 in Cook County, and their numbers were growing. Political inroads, combined with a growing Latino population, made many Latinos cautiously optimistic that in the near future Latinos will progress in Chicago. Some excitedly predicted that someday soon Chicago will elect its first Latino mayor. Other Latinos were even more optimistic about the future. For instance, Mexican businessman Arthur R. Velasquez says, "I think Latinos are going to be key in leading the educational system in this city. We're going to be key in leading the Catholic Church. We're going to be key politically. Heck, in about ten to fifteen years, Latinos will own this town."[4] Whether Latinos will even own the town is open to debate. But there is no denying that like European and African American immigrants groups before them, diverse Latino groups have made—and continue to make—important contributions to the political, educational, social, and cultural institutions of Chicago. Latinos were no longer content to be bit players looking on from the sidelines. Unlike the past, Latinos could no longer be ignored by major businesses, policy makers, and politicians.

Notes

Introduction

1. Frank James, "U.S. Hispanic Population Grows by 58%." *ChicagoTribune,* March 8, 2001, 1. Scott Fornek, "City Population Up As Suburbs Surge." *Chicago Sun-Times,* March 15, 2001, 12.

2. Felix Padilla, *Latino Ethnic Consciousness: The Case of Mexican Americans and Puerto Ricans in Chicago* (Notre Dame, IN: University of Notre Dame Press, 1985).

Chapter One: Mexicans

1. Author interview with Frank and Jovita Duran, March 30, 1998, Chicago.

2. Jorge Casuso and Eduardo Camacho, "Latino Chicago", in Melvin G. Holli and Peter d'A. Jones, eds., *Ethnic Chicago A Multicultural Portrait* (Grand Rapids, Mich: William B. Eerdmans, 1995), 353.

3. U. S. Census Bureau. "Hispanic Population By Type For Regions, States, and Puerto Rico: 1990 and 2000," (Washington D. C.: Government Printing Office, 2000). See also David Mendell, "New Numbers Add Up to Decade of Diversity, Minority boom, Aging population Reshape Chicago," *Chicago Tribune*, August 12, 2001, 1. Martha Irvine, "Hispanic Influx Shaping Chicago," *Chicago Sun-Times*, March 11, 2001, 1.

4. Louise Año Nuevo-Kerr, "The Chicano Experience in Chicago, 1920-1970," (Ph.D. dissertation, University of Illinois at Chicago, 1976), 19.

5. Paul S. Taylor, *Mexican Labor in the United States: Chicago and the Calumet Region* (Berkeley: University of California Press, 1932), 32.

6. Author interview with Dennis Prieto, September 15, 1998, Chicago.

7. Zargosa Vargas. *Proletarians of the North: A History of Mexican Industrial Workers in Detroit and the Midwest, 1917-1933* (Berkeley: University of California Press, 1999) 38-40.

8. Louise Año Nuevo-Kerr, "The Chicano Experience in Chicago, 1920-1970," 26.

9. Zaragosa Vargas, *Proletarians of the North*, 29.

10. Francisco A. Rosales and Daniel T. Simon. "Chicano Steel Workers and Unionism in the Midwest, 1919-1945," *Aztlán* 6 (1975), 268.

11. Willaim M. Tuttle Jr. *Race Riot: Chicago in the Red Summer of 1919* (New York: Atheneum Publishers, 1970).

12. Mark Reisler, *By the Sweat of Their Brow: Mexican Immigrant Labor in the United States, 1900-1940* (Westport CT: Greenwood Press, 1973), 103.

13. Mark Reisler, *By the Sweat of Their Brow*, 103.

14. Mark Reisler, "Always the Laborer, Never the Citizen: Anglo Perceptions of the Mexican Immigrant During the 1920's," *Pacific Historical Review* 37 (May 1976), 233.

15. Paul S. Taylor, *Mexican Labor in the United States*, 113

16. Louise Año Nuevo-Kerr, "Mexican Chicago: Chicano Assimilation Aborted, 1939-1954," in Melvin G. Holli and Peter d'A. Jones, eds., *The Ethnic Frontier: Essays in the History of Group Survival in Chicago and the Midwest* (Grand Rapids, Mich: Williams B. Eerdmans, 1977) 294.

17. Anita Edgar Jones, "Mexican Colonies in Chicago," *Social Service Review* 2 (December 1928), 586.

18. Abraham Hoffman, *Unwanted Mexican Americans in the Great Depression: Repatriation Pressures, 1929-1939* (Tucson, Arizona: The University of Arizona Press, 1974).

19. Louise Año Nuevo-Kerr, "The Chicano Experience in Chicago: 1920-1970," 75.

20. Raymond A. Mohl and Neil Betten, "Discrimination and Repatriation: Mexican Life in Gary," 167. See also Francisco Arturo Rosales and Daniel T. Simon, "Mexican Experience in the Urban Midwest: East Chicago, Indiana, 1919-1945," *Indiana Magazine of History* 77 (December 1981).

21. Paul S. Taylor, *Mexican Labor in the United States*, 154.

22. Richard B. Craig, *The Bracero Program* (Austin, TX: University of Texas Press, 1971).

23. Anita Edgar Jones, "Conditions Surrounding Mexicans in Chicago," (M.A. thesis, University of Chicago, August 1923), 59.

24. Author interview with Jorge and Luz Maria Prieto, November 21, 1997, Chicago. See also Wilfredo Cruz, "Dedicated Doctor, Prieto Advocates Health Care for Poor," *The Chicago Reporter* 10 (October 1981).

25. Jorge Prieto, *Harvest of Hope: The Pilgrimage of a Mexican American Physician* (Notre Dame, IN: University of Notre Dame, 1989). Jorge Prieto, *The Quarterback Who Almost Wasn't* (Houston, TX: Arte Publico Press, 1994).

26. Jon Handley, "A New Chapter," *Chicago Tribune*, August 20, 2000, 1.

27. Mark Reisler, "The Mexican Immigrant in the Chicago Area during the 1920's," *Illinois State Historical Association Journal* 66 (Summer 1973), 148.

28. Author interview with Dolores and Emilio Reyes, September 15, 1998, Chicago.

29. Francisco A. Rosales and Daniel T. Simon, "Chicano Steel Workers and Unionism in the Midwest, 1919-1945," 272.

30. Zaragosa Vargas, *Proletarians of the North*, 42.

31. Jorge Hernandez-Fujigake, "Mexican Steelworkers and the United Steelworkers of America in the Midwest: the Island Steel Experience, 1936-1979," (Ph. D. dissertation, The University of Chicago, 1991), 175-179.

32. Rodolfo Acuña, *Occupied America: a History of Chicanos* (New York: HarperCollins, 1988), 316.

33. William Kornblum, *Blue Collar Community* (Chicago: University of Chicago Press, 1974), 22

34. David Bensman and Roberta Lynch, *Rusted Dreams: Hard Times in a Steel Community* (New York: McGraw-Hill, 1987), 2.

35. Author interview with Abram and Rose Jacinto, March 21, 1998, Chicago.

36. David Bensman and Roberta Lynch, *Rusted Dreams: Hard Times in a Steel Community*, 99. See also "Chicago Steelworkers: The Cost of Unemployment," *Steelworkers Research Project* (January 1985).

37. Jennifer Peltz, "Landlord Gets Prison in Slaying of Activist," *Chicago Tribune*, March 8, 2000, 3.

38. Paul S. Taylor, *Mexican Labor in the United States*, 131.

39. Ibid., 134

40. Juan R. Garcia and Angel Cal, "El Circulo De Obreros Catolicos "San Jose," 1925-1930," in James B. Lane and Edward J. Escobar, eds. *Forging a Community: the Latino Experience in Northwest Indiana, 1919-1975* (Chicago: Cattails Press, 1987).

41. Louise Año Nuevo- Kerr, "The Chicano Experience in Chicago: 1920-1970," 52.

42. Ibid., 50

43. Paul S. Taylor, *Mexican Labor in the United States*, 170.

44. Author interview with Carmen Martinez Arias, March 18, 1998, Chicago.

45. Will Hogan and Lilia Villanueva, "Lower West Side," in The Chicago Fact Book Consortium, eds., *Local Community Fact Book Chicago Metropolitan Area, 1990* (Chicago: Academy, 1995), 113.

46. Author interview with Mario Castillo, November 20, 1998, Chicago.

47. Victor A. Sorell and Mark Rogovin, "The Barrio Murals/Murales Del Barrio," *Mexican Fine Arts Center Museum*, 1987.

48. Wilfredo Cruz, "Anti-Immigrant Attitudes Hurting Chicago's Mexican American Community," *One City*, Spring 1997.

49. Author interview with Mary Gonzáles, December 16, 1998, Chicago. See also Wilfredo Cruz, "Mary Gonzáles: You Can't Sit Back and do Nothing," in Peg Knoeplfe, ed., *After Alinsky: Community Organizing in Illinois* (Springfield IL: Sangamon State University, 1990), 16.

50. Leonard Aronson, "Claim-jumpers Eye Pilsen Gold," *Chicago Today*, July 24, 1973, 1.

51. Gary Washburn, "Study Criticizes Chicago TIFs," *Chicago Tribune*, March 12, 2002, 2.

52. Wilfredo Cruz, "UNO: Organizing at the Grass Roots," *Illinois Issues*, April 1988.

53. Wilfredo Cruz, "From Blue Jeans to Pinstripes: Danny Solis Has Traded Confrontation Politics for a Seat at the Tables of Power," *Illinois Issues*, December 1993.

54. Author interview with Juan Rangel, September 21, 1998, Chicago.

55. Kari Lydersen, "Party Pooper, is Danny Solis Responsible for Keeping Fiesta del Sol From its Traditional Site?" *The Chicago Reader*, July 30, 1999, 5.

56. Author interview with Carlos Tortolero, October 21, 1998, Chicago.

57. Will Hogan and Magdalena Cortes, "South Lawndale," in The Chicago Fact Book Consortium, eds., *Local Community Fact Book Chicago Metropolitan Area 1990*, 110. –

58. Author interview with Norma Seledon, July 29, 1998, Chicago.

59. Mujeres Latinas En Acción , "Latinas in Chicago: A Portrait," Mujeres Latinas En Acción, October 1996.

60. Author interview with Ron Baltierra, October 8, 1998, Chicago.

61. Author interview with Juan Ochoa, September 2, 1998, Chicago.

62. Author interview with Dennis Prieto, September 15, 1998, Chicago.

63. Author interview with Esperanza Torres, August 7, 1998, Chicago.

64. Fran Spielman, "Food Vendors Face Regulation," *Chicago Sun-Times*, September 19, 2000, 12.

65. Author interview with Dennis Prieto, September 15, 1998, Chicago.

Chapter Two: Mexicans

1. Author interview with Rev. Peter Rodríguez, April 17, 1998, Chicago.

2. Dominic A. Pacyga, "New City", in The Chicago Fact Book Consortium, eds., *Local Community Fact Book Chicago Metropolitan Area 1990* (Chicago: Academy, 1995), 178.

3. Robert A. Slayton, *Back of the Yards The Making of a Local Democracy* (Chicago: University of Chicago Press, 1986), 180.

4. Frank X. Paz, "Mexican Americans in Chicago, a General Survey," *Welfare Council of Metropolitan Chicago*, January 1948, 7.

5. Robert A. Slayton, *Back of the Yards*, 186. See also Eunice Felter "The Social Adaptations Of The Mexican Churches In The Chicago Area," (M.A. thesis, University of Chicago, June 1941).

6. "A Butcher Shop Their Church—An Ice Box Serves as Altar," *The New World*, March 4, 1941, 2.

7. Dominic A. Pacyga, "New City," 178.

8. Ellen Skerrett, Edward R. Kantowicz, and Steven M. Avella, *Catholicism, Chicago Style* (Chicago: Loyola University Press, 1993), 140.

9. Edward R. Kantowicz, "The Ethnic Church," in Melvin G. Holli and Peter d'A. Jones, eds., *The Ethnic Frontier: Essays in the History of Group Survival in Chicago and the Midwest* (Grand Rapids, Mich: Williams B. Eerdmans, 1977), 602.

10. David A. Badillo, "Midwestern Catholicism and the Early Mexican Parishes, 1910-930," in Jay P. Dolan and Gilberto Hinojosa, eds., *Mexican Americans and the Catholic Church, 1900-1965* (Notre Dame, IN: University of Notre Dame Press, 1994), 256.

11. Ibid., 256.

12. Author telephone interview with Rev. James Maloney, June 2, 2000, Chicago.

13. RoseAnna M. Mueller, "Pilsen Rallies Around Cultural Symbol of Mexican

Immigrants: Virgin of Guadalupe, *Chicago Tribune*, December 9,1999, 8.

14. Author interview with Mary Quiroz Flores, September 14, 1998, Chicago.

15. Author interview with Rev. David Staszak, February 18, 1998, Chicago.

16. Archdiocese of Chicago. "Archdiocesan Pastoral Plan for Hispanic Ministry," *Archdiocese of Chicago*, June 1997, 3.

17. Teresa Puente and Ray Quintanilla, "Bringing It Together," *Chicago Tribune*, April 13, 1997, 1.

18. Jon Schmid, "Near W. Side Church Celebrates 2 Rebirths," *Chicago Sun-Times*, April 8, 1996, 4.

19. Archdiocese of Chicago, "Office of Hispanic Ministry, *Archdiocese of Chicago*, December 11, 2000.

20. Archdiocese of Chicago, "Archdiocesan Pastoral Plan for Hispanic Ministry," 9.

21. Author interview with Jesus Zeferino Ochoa, August 31, 1999, Chicago.

22. Bill Rumbler, "Helping Hands, Throughout Chicago's Neglected Neighborhoods, Church Groups Lead a Housing Revival," *Chicago Sun-Times*, June 18, 1999, 1.

23. Author interview with Rev. Juan Huitrado, August 28, 1998, Chicago.

24. Stephen C. Holler, "Exploring The Popular Religion of U.S. Hispanic/Latino Ethnic Groups," *Latino Studies Journal* 6 (September 1995), 20.

25. Constanza Montana, "Some Latinos Spare No Expense When Their Daughters Come Of Age," *Chicago Tribune*, June 19, 1990, 1. See also Karen Mary Davalos, "Ethnic Identity Among Mexican and Mexican American Women In Chicago, 1920-1991," (Ph. D. Dissertation, Yale University, 1993).

26. Author interview with Teresa Fraga, November 17, 1998, Chicago.

27. Chicago Public Schools, "Racial/Ethnic Survey of Students," *Chicago Public Schools*, September 30, 1997, xi.

28. Wilfredo Cruz, "Dilapidated and Dangerous: Board Still Crowds Minority Pupils Into Mobile Classrooms," *The Chicago Reporter*, December 1981, 1.

29. Author interview with Carmen Velasquez, December 7, 1998, Chicago.

30. Greg Burke and Phil Greer, "Viva Velasquez, Making the American Dream Come True and Sharing It," *Chicago Tribune Magazine*, February 28, 1988, 1.

31. Author interview with Martin and Edgar Jaimes, January 14, 1999, Chicago.

32. Wilfredo Cruz, "Chicago Schools Employ Few Latino Administrators," *The Chicago Reporter*, June 1981, 1.

33. Chicago Public Schools, "Racial/Ethnic Survey of Staff," *Chicago Public Schools*, September 30, 1997, 5.

34. Author interview with Gery Chico, November 7, 1998, Chicago.

35. Gary Washburn, "Daley Backs School Board Chief Sees No Conflict In Chico's Lobbying And His Position," *Chicago Tribune*, March 15, 2000, 3.

36. Virginia Valdez, "Progress Report: An Evaluation of the Chicago Public Schools' Efforts to Relieve Overcrowding at Elementary Schools," *Mexican American Legal Defense And Educational Fund*, April 2000, 2.

37. The Neighborhood Capital Budget Group, "Rebuilding Our Schools Brick By Brick," *The Neighborhood Capital Budget Group*, November 1999, 9.

38. Ray Quintanilla, "Hispanic Area May Get 2 High Schools," *Chicago Tribune*, August 21, 2001, 1.

39. Rui Kaneya, "Dropout Rates Still Plague Public Schools," *The Chicago Reporter*, May 1998, 3.

40. Andrew Herman, "Innovative Catholic High to Open In Pilsen/Little Village This Fall," *Chicago Sun-Times*, January 19, 1996, 13.

41. Author interview with Ramon and Socorro Abrego, March 4, 1998, Chicago.

42. Author interview with Arthur R. Velasquez, July 27, 1998, Chicago.

43. Susy Schultz, "Legislators Threaten UIC's Budget, Hearings Set on Minority Hiring, Enrollment," *Chicago Sun-Times*, January 23, 1998, 16

44. J. Linn Allen, "Hispanic Students Gain Influence to Match Their Growing Numbers," *Chicago Tribune*, June 18, 2000, 1.

45. Illinois State Board of Higher Education, "Report to the Governor and General Assembly on Underrepresented Groups in Illinois in Public Institutions of Higher Education," *Illinois State Board of Higher Education*, March 1998, i.

46. "Latinos Face To Face/Latinos Cara A Cara," *Latino Institute*, October 1994, 16. The Latino Institute, formerly located in downtown Chicago, was one of a few organizations that advocated for the civil rights of all Latino groups in Chicago. The organization produced excellent research on the needs of Latinos. But after twenty-five years of service, the organization folded in 1998, due to financial problems.

47. Author interview with Maria Sánchez, September 10, 1998, Chicago.

48. Author interview with Luis J. Rodríguez, October 23, 1998, Chicago.

49. Luis J. Rodríguez, *Always Running La Vida Loca: Gang Days in L. A.* (New York: Touchstone, 1993).

50. Robert Davis, "Hispanics Ask Apology For Marzullo Comment," *Chicago Tribune*, January 13, 1983, 2.

51. Ben Joravsky, "Juan A. Velazquez, Pilsen Street Hustler Takes on Old Guard at City Hall," *The Chicago Reporter*, November 1984, 3.

52. Author interview with Jesus Garcia, October 13, 1998, Chicago.

53. David K. Fremon, *Chicago Politics Ward By Ward* (Bloomington, IN: Indiana University Press, 1988), 148.

54. Manuel Galvan, "Lozano's Slaying Called Political Assassination," *Chicago Tribune*, June 10, 1983, 2.

55. Taller de Estudios Comunitarios. *Rudy Lozano, His Life, His People* (Chicago: Taller de Estudios Comunitarios, 1984).

56. Manuel Galvan, "Hispanic Voting Bloc Goes Strong For Washington," *Chicago Tribune*, May 23, 1983, 4.

57. Ben Joravsky and Jorge Casuso, "Hispanic Vote Emerges as New Battlefront in Council Wars," *The Chicago Reporter*, September 1984, 8.

58 .David K. Fremon, *Chicago Politics Ward by Ward*, 166.

59. Author interview with Danny Solis, November 13, 1998, Chicago.

60. Author interview with Sonia Silva, October 20, 1998, Chicago.

61. Gary Washburn, "City Ward Remap Okd by 48-1 Vote," *Chicago Tribune*, December 20, 2001, 3.

62. Author interview with Patricia Mendoza, December 17, 1998, Chicago.

63. Institute for Latino Studies. "Bordering the Mainstream: a Needs Assessment of Latinos in Berwyn and Cicero, Illinois," *Institute For Latino Studies*, January 2002, 3.

64. Ibid., 5.

65. Ibid., 7

Chapter Three: Puerto Ricans

1. Author interview with Raul and Felix Cardona, October 1, 1998, Chicago.

2. U. S. Census Bureau, "Hispanic Population by Type for Regions, States, and Puerto Rico: 1990 and 2000," *Government Printing Office*, 2000. See also Dan Mihalopoulus and Evan Osnos, "Chicago: a Hub for Mexicans," *Chicago Tribune*, May 10, 2001, 18.

3. Carmen Teresa Whalen, *From Puerto Rico to Philadelphia: Puerto Rican Workers and Postwar Economies* (Philadelphia: Temple University Press, 2001), 49.

4. Elena Padilla, "Puerto Rican Immigrants in New York and Chicago: A Study in Comparative Assimilation," (M.A. thesis, University of Chicago, June 1947), 84.

5. Manuel Martínez, *Chicago: Historia de Nuestra Comunidad Puerrtorriqueña, Photographic Documentary*, (Chicago: Reyes & Sons, 1989), 103.

6. Ibid., 87.

7. Edwin Maldonado, "Contract Labor and the Origins of Puerto Rican Communities in the United States," in James B. Lane and Edward J. Escobar, eds., *Forging a Community: the Latino Experience in Northwest Indiana, 1919-1975* (Chicago: Cattails Press, 1987), 206.

8. Author interview with Cesareo and Luz Maria Rivera, June 23, 1998, Chicago.

9. History Task Force Centro de Estudios Puertorriqueños, *Labor Migration Under Capitalism: The Puerto Rican Experience* (New York: Monthly Review Press 1979), 15.

10. Author interview with Wilfredo Ortiz, September 23, 1998, Chicago.

11. Author telephone interview with Eduardo Ortiz, February 9, 2000, Chicago.

12. John J. Betancur, Teresa Cordova and María de los Angeles Torres, "Economic Restructuring and the Process of Incorporation of Latinos into the Chicago Economy," in Rebecca Morales and Frank Bonilla, eds., *Latinos in a Changing U.S. Economy: Comparative Perspectives on Growing Inequality* (Newbury Park, CA: Sage Publications, 1993), 124.

13. The Woodstock Institute, "A Rising Tide...But Some Leaky Boats," *The Woodstock Institute*, November 1998, 3.

14. John J. Betancur, Teresa Cordova and María de los Angeles Torres, "Economic Restructuring,"

15. Michael Norkewicz, "A Profile of Nine Latino Groups in Chicago," *Latino Institute*, October 1994, 6.

16. Felix M. Padilla, *Puerto Rican Chicago* (Notre Dame, IN: University of Notre Dame Press, 1987), 113.

17. John J. Betancur, "The Settlement Experience of Latinos in Chicago: Segregation, Speculation, and the Ecology Model," in Adalberto Aguirre, Jr. and David V. Baker, *Structured Inequality in the United States* (Englewood, Cliffs, NJ: Prentice Hall, 2000), 253.

18. David B. Miller, "Lincoln Park," in *Local Community Fact Book Chicago Metropolitan Area 1990*. The Chicago Fact Book Consortium (Chicago: Academy, 1995), 54. See also Majorie DeVault, Arny Reichler and H. M.W., "Near North Side," in *Local Community Fact Book Chicago Metropolitan Area 1990*, 57.

19. Julio Morales, *Puerto Rican Poverty and Migration: We Just Had to Try Elsewhere* (New York: Praeger, 1986), 78.

20. Carmen Teresa Whalen, *From Puerto Rico to Philadelphia*, 49.

21. Author interview with Eligio Quiñones, June 24, 1998, Chicago.

22. Roberto Rey, "Humboldt Park," in *Local Community Fact Book Chicago Metropolitan Area 1990*, 89.

23. Author interview with Noel and Marcia Ruiz, July 6, 1998, Chicago.

24. Wilfredo Cruz, "Minorities Find Washburne's Legacy of Exclusion Solidly Built," *The Chicago Reporter*, May 1983, 1.

25. Nilda Flores-Gonzáles, "Paseo Boricua: Claiming a Puerto Rican Space in Chicago," in *Centro: Journal of the Center for Puerto Rican Studies*, 13 (Fall 2001), 17.

26. Author interview with Angelo Sánchez, July 20, 1998, Chicago.

27. John J. Betancur, "The Settlement Experience of Latinos in Chicago," 258.

28. Ibid., 258.

29. Author interview with Mirta Ramirez, June 6, 1998, Batavia, Illinois.

30. Maura I. Toro-Morn, "Yo Era Muy Arriesgada: a Historical Overview of the Work Experiences of Puerto Rican Women in Chicago," in *Centro: Journal of the Center for Puerto Rican Studies*, 13 (Fall 2001), 37.

31. Author interview with Rev. Leo T. Mahon, February 20, 1998, Chicago.

32. Felix M. Padilla, *Puerto Rican Chicago*, 129.

33. "Crowd Burns 2 Police Cars in N.W. Side Disturbance," *Chicago Sun-Times*, June 13, 1966, 1.

34. Author interview with Victor and Migalia Flores, September 22, 1998, Chicago.

35. Chicago Commission on Human Relations, "The Puerto Rican Residents of Chicago, A Report On An Open Hearing, July 15 and 16, 1966," *Chicago Commission on Human Relations.*

36. John Adam Moreau, "Puerto Rican Young Lords Emulate the Black Panthers," *Chicago Sun-Times,* June 5, 1969, 14.

37. Author interview with Rev. Jorge Morales, September 24, 1998, Chicago.

38. Wilfredo Cruz and Alan Neff, "Million-Dollar Fiasco: Latino Group's Collapse Shatters Rehab Plans in Humboldt Park," *The Chicago Reporter,* November 1983, 1.

39. Wilfredo Cruz, "All Politics is Local: a Furor Over Puerto Rican Nationalism Masks the Real Issues at Stake in Chicago's School Reform," *In These Times,* April 14, 1997, 19.

40. Author interview with Josefina Rodríguez, October 29, 1998, Chicago.

41. José E. Cruz, "Pushing Left to Get to the Center: Puerto Rican Radicalism in Hartford, Connecticut," in Andrés Torres and José E. Velázquez, eds., *The Puerto Rican Movement: Voices From The Diaspora* (Philadelphia: Temple University Press, 1998), 81.

42. Author interview with José López, November 1, 1999, Chicago.

43. José E. Cruz, "Pushing Left to Get to the Center," 76.

44. Teresa Puente, "Latino Radio Pioneer is one of the Family," *Chicago Tribune,* December 13, 1998, 1.

45. Diana Elranova, "Rafael Cruz Y Julio Osorio Piden Justicia Desde La Tumba," *La Raza,* May 2-8, 1984, 24.

46. Author interview with Daniel Ramos, July 31, 1998, Chicago.

47. Author interview with David Hernandez, October 16, 1998, Chicago.

48. Author interview with Oscar Martinez, November 4, 1998, Chicago.

49. Jeff Huebner, "Rogue Gallery," *Chicago Reader,* October 9, 1998, 18.

Chapter Four: Puerto Ricans

1. Author interview with Martha Hernandez, August 4, 1998, Chicago.

2. Jaime R. Vidal, "Beyond New York," in Jay P. Dolan and Jaime R. Vidal, eds., *Puerto Rican and Cuban Catholics in the U.S., 1900-1965* (Notre Dame, IN: University

of Notre Dame Press, 1994), 127.

3. Ibid., 131.

4. Jaime R. Vidal, "The Rejection of the Ethnic Parish Model," in Jay P. Dolan and Jaime R. Vidal, eds., *Puerto Rican and Cuban Catholics in the U.S., 1900-1965*, 87.

5. Edward R. Kantowicz, "The Ethnic Church," in Melvin G. Holli and Peter d'A. Jones eds., *Ethnic Chicago, a Multicultural Portrait* (Grand Rapids, Mich.: William B. Eerdmans, 1995), 602.

6. Author interview with Rev. Leo T. Mahon, February 20, 1998, Chicago.

7. Stephen C. Holler, "Exploring the Popular Religion of U.S. Hispanic/Latino Ethnic Groups," in *Latino Studies Journal* 6 (September 1995), 20.

8. Allen Figueroa Deck, S.J., "The Challenge of Evangelical/Pentecostal Christianity to Hispanic Catholicism," in Jay P. Dolan and Allen Figueroa Deck, S.J., eds., *Catholic Culture in the U.S. Issues and Concerns* (Notre Dame, IN: University of Notre Dame Press, 1994), 410.

9. Ibid., 425.

10. Author interview with Rev. Tomas V. Sanabria, July 23, 1998, Chicago.

11. Jorge Casuso and Michael Hirsley, "Troubled Hispanics Find Haven Within Strict Pentecostal Rules," *Chicago Tribune*, January 8, 1990, 1.

12. Author interview with Lucia Martinez, December 31, 1998, Chicago.

13. Jorge Casuso and Michael Hirsley, "Troubled Hispanics Find Haven Within Strict Pentecostal Rules," 6.

14. Melita Marie Garza, "Humboldt Power Play," *Chicago Tribune*, July 1, 1999, 1.

15. Jorge Casuso and Michael Hirsley, "Troubled Hispanics Find Haven Within Strict Pentecostal Rules," 6.

16. Author interview with Jose Velgara, October 10, 1998, Chicago.

17. María Elizabeth Pérez y González, "Latina Women in a Traditionally Male-Dominated Institutions-The Church," in *Latino Studies Journal* 8 (Fall, 1997), 25.

18. Ana María Díaz-Stevens, "Aspects of Puerto Rican Religious Experience: a Sociohistorical Overview," in Gabriel Haslip-Viera and Sherrie L. Baver, eds., *Latinos in New York: Communities in Transition* (Notre Dame, IN: University of Notre Dame Press, 1996), 168.

19. Lois Wille, "The Puerto Rican 'Doodlers'," *Chicago Daily News*, June 23, 1966, 2.

20. Author interview with David Hernández, October 16, 1998, Chicago.

21. Author interview with Miguel del Valle, November 12, 1998, Chicago.

22. Chicago Board of Education, "Puerto Rican Culture as it Affects Puerto Rican Children in Chicago Classrooms," *Chicago Board of Education*, September 30, 1970, 11.

23. Author interview with Mirna Diaz Ortiz, December 14, 1998, Chicago.

24. Wilfredo Cruz, "All Politics is Local," *In These Times*, April 14, 1997, 20.

25. Author interview with Gery Chico, November 19, 1998, Chicago.

26. Isidro Lucas, "El Problema Educativo del 'Dropout'," *The Rican: A Journal of Contemporary Puerto Rican Thought* 1 (May 1974), 5.

27. Author interview with Aracelis Figueroa, August 7, 1998, Chicago.

28. "30 Seized in Tuley Melee: 6 Cops Hurt," *Chicago Sun-Times*, February 1, 1973, 1.

29. Author interview with Aida Sánchez, December 15, 1998, Chicago.

30. Author interview with Maximino DeJesus Torres, July 10, 1998, Chicago.

31. Author interview with Samuel Betances, November 31, 1998, Chicago.

32. Author interview with Angela Rodríguez, December 4, 1998, Chicago.

33. Author interview with Ricky DeJesus, September 16, 1998, Chicago.

34. Author interview with Kenny Ruiz, December 1, 1998, Chicago.

35. Wilfredo Cruz, "Arrests Jump Sharply, Minority Leaders Charge Police with 'Disorderly Conduct,'" *The Chicago Reporter*, October 1982, 1.

36. David K. Fremon, *Chicago Politics Ward by Ward* (Bloomington, IN: Indiana University Press, 1988), 205.

37. Author interview with Miguel del Valle, November 12, 1998, Chicago.

38. Wilfredo Cruz, "Latinos Give the Party a Chance as Independent Efforts Falter," *The Chicago Reporter*, December 1982, 2.

39. Wilfredo Cruz, "Joseph Jose Martinez: God Made Family, Marriage, Government," *The Chicago Reporter*, January 1982, 2.

40. Ben Joravsky and Tom Brune, "Washington's Victory: All Blacks, Most Latinos, 17% Whites," *The Chicago Reporter*, May 1983, 3.

41. Jorge Casuso and Ben Joravsky, "What Makes Luis Run? Ambition, Guts and, Some Say, Opportunism Drive Alderman Gutierrez," *Chicago Tribune Magazine*, June 4, 1989, 20.

42. John Kass, "Gutierrez's Tax Bill Proves that Miracles Still do Happen," *Chicago Tribune*, August 2, 1998, 3.

43. Author interview with Billy Ocasio, August 6, 1998, Chicago.

44. Author interview with Edgar López, October 30, 1998, Chicago.

45. Wilfredo Cruz, "All Politics is Local," 20.

46. Carlos Hernández Gómez, "Latino Leadership, Population Soars, but Political Power Lags," *The Chicago Reporter*, September/October 2001, 5.

47. William Neikirk, "Gutierrez Unhappy With 'Old Boss' Daley," *Chicago Tribune*, March 12, 2000, 10.

48. Lynn Sweet, "Daley, Gutierrez Patch it up Mayor Pledges Support for Congressman's Re-election after June Talks Irons out Differences," *Chicago Tribune*, July 26, 2001, 35.

49. Scott Fornek, "Blagojevich Aims Ad at Hispanics, Gutierrez Appears in Spot for Governor Hopeful," *Chicago Sun-Times*, January 8, 2002, 8.

Chapter Five: Guatemalans and Salvadorans

1. Antonio Martinez, "Guatemalan Americans," in Cynthia Linton, ed., *The Ethnic Handbook: a Guild to the Cultures and Traditions of Chicago's Diverse Communities* (Schiller Park, IL: The Illinois Ethnic Coalition, 1996), 75.

2. Yanira Hernández Cabiya, "En El Norte Los Guatemaltecos En Chicago," *Exito*, July 20, 2000, 14.

3. U. S. Census Bureau, "Hispanic Population by Type for Regions, States, and Puerto Rico: 1990 and 2000," (Washington D.C.: Government Printing Office, 2000).

4. Jorge Casuso and Eduardo Camacho, "Hispanics in Chicago," *The Community Renewal Society*, July 1985, 22.

5. Nora Hamilton and Norma Stoltz Chinchilla, *Seeking Community in a Global City: Guatemalans and Salvadorans in Los Angeles* (Philadelphia: Temple University Press, 2001), 222.

6. Juan Gonzales, *Harvest of Empire, A History of Latinos in America* (New York: Penguin Books, 2000), 59.

7. Author interview with Guillermo and Maria Mendizabal, July 20, 1998, Chicago.

8. Author interview with Adriana Portillo Bartow, July 16, 1998, Chicago.

9. Nora Hamilton and Norma Stoltz Chinchilla, *Seeking Community in a Global City*, 71.

10. Teresa Puente and Stephen Franklin, "Janitors' 1-Day Strike Moves to Suburbs," *Chicago Tribune*, April 18, 2000, 1.

11. Rebekah Levin, and Robert Ginsburg, "Sweatshops in Chicago: A Survey on Working Conditions in Low-Income and Immigrant Communities," *The Sweatshop Working Group*, January 13, 2000, 3.

12. Chirag Mehta et al., "Chicago's Undocumented Immigrants: An Analysis of Wages, Working Conditions, and Economic Contributions," *Center for Urban Economic Development at UIC*, February 2002, vi.

13. Heather Dalmage, "Factors of Integration: the Guatemalan Experience in Chicago," *Latino Studies Journal* 4 (January 1993), 34.

14. Teresa Puente, "Guatemalan's Visit Protested, Some Suspicious of Country's Chief Despite Peace Accord," *Chicago Tribune*, June 12, 1998, 3.

15. Author interview with Catalina de Garcia, January 12, 2000, Chicago.

16. Author interview with Julio Revolorio, July 28, 1998, Chicago.

17. Rigoberta Menchú, *I, Rigoberta Menchú: An Indian Woman in Guatemala* (London: Verso, 1984).

18. Lynda Gorov, "Living in Fear: Guatemalans Seek Refuge, Community in Chicago," *The Chicago Reporter*, January 1990, 4.

19. Author interview with Maricela Garcia, August 13, 1998, Chicago.

20. Claudia Dorrington, "Central American Refugees in Los Angeles: Adjustment of Children and Families," in Ruth E. Zambrana, ed., *Understanding Latino Families: Scholarship, Policy, and Practice* (London: Sage Publications, 1995), 114.

21. Nora Hamilton and Norma Stoltz Chinchilla, "Central American Migration: a Framework for Analysis," in Mary Romero, Pierrette Hondagneu-Sotelo, and Vilma Ortiz, eds., *Challenging Fronteras: Structured Latina and Latino Lives in the U.S.* (New York: Routledge, 1997), 91.

22. "Latinos Face To Face/ Cara A Cara," *Latino Institute*, October 1994, 5.

23. Author interview with Daisy Funes, September 8, 1998, Chicago.

24. Nora Hamilton and Norma Stoltz Chinchilla, "Central American Migration: a

Framework for Analysis," 89.

25. David Mendell and Darnell Little, "Rich '90s Failed to Lift all, Income Disparity Between Races Widened Greatly, Census Analysis Shows," *Chicago Tribune*, August 20, 2002.

26. Manuel Galvan, "Refugee Underground Leads to Chicago Area," *Chicago Tribune*, May 30, 1983, 3.

27. Manuel Galvan, "Alien 'Sanctuaries' Pit Church, U.S.," *Chicago Tribune*, May 29, 1983, 1.

28. Author interview with Rev. David Chevrier, October 15, 1998, Chicago.

29. Author interview with Rev. Donald Headley, May 6, 1998, Chicago.

30. Author interview with Theresita Perez, July 14, 1998, Chicago.

31. Author interview with Judith Alvarado, July 26, 1998, Chicago.

Chapter Six: Cubans

1. Author interview with Elias Sánchez, October 23, 1998, Chicago.

2. José Llanes, *Cuban Americans: Masters of Survival* (Cambridge, MA: Abt Books, 1982), 8.

3. Jorge Casuso and Eduardo Camacho, "Latino Chicago," in Melvin G. Holli and Peter d'A. Jones, eds., *Ethnic Chicago, a Multicultural Portrait* (Grand Rapids, Mich.: William B. Eerdmans, 1995), 370.

4. Dan Mihalopoulus and Evan Osnos, "Chicago: a Hub for Mexicans," *Chicago Tribune*, May 10, 2001, 18.

5. Joan Moore and Raquel Pinderhuges, "The Latino Population: the Importance of Economic Restructuring," in Margaret L. Anderson, and Patricia Hill Collins, eds., *Race, Class and Gender* (New York: Wadsworth, 1998), 259.

6. José Llanes, *Cuban Americans: Masters of Survival*, 8.

7. María Cristina García, *Havana USA: Cuban Exiles and Cuban Americans in South Florida, 1959-1994* (Berkeley: University of California Press, 1996), 22.

8. Author interview with Jesus Zeferino Ochoa, August 31, 1999, Chicago.

9. Author interview with Ann Alvarez, February 11, 1999, Chicago.

10. María Cristina García, *Havana USA:*, 6.

11. Jorge Casuso and Eduardo Camacho, "Hispanics in Chicago," *The Community Renewal Society.*

12. George de Lama, "He Wanted Cuban Unity, Found Death," *Chicago Tribune,* July 5, 1981, 3.

13. George de Lama, "2,000 Cuban Refugees Find a Harsh Life in Chicago," *Chicago Tribune,* August 24, 1980, 1.

14. Author interview with Jesus Zeferino Ochoa, August 31, 1999, Chicago.

15. Author interview with María Cardenas, September 20, 1998, Chicago.

16. Author interview with Angelica Garcia, September 16, 1998, Chicago.

17. Author interview with Candido Bouso, September 12, 1999, Chicago.

18. George Brandon, *Santeria From Africa to the New World, The Dead Sell Memories* (Bloomington, IN: Indiana University Press, 1997), 108.

19. Author interview with Luis Carlos, September 14, 1999, Chicago.

20. Ernest Tucker, "For Cubans, it's a Matter of Faiths," *Chicago Sun-Times,* January 21, 1998, 6.

21. María Elizabeth Pérez y González, "Latina Women in a Traditionally Male-Dominated Institution—The Church," *Latino Studies Journal* 8, (Fall 1997), 30.

22. George Brandon, *Santeria From Africa to the New World,* 106.

23. Helen I. Safa, "Migration and Identity: a Comparison of Puerto Rican and Cuban Migrants in the United States," in Edna Acosta-Belén and Barbara R. Sjostrom, eds., *The Hispanic Experience in the United States: Contemporary Issues and Perspectives* (Westport, CT: Praeger, 1988), 144.

24. Author interview with José Garcia, July 13, 1998, Chicago.

25. John J. Betancur, Teresa Cordova and María de los Angeles Torres, "Economic Restructuring and the Process of Incorporation of Latinos Into the Chicago Economy," In Rebecca Morales and Frank Bonilla, eds., *Latinos in a Changing U.S. Economy: Comparative Perspectives on Growing Inequality* (Newbury Park, CA: Sage Publications, 1993), 122.

26. "Lourdes Monteagudo Fueled by the Belief Than one Can Make a Difference," *Chicago Tribune,* September 2, 1990, 3.

27. Author interview with Daniel Alvarez, April 6, 1998, Chicago.

28. Magaly Queralt, "Understanding Cuban Immigrants: a Cultural Perspective," *Social Work* 29, (March-April 1984), 116.

29. María de los Angeles Torres and Achy Obejas, "Freedom Means a Cuban Orchestra Should Perform," *Chicago Tribune*, April 14, 1989, 19.

30. Author interview with Achy Obejas, November 18, 1998, Chicago.

31. "Cuba, Inside and Out," *Chicago Tribune Magazine*, February 3, 2003.

32. Monica Eng, "Victor Parra: Mad About Mambo, Cuban Music Weaves a Permanent Spell," *Chicago Tribune*, July 28, 1999, 1.

33. Author interview with Angelina Pedroso, October 7, 1998, Chicago.

34. Author interview with María de los Angeles Torres, November 11, 1998, Chicago.

Epilogue

1. Mark Skertic. "White Ethnic Groups Fade." *Chicago Sun-Times*, August 21, 2002, 1.

2. Teresa Puente. "Columbia Strife Inflicts Far-Reaching Pain." *Chicago Tribune*, January 2, 2001, 1.

3. David Mendell and Darnell Little. "Rich '90s Failed to Lift all, Income Disparity Between Races Widened Greatly, Census Analysis Shows." *Chicago Tribune*, August 20, 2002, 1.

4. Author interview with Arthur R. Velasquez, July 27, 1998, Chicago.

Bibliography

Interviews

Abrego, Ramon and Socorro. Interview by author. March 4, 1998.
Chicago. Tape recording.

Alvarado, Judith. Interview by author. July 26, 1998. Chicago. Tape recording.

Alvarez, Ann. Interview by author. February 11, 1999. Chicago. Tape recording.

Alvarez, Daniel. Interview by author. April 6, 1998. Chicago. Tape recording.

Anglada, Rafael and Olga. Interview by author. August 11, 1998. Chicago. Tape recording.

Aquilar, Martha. Interview by author. December 24, 1998. Chicago. Tape recording.

Arias, Carmen Martinez. Interview by author. March 18, 1998. Chicago. Tape recording.

Baltierra, Ron. Interview by author. October 8, 1998. Chicago. Tape recording.

Bartow, Adriana Portillo. Interview by author. July 16, 1998. Chicago. Tape recording.

Betances, Samuel. Interview by author. November 13, 1998. Chicago. Tape recording.

Bouso, Candido. Interview by author. September 12, 1999. Chicago. Written transcript.

Bugarin, Rudy. Interview by author. September 13, 1999. Chicago. Written transcript.

Calixto, Freddy. Interview by author. August 13, 1998. Chicago. Tape recording.

Campos, Ed. Interview by author. August 18, 1998. Chicago. Written transcript.

Cardenas, Henry. Interview by author. October 27, 1998. Chicago. Tape recording.

Cardenas, Maria. Interview by author. September 20, 1998. Chicago. Tape recording.

Cardona, Raul and Felix. Interview by author. October 1, 1998. Chicago. Tape recording.

Carlos, Luis. Interview by author. September 14, 1999. Chicago. Tape recording.

Castillo, Mario. Interview by author. November 20, 1998. Chicago. Tape recording.

Chevrier, David. Interview by author. October 15, 1998. Chicago. Tape recording.

Chico, Gery. Interview by author. November 19, 1998. Chicago. Tape recording.

de Garcia, Catalina. Interview by author. January 12, 2000. Chicago. Tape recording.

DeJesus, Ricky. Interview by author. September 16, 1998. Chicago. Tape recording.

del Valle, Miguel. Interview by author. November 12, 1998. Chicago. Tape recording.

Duran, Frank and Jovita. Interview by author. March 30, 1998. Chicago. Tape recording.

Figueora, Aracelis. Interview by author. August 7, 1998. Chicago. Tape recording.

Flores, Mary Quiroz. Interview by author, 17 April 1998, Chicago. Tape recording.

Flores, Victor and Migalia. Interview by author. September 22, 1998. Chicago. Tape
    recording.
Fraga, Teresa. Interview by author. November 17, 1998. Chicago. Tape recording.
Funes, Daisy. Interview by author. September 8, 1998. Chicago. Tape recording.
Garcia, Angelica. Interview by author. September 16, 1998. Chicago. Tape
    recording.
Garcia, Jesus. Interview by author. October 13, 1998. Chicago. Tape recording.
Garcia, Jose. Interview by author. July 13, 1998. Chicago. Tape recording.
Garcia, Maricela. Interview by author. August 13, 1998. Chicago. Tape recording.
Gomez, Armando and Leona. Interview by author. May 18, 1998. Chicago. Tape
    recording.
Gonzáles, Mary. Interview by author. December 16, 1998. Chicago. Tape recording.
Gutierrez, Robert. Interview by author. September 30, 1998. Chicago. Tape
    recording.
Headley, David. Interview by author. May 6, 1998. Chicago. Tape recording.
Hernandez, David. Interview by author. October 16, 1998. Chicago. Tape recording.
Hernandez, Marisel Ayabarreno. Interview by author. December 30, 1998 Chicago.
Tape
    recording.
Hernandez, Martha. Interview by author. August 4, 1998. Chicago. Tape recording.
Huitrado, Juan. Interview by author. August 28, 1998. Chicago. Tape recording.
Jacinto, Abram and Rose. Interview by author. March 21, 1998. Chicago. Tape
    recording
Jaimes, Martin and Edgar. Interview by author. January 14, 1999. Chicago. Tape
    recording.
Lebrón, Carlos. Interview by author. December 1, 1998. Chicago. Tape recording.
López, Edgar. Interview by author. October 30, 1998. Chicago. Tape recording.
López, José. Interview by author. November 1, 1999. Chicago. Tape recording.
Mahon, Leo T. Interview by author. February 20, 1998. Chicago. Tape recording
Maloney, James. Interview by author. June 2, 2000. Chicago. Written transcript.
Martinez, Lucia. Interview by author. December 31, 1998. Chicago. Tape recording.
Martinez, Oscar. Interview by author. November 4, 1998. Chicago. Tape recording.
Mendizabal, Guillermo and Maria. Interview by author. July 20, 1998. Chicago.
    Tape recording.
Mendoza, Patricia. Interview by author. December 17, 1998. Chicago. Tape
    recording.
Morales, Jorge. Interview by author. September 24, 1998. Chicago. Tape recording.
Munar, David Ernesto, Interview by author. October 13, 1998. Chicago. Tape
    recording.
Obejas, Achy. Interview by author. November 18, 1998. Chicago. Tape recording.
Ocasio, Billy. Interview by author. August 6, 1998. Chicago. Tape recording.
Ochoa, Jesus Zeferino. Interview by author. August 31, 1999. Chicago. Tape
    recording.
Ochoa, Juan. Interview by author. September 2, 1998. Chicago. Tape recording.
Ortiz, Eduardo. Interview by author. February 9, 2000. Chicago. Written transcript.
Ortiz, Mirna Diaz. Interview by author. December 14, 1998. Chicago. Tape
    recording.
Ortiz, Wilfredo. Interview by author. September 23, 1998. Chicago. Tape recording.
Pedroso, Angelina. Interview by author. October 7, 1998. Chicago. Tape recording.
Perez, Theresita. Interview by author. July 14, 1998. Chicago. Tape recording.

Plazas, Carlos. Interview by author. November 24, 1998. Chicago. Tape recording.

Prieto, Dennis. Interview by author. September 15, 1998. Chicago. Tape recording.

Prieto, Jorge and Luz Maria. Interview by author. November 21, 1997. Chicago. Tape recording.

Quiñones, Eligio. Interview by author. June 24, 1998. Chicago. Tape recording.

Ramirez, Mirta. Interview by author. June 6, 1998. Chicago. Tape recording.

Ramos, Analicia. Interview by author. August 19, 1998. Chicago. Tape recording.

Ramos, Daniel. Interview by author. July 31, 1998. Chicago. Tape recording.

Ramos, Teresa. Interview by author. August 18, 1998. Chicago. Tape recording.

Rangel, Juan. Interview by author. September 21, 1998. Chicago. Tape recording.

Revolorio, Julio. Interview by author. July 28, 1998. Chicago. Tape recording.

Reyes, Dolores Garcia and Emilio. Interview by author. April 29, 1998. Chicago. Tape recording.

Rivera, Luz and Cesareo. Interview by author. June 23, 1998, Chicago. Tape recording.

Rodríguez, Angela. Interview by author. December 4, 1998. Chicago. Tape recording.

Rodríguez, Josefina. Interview by author. October 12, 1998. Chicago. Tape recording.

Rodríguez, Luis J. Interview by author. October 23, 1998, Chicago. Tape recording.

Rodríguez, Peter. Interview by author. April 17, 1998. Chicago. Tape recording.

Rossi, Luis, Interview by author. February 3, 1999. Chicago. Tape recording.

Ruiz, Kenny. Interview by author. December 1, 1998. Chicago. Tape recording.

Ruiz, Noel and Marcia. Interview by author. July 6, 1998. Chicago. Tape recording

Sanabria, Tomas V. Interview by author. July 23, 1998. Chicago. Tape recording.

Sánchez, Aida. Interview by author. December 15, 1998. Chicago. Tape recording.

Sánchez, Angelo. Interview by author. July 20, 1998. Chicago. Tape recording.

Sánchez, Elias. Interview by author. October 23, 1998. Chicago. Tape recording.

Sánchez, Maria. Interview by author. September 10, 1998. Chicago. Tape recording.

Seledon, Norma. Interview by author. July 29, 1998. Chicago. Tape recording.

Silva, Sonia. Interview by author. October 20, 1998. Chicago. Tape recording.

Solis, Danny. Interview by author. November 13, 1998. Chicago. Tape recording.

Staszak, David. Interview by author. February 18, 1998. Chicago. Tape recording.

Torres, Esperanza. Interview by author. August 7, 1998. Chicago. Written transcript.

Torres, María de los Angeles. Interview by author. November 11, 1998 Chicago. Tape recording.

Torres, Maximino DeJesus. Interview by author. July 10, 1998. Chicago. Tape recording.

Tortolero, Carlos. Interview by author. October 21, 1998. Chicago. Tape recording.

Vargas, Jose. Interview by author. November 25, 1998. Chicago. Tape recording.

Velasquez, Arthur R. Interview by author. July 27, 1998. Chicago. Tape recording.

Velasquez, Carmen. Interview by author. December 7, 1998. Chicago. Tape recording.

Velgara, Jose. Interview by author. October 10, 1998. Chicago. Tape recording.

Zayas, Hiram. Interview by author. September 28, 1998. Michigan. Tape recording.

Works Cited

"A Butcher Shop Their Church--An Ice Box Serves as Altar."1941. *The New World*, March 4.

Acosta-Belén, Edna, and Barbara R. Sjostrom, eds. 1988. *The Hispanic Experience in the United States: Contemporary Issues and Perspectives.* Westport, CT: Praeger.

Acosta-Belén, Edna; et al. 2000. *"Adios Borinquen Querida": The Puerto Rican Diaspora, its History, and Contributions.* New York: University at Albany, SUNY.

Acuña, Rodolfo. 1988. *Occupied America: a History of Chicanos.* New York: HarperCollins.

Aguirre, Adalberto Jr., and David V. Baker. 2000. *Structured Inequality in the United States.* Englewood Cliffs, NJ: Prentice-Hall.

Aguirre, Adalberto Jr., and Jonathan H. Turner. 1995. *American Ethnicity, the Dynamics and Consequences of Discrimination.* New York: McGraw-Hill.

Aguirre, Adalberto, Jr., and David V. Baker, eds. 1998. *Sources: Notable Selections in Race and Ethnicity.* Guilford, CT: Dushkin/McGraw-Hill.

Allen, J. Linn. 2000. "Hispanic Students Gain Influence to Match Their Growing Numbers." *Chicago Tribune*, June 18.

Anderson, Margaret L., and Patricia Hill Collins, eds. 1998. *Race, Class and Gender.* New York: Wadsworth.

Año Nuevo-Kerr, Louise. 1976. "The Chicano Experience in Chicago: 1920-1970." Ph.D. diss., University of Illinois at Chicago.

———— . 1977. "Mexican Chicago: Chicano Assimilation Aborted, 1939-1954." In *The Ethnic Frontier: Essays in the History of Group Survival in Chicago and the Midwest*, eds. Melvin G. Holli and Peter d'A. Grand Rapids, Mich: Williams B. Eerdmans.

Archdiocese of Chicago. June 1997. *Archdiocesan Pastoral Plan for Hispanic Ministry.* Chicago: Archdiocese of Chicago.

Archdiocese of Chicago. December 2000. *Office of Hispanic Ministry.* Chicago: Archdiocese of Chicago.

Aronson, Leonard. 1973. "Claim-jumpers Eye Pilsen Gold." *Chicago Tribune*, July 24.

Badillo, David A. 1994. "Midwestern Catholicism and the Early Mexican Parishes, 1910-1930." In *Mexican Americans and the Catholic Church, 1900- 1965*, eds. Jay P. Dolan and Gilberto Hinojosa. Norte Dame, IN: University of Notre Dame Press.

Bauer, Edward Jackson. 1938. "Delinquency Among Mexican Boys in South Chicago." M.A. thesis, University of Chicago.

Bean, Frank D., and Marta Tienda. 1990. *The Hispanic Population of the United States.* New York: Russell Sage Foundation.

Bensman, David, and Roberta Lynch. 1987. *Rusted Dreams: Hard Times in a Steel Community.* New York: McGraw-Hill.

Betancur, John J. 2000. "The Settlement Experience of Latinos in Chicago: Segregation, Speculation and the Ecology Model." In *Structured Inequality in the United States,"* eds. Adalberto Aguirre, Jr., and David V. Baker. Englewood Cliffs, NJ: Prentice-Hall.

Betancur, John J., Teresa Cordova, and María de los Angeles Torres. 1993.

"Economic Restructuring and the Process of Incorporation of Latinos into the Chicago Economy." In *Latinos in a Changing U.S. Economy: Comparative Perspectives on Growing Inequality*, eds. Rebecca Morales and Frank Bonilla. Newbury Park, CA: Sage Publications.

Brandon, George. 1997. *Santeria from Africa to the New World, the Dead Sell Memories*. Bloomington, IN: Indiana University Press.

Brandon, Karen. 1998. "Many With HIV Lack Regular Care." *Chicago Tribune*, December 24.

Burke, Greg, and Phil Greer. 1988. "Viva Velasquez, Making the American Dream Come True and Sharing It." *Chicago Tribune Magazine*, February 28.

Burns, Allan F. 1993. *Maya in Exile, Guatemalans in Florida*. Philadelphia: Temple University Press.

Cabiya Hernández, Yanira. 2000. "En El Norte Los Guatemaltecos En Chicago." *Exito*, July 20.

Casuso, Jorge. 1986. "Hispanic Hopefuls Scramble to Organize for Special Elections." *The Chicago Reporter*. February.

Casuso, Jorge, and Eduardo Camacho. July 1985. *Hispanics in Chicago*. Chicago: The Community Renewal Society.

———. 1995. "Latino Chicago." In *Ethnic Chicago a Multicultural Portrait*, eds. Melvi G. Holli and Peter d'A. Jones. Grand Rapids, Mich: Williams B. Eerdmans.

Casuso, Jorge, and Michael Hirsley. 1990. "Troubled Hispanics Find Haven Within Strict Pentecostal Rules." *Chicago Tribune*, January 8.

Casuso, Jorge, and Ben Joravsky. 1989. "What Makes Luis Run? Ambition, Guts and, Some Say, Opportunism Drive Alderman Gutierrez." *Chicago Tribune Magazine*, June 4.

Chicago Commission on Human Relations. November 10. 1966. *The Puerto Rican Residents of Chicago: A Report on an Open Hearing, July 15 and 16,1966*. Chicago: Chicago Commission on Human Relations.

Chicago Fact Book Consortium. 1995. *Local Community Fact Book Chicago Metropolitan Area, 1990*. Chicago: University of Illinois Chicago.

Chicago Public Schools. 1969. *Puerto Rican Culture as it Affects Puerto Rican Children in Chicago Classrooms*. Chicago: Chicago Board of Education.

Chicago Public Schools. September 30, 1997. *Racial/Ethnic Survey of Staff*. Chicago: Chicago Board of Education.

Chicago Public Schools. September 30, 1997. *Racial/Ethnic Survey of Students*. Chicago: Chicago Board of Education.

Chicago Urban League, Latino Institute, and Northern Illinois University. December 1993. *Making Work Pay, State and Local Responses to the Problems of the Working Poor*. Chicago: Chicago Urban League.

Chicago Urban League, Latino Institute and Northern Illinois University. 1994. *The Changing Economic Standing of Minorities and Women in the Chicago Metropolitan Area 1970-1990*. Chicago: Chicago Urban League.

City of Chicago. 1983. *Chicago Statistical Abstract Community Area Profiles, 1980*. Chicago: City of Chicago.

Cole, Patrick. 2000. "Day Laborers Could Come In From Cold, Alderman Sees Way to Get Men Off Street." *Chicago Tribune*, January 31.

Craig, Richard B. 1971. *The Bracero Program, Interest Groups and Foreign Policy*. Austin, TX: University of Texas Press.

"Crowd Burns 2 Police Cars in N.W. Side Disturbance." 1966. *Chicago Sun-Times*,

June 13.

Cruz, José E. 1988. "Pushing Left to Get to The Center: Puerto Rican Radicalism in Hartford, Connecticut." In *The Puerto Rican Movement: Voices From the Diaspora*, Andrés Torres and José E. Velázquez, eds. Philadelphia: Temple University Press.

Cruz, Wilfredo. 1981. "Population Growth Fuels Latino Drive for Political Power." *The Chicago Reporter*, July.

————. 1981. "Chicago Schools Employ Few Latino Administrators." *The Chicago Reporter*, June.

————. 1981. "Dilapidated and Dangerous: Board Still Crowds Minority Pupils into Mobile Classrooms." *The Chicago Reporter*, December.

————. 1981. "Dedicated Doctor, Prieto Advocates Health Care For Poor." *The Chicago Reporter*, December.

————. 1982 "Latinos Give the Party a Chance as Independent Efforts Falter." *The Chicago Reporter*, December.

————. 1982. "Arrests Jump Sharply, Minority Leaders Charge Police with Disorderly Conduct.'" *The Chicago Reporter*, October.

————. 1982. "Joseph Jose Martinez: God Made Family, Marriage, Government." *The Chicago Reporter*, January.

————. 1983. "Minorities Find Washburne's Legacy of Exclusion Solidly Built." *The Chicago Reporter*, May.

————. 1987. "The Nature of Alinsky-Style Community Organizing in the Mexican American Community of Chicago." Ph.D. diss., University of Chicago.

————. 1988. "UNO: Organizing at the Grass Roots." *Illinois Issues*, April.

————. 1990. "Mary Gonzales: You Can't Sit Back and do Nothing." In *After Alinsky: Community Organizing In Illinois*, ed. Peg Knoeplfe. Springfield, IL: Sangamon State University.

————. 1993. "From Blue Jeans to Pinstripes: Danny Solis Has Traded Confrontation Politics for a Seat at the Tables of Power." *Illinois Issues*, December.

————. 1997. "Anti-Immigrant Attitudes Hurting Chicago's Mexican American Community." *One City*, Spring.

————. 1997. "All Politics is Local: a Furor Over Puerto Rican Nationalism Masks the Real Issues at Stake in Chicago's School Reform." *In These Times*, April 14-27.

————. 2004. *Puerto Rican Chicago*. Charleston, SC: Arcadia Publishing.

Cruz, Wilfredo, and Alan Neff. 1983. "Million-Dollar Fiasco: Latino Group's Collapse Shatters Rehab Plans in Humboldt Park." *The Chicago Reporter*, November.

"Cuba, Inside and Out." 2003. *Chicago Tribune Magazine*, February 3.

Dalmage, Heather. 1993. "Factors of Integration: The Guatemalan Experience in Chicago." *Latino Studies Journal* 4: 23-40.

Darder, Antonia, and Rodolfo D. Torres, eds. 1998. *The Latino Studies Reader, Culture, Economy and Society*. Malden, MA: Blackwell Publishers.

Davalos, Karen Mary. 1993. "Ethnic Identity Among Mexican and Mexican American Women in Chicago, 1920-1991." Ph.D. diss., Yale University.

Davis, Robert. 1983. "Hispanics Ask Apology for Marzullo Comment." *Chicago Tribune*, January 13.

de la Garza, Paul. 1999. "Guatemala Atrocities Blamed on Military." *Chicago Tribune*, February 26.

de Lama, George. 1981. "He Wanted Cuban Unity, Found Death." *Chicago Tribune*, July 5.

———. "2000 Cuban Refugees Find a Harsh Life in Chicago." *Chicago Tribune*, August 24, 1980.

Deck S.J., Allan Figueroa. 1994. "The Challenge of Evangelical/Pentecostal Christianity to Hispanic Catholicism." In *Catholic Culture in the U.S. Issues and Concerns*, eds. Jay P. Dolan and Allan Figueroa Deck, S.J. Notre Dame, IN: University of Notre Dame Press.

DeVault, Majorie, Amy Reicher, and H. M.W. 1995. "Near North Side." In *Local Community Fact Book Chicago Metropolitan Area 1990*, eds. The Chicago Fact book Consortium. Chicago: Academy.

Díaz-Stevens, Ana María. 1996. "Aspects of the Puerto Rican Religious Experience: a Sociohistorical Overview." In *Latinos in New York: Communities in Transition*, eds. Gabriel Haslip-Viera and Sherrie L. Baver. Notre Dame, IN: University of Notre Dame Press.

Dolan, Jay P., and Gilberto Hinojosa, eds. 1994. *Mexican Americans and the Catholic Church, 1900-1965*. Notre Dame, IN: University of Notre Dame Press.

Dolan, Jay P., and Allan Figueroa Deck, S.J. 1994. *Hispanic Catholic Culture in the U.S. Issues and Concerns*. Notre Dame, IN: University of Notre Dame Press.

Dolan, Jay P., and Jaime R. Vidal, eds. 1994. *Puerto Rican and Cuban Catholics in the U.S., 1900-1965*. Notre Dame, IN: University of Notre Dame Press.

Dorrington, Claudia. 1995. "Central American Refugees in Los Angeles: Adjustment of Children and Families." In *Understanding Latino Families: Scholarship, Policy and Practice*, ed. Ruth E. Zambrana. London: Sage Publications.

Ellison, Christopher G., and W. Allen Martin, eds. 1999. *Race and Ethnic Relations in the United States, Readings for the 21st Century*. Los Angeles: Roxbury.

Elranova, Diana. 1984. "Rafael Cruz Y Julio Osorio Piden Justicia Dese La Tumba," *La Raza*, May 2-8.

Eng, Monica. 1999. "Victor Parra: Mad About Mambo, Cuban Music Weaves a Permanent Spell." *Chicago Tribune*, July 28..

Felter, Eunice. 1941. "The Social Adaptations of the Mexican Churches in the Chicago Area." M.A. thesis, University of Chicago.

Fitzpatrick, Joseph P. 1987. *Puerto Rican Americans the Meaning of Migration to the Mainland*. Englewood Cliffs, NJ: Prentice-Hall.

Flores-Gonzáles, Nilda. 2001. "Paseo Boricua: Claiming a Puerto Rican Space n Chicago." *Centro: Journal of the Center for Puerto Rican Studies* 13 (2): 6-21.

Fornek, Scott. 2001. "City Population Up As Suburbs Surge." *Chicago Sun-Times*, March 15.

———. 2002 "Blagojevich Aims Ad at Hispanics, Gutierrez Appears in Spot for Governor Hopeful." *Chicago Sun-Times*, January 8.

Fremon, David K. 1988. *Chicago Politics Ward by Ward*. Bloomington, IN: Indiana University Press.

Furer, Howard B. 1974. *Chicago, A Chronological & Documentary History 1784-1970*. Dobbs Ferry, New York.

Galvan, Manuel. 1983. "Hispanic Voting Bloc Goes Strong for Washington." *Chicago Tribune*, May 23.

————. 1983. "Alien 'Sanctuaries' Pit Churches, U.S." *Chicago Tribune,* May 29.

————. 1983. "Refugee Underground Leads To Chicago." *Chicago Tribune.* May 30.

————. 1983. Lozano's Slaying Called Political Assassination." *Chicago Tribune,* June 10.

Garcia, F. Chris, ed. 1988. *Latinos and the Political System.* Notre Dame, IN: University of Notre Dame Press.

Garcia, Juan R., and Angel Cal. 1987. "El Circulo De Obreros Catolicos "San Jose" 1925-1930." In *Forging a Community the Latino Experience in Northwest Indiana, 1919-1975,* eds. James B. Lane and Edward J. Escobar. Chicago: Cattails Press.

García, María Christina. 2000. "Hardliners V. "Dialogueros": Cuban Exile Political Groups and United States-Cuban Policy." In *Race and Ethnic Relations Annual Editions,* ed. John A. Kromkowski. Guilford, Conn: Dushkin/McGraw-Hill.

————. 1996. *Havana USA: Cuban Exiles and Cuban Americans in South Florida, 1959-1994.* Berkeley: University of California Press.

Garza, Marie, Melita. 1999. "Humboldt Power Play'" *Chicago Tribune,* July 1.

Goering, Laurie. 2000. "Torn and Isolate, Miami's Cubans Brace for Endgame." *Chicago Tribune,* April 9.

Gómez, Carlos Hernández. 2000. "State Representative Edgar López has the Support of Everyone From Michael Madigan to George Ryan. So Why's a Challenge From Cynthia Soto Making Him Sweat?" *The Chicago Reader,* March 17.

————. 2001. "Latino Leadership, Population Soars, but Political Power Lags," *The Chicago Reporter,* September/October.

Gonzales, Juan. 2001. *Harvest of Empire, a History of Latinos in America.* New York: Penguin.

Goodwin, Paul B. 1998. *Latin America.* Guilford, CT: Dushkin/McGraw-Hill.

Gorov, Lynda. 1990 "Living in Fear: Guatemalans Seek Refuge, Community in Chicago." *The Chicago Reporter,* January.

Grenier, Guillermo J. and Alex Stepick. 1998. "The Rise of Miami's Cubans." In *Race and Ethnicity in the United States, an Institutional Approach,* ed. William Vélez, New York: General Hall.

Grossman, James R. 1991. *Land of Hope, Chicago, Black Southerners, and the Great Migration.* Chicago: University of Chicago Press.

Grossman, James R., Ann Durkin Keating and Janice L. Reiff 2004. *The Encyclopedia of Chicago.* Chicago: University of Chicago Press.

Hagan, Jacqueline Maria. 1994. *Deciding to be Legal, a Maya Community in Houston.* Philadelphia: Temple University Press.

Hamilton, Nora, and Norma Stoltz Chinchilla. 2001. *Seeking Community in a Global City: Guatemalans and Salvadorans in Los Angeles.* Philadelphia: Temple University Press.

————. 1997. "Central American Migration: A Framework for Analysis." In *Challenging Fronteras, Structured Latina and Latino Lives in the U.S.,* eds. Mary Romero, Pierrette Hondaguey-Sotelo, and Vilma Ortiz. New York: Routledge.

Handley, Jon. 2000. "A New Chapter." *Chicago Tribune,* August 20.

Herman, Andrew. 1996. "Innovative Catholic High to Open in Pilsen/Little Village This Fall." *Chicago Sun-Times,* January 19.

Hernandez-Fujigake, Jorge. 1991. "Mexican Steelworkers and the United

Steelworkers of America in the Midwest: the Island Steel Experience, 1936-1979." Ph.D. diss., University of Chicago.

Hirsley, Michael, and Jorge Casuso. 1990. "Changing Faith of Hispanics." *Chicago Tribune*, January 7.

———. 1990 "Catholics Fighting Back to Hold Onto Hispanics." *Chicago Tribune*, January 9.

History Task Force Centro de Estudios Puertorriqueños. 1979. *Labor Migration Under Capitalism: The Puerto Rican Experience.* New York: Monthly Review Press. History Task Force Centro de Estudios Puertorriqueños. 1982. *Sources for the Study of Puerto Rican Migration-1879-1930.* New York: City University of New York.

Hogan, Will, and Magdalena Cortes. 1995. "South Lawndale." In *Local Community Fact Book Chicago Metropolitan Area 1990*, eds. The Chicago Fact Book Consortium. Chicago: Academy.

Hogan, Will, and Lilia Villanyeva. 1995. "Lower West Side." In *Local Community Fact Book Chicago Metropolitan Area 1990*, eds. The Chicago Fact Book Consortium. Chicago: Academy.

Hoffman, Abraham. 1974. *Unwanted Mexican Americans in the Great Depression: Repatriation Pressures, 1929-1939.* Tucson, Arizona: University of Arizona Press.

Holler, Stephan C. 1995. "Exploring the Popular Religion of U.S. Hispanic/Latino Ethnic Groups." *Latino Studies Journal.* 6: 3-29.

Holli, Melvin G. and Jones, Peter d'A., eds., 1995. *Ethnic Chicago, a Multicultural Portrait.* Grand Rapids, Mich.: Williams B. Eerdmans.

Holston, Lisa. 1990. "Church Divided Over Quinceanera." *Chicago Sun-Times*, July 8.

Huebner, Jeff. 1998. "Rogue Gallery." *Chicago Reader*, October 9.

Iglesias César Andreu, ed. 1984. *Memoirs of Bernardo Vega, a Contribution to the History of the Puerto Rican Community in New York.* New York: Monthly Review Press.

Illinois State Board of Higher Education. 1998. *Report to the Governor and General Assembly on Underrepresented Groups in Illinois in Public Institutions of Higher Education.* Chicago: Illinois State Board of Higher Education.

Institute For Latino Studies. January 2002. *Bordering the Mainstream: a Needs Assessment of Latinos in Berwyn and Cicero, Illinois.* Norte Dame, IN: Norte Dame University.

Irvine, Martha. 2001. "Hispanic Influx Shaping Chicago." *Chicago Sun-Times*, March 11.

James, Frank. 2001. "U.S. Population Grows by 58%." *Chicago Tribune*, March 8.

Jennings, James, and Monte Rivera, eds. 1984. *Puerto Rican Politics in Urban America.* Westport, CT: Greenwood Press.

Jones, Anita Edgar. 1928. "Conditions Surrounding Mexicans in Chicago." M.A. thesis, University of Chicago.

———. 1928. "Mexican Colonies in Chicago," *The Social Service Review* 1: 579-97.

Joravsky, Ben. 1984. "Juan A. Velazquez, Pilsen, Street Hustler Takes on Old Guard at City Hall." *The Chicago Reporter*, November.

Joravsky, Ben, and Tom Brune. 1983. "Washington's Victory: all Blacks, Most Latinos, 17% Whites." *The Chicago Reporter*, May.

Joravsky, Ben, and Jorge Casuso. 1984. "Hispanic Vote Emerges as New Battlefront in Council Wars." *The Chicago Reporter*, September.

Kaneya, Rui. 1988. "Dropout Rates Still Plague Public Schools." *The Chicago Reporter*, May.

Kantowicz, Edward R. 1995. "The Ethnic Church." In *Ethnic Chicago, a Multicultural Portrait*, eds. Melvin G. Holli and Peter d'A. Jones. Grand Rapids, Mich.: William B. Eerdmans.

Kass, John. 1998. "Gutierrez's Tax Bill Proves that Miracles Still do Happen." *Chicago Tribune*, August 2.

Kirby, Joseph. 1992. "Walls Become Canvas for Masterpieces." *Chicago Tribune*, September 16.

Kitagawa, Evelyn M., and Karl E. Taeuber, eds. 1963. *Local Community Fact Book Chicago Metropolitan Area, 1960*. University of Chicago.

Koenig, Harry C., ed. 1980. *A History of the Parishes of the Archdiocese of Chicago*. Chicago: Archdiocese of Chicago.

Kornblum, William. 1974. *Blue Collar Community*. Chicago: University of Chicago Press.

Kromkowski, John A., ed. 2000. *Race and Ethnic Relations, Annual Editions*. Guilford, CT: Dushkin/McGraw-Hill.

Lane, James B. and Edward J. Escobar, eds. 1987. *Forging a Community: the Latino Experience in Northwest Indiana, 1919-1975*, Chicago: Cattails Press.

Latino Institute. September 1986. *Al Filo/At the Cutting Edge, the Empowerment of Chicago's Latino Electorate*. Chicago: Latino Institute.

Latino Institute. October 1994. *Latinos Face to Face/Cara a Cara*. Chicago: Latino Institute.

Latino Institute. 1983. *Latinos in Metropolitan Chicago: a Study of Housing and Employment*. Chicago: Latino Institute.

Latino Institute. 1983. *Suburban Latinos: the Working Poor?* Chicago: Latino Institute.

Levin, Rebekah, and Robert Ginsburg. January 13, 2000. *Sweatshops in Chicago: a Survey on Working Conditions in Low-Income and Immigrant Communities*. Chicago: The Sweatshop Working Group.

Lindberg, Richard. 1997. *Ethnic Chicago, a Complete Guide to the Many Faces and Cultures of Chicago*. Lincolnwood, IL: Passport Books.

Linton Cynthia, ed. 1996. *The Ethnic Handbook: a Guild to the Cultures and Traditions of Chicago*. Schiller Park, IL: The Illinois Ethnic Coalition.

Llanes, José. 1982. *Cuban Americans: Masters of Survival*. Cambridge, MA: bt Books.

"Lourdes Monteagudo, Fueled by the Belief that one Can Make a Difference." 1990. *Chicago Tribune*, September 2.

Love, Judy, and Al Romero. 1980. "7 Arrested As 'Disrupters' During Parade on 26th St." *W.S. Times-Lawndale News*, September 21.

Lucas, Isidro. 1974. "El Problema Educativo del "Dropout." *The Rican: A Journal of Contemporary Puerto Rican Thought*. 1: 5-19.

Lutton, Linda. 1998. "War on Independents." *The Chicago Reader*, September 4.

———."Will Development Bury the Barrio?" *The Chicago Reader*, April 24, 1998.

Lydersen, Kari. 1999. "Party Pooper, is Danny Solis Responsible for Keeping Fiesta del Sol from Its Traditional Site?" *The Chicago Reader*, July 30.

Maldonado, Edwin. 1987. "Contract Labor and the Origins of Puerto Rican Communities in the United States." In *Forging a Community The Latino Experience in Northwest Indiana, 1919-1975*, eds. James B. Lane and Edward

J. Escobar. Chicago: Catails.

Maldonado, Rita M. 1976. "Why Puerto Ricans Migrated to the United States in 1943-73." *Monthly Labor Review* 9: 7-19.

Martinez, Antonio. 1996. "Guatemalan Americans." In *The Ethnic Handbook: a Guild to the Culture and Traditions of Chicago's Diverse Communities*, ed. Cynthia Linton. Shiller Park, IL: The Illinois Ethnic Coalition.

Martínez, Manuel. 1989. *Chicago: Historia de Nuestra Comunidad Puertorriqueña, Photographic Documentary*. Chicago: Reyes & Sons.

Menchú, Rigoberta. 1984. *I, Rioberta Menchú: An Indian Woman in Guatemala*. London:Verso.

Mendell, David. 2001. "New Numbers Add Up To Decade of Diversity, Minority Boom, Aging Population Reshape Chicago." *Chicago Tribune*, August 12.

Mendell, David, and Darnell Little. 2002. "Rich 90s Failed to Lift all, Income Disparity Between Races Widened Greatly, Census Analysis Shows." *Chicago Tribune*, August 20.

Mendieta, Ana. 1999. "With Division Street Stretch all Spiffed up, Puerto Rican Merchants Wonder Where all the Customers Are. All Dressed and Ready to Grow." *Chicago Sun-times*, October 5.

———. 2000. "The Energy Behind Logan Square, Developer, Alderman see Neighborhood Transforming." *Chicago Sun-Times*, February 29.

———. 1998. "Celebrating 75 years of Faith." *Chicago Sun-Times*, September 14.

———. 1999. "Daley Allies Push to Unseat Independent in 22nd Ward." *Chicago Sun-Times*, February 15.

Mehta, Chirag, Nik Theodore, Iliana Mora, and Jennifer Wade. February 2002. *Chicago's Undocumented Immigrants: an Analysis of Wages, Working Conditions, and Economic Contributions*. Chicago: Center for Urban Economic Development at UIC.

Mihalopoulus, Dan, and Evan Osnos. 2001. "Chicago: a Hub for Mexicans." *Chicago Tribune*, May 10.

Miller, David B. 1995. "Lincoln Park." In *Local Community Fact Book Chicago Metropolitan Area 1990*, eds. The Chicago Fact Book Consortium. Chicago: Academy.

Mohl, Raymond A., and Neil Betten. 1987. "Discrimination and Repatriation, Mexican Life in Gary." In *Forging a Community the Latino Experience in Northwest Indiana, 1919-1975*, eds. James B. Lane and Edward J. Escobar. Chicago: Cattails Press.

Montana, Constanza. 1990. "Some Latinos Spare no Expense When Their Daughters Come of Age." *Chicago Tribune*, June 19.

Moore, Joan and Raquel Pinderhuges, eds. 1993. *In the Barrios: Latinos and the Underclass Debate*. New York: Russell Sage.

———. 1998. "The Latino Population: The Importance of Economic Restructuring." In *Race Class and Gender*, eds. Margaret L. Anderson and Patricia Hill Collins. New York: Wadsworth.

Morales, Julio. 1986. *Puerto Rican Poverty and Migration: We Just Had to Try Elsewhere*. New York: Praeger.

Morales, Rebecca and Frank Bonilla, eds. 1993. *Latinos in a Changing U.S. Economy: Comparative Perspectives on Growing Inequality*. Newbury CA: Sage Publications.

Moreau, John Adam. 1969. "The Puerto Ricans: Who Are They?" *Midwest Magazine of the Chicago Sun-Times*, September 21.

————. 1969. "Puerto Rican Young Lords Emulate the Black Panthers." *Chicago Sun- Times*, June 5.

Morin, Raul. 1966. *Among the Valiant: Mexican Americans in World War II and Korea*. Alhambra, CA: Border.

Mujeres Latinas En Acción and Latino Institute. October 1996. *Latinas in Chicago: a Portrait*. Chicago: Mujeres Latinas En Acción.

Muller, RoseAnna M. 1999. "Pilsen Rallies Around Cultural Symbol of Mexican Immigrants: Virgin of Guadalupe." *Chicago Tribune*, December 9.

Nathan, Debbie. 1984. "Indigence and Bliss: can Pentecostal Hispanics Escape from Escapism?" *The Chicago Reader*, May 11.

Neikirk, William. 2000. "Gutierrez Unhappy With 'Old Boss' Daley." *Chicago Tribune*, March 12.

Nelli, Humbert S. 1970. *Italians in Chicago: 1880-1930: A Study in Ethnic Mobility*. New York: Oxford University Press.

"News Analysis, Latinos Brush Up On Politics 101." 1998. *Chicago Sun-Times*, January 27.

Norkewicz, Michael. October 1994. *A Profile of Nine Latino Groups in Chicago*. Chicago: Latino Institute.

Ortiz, Altagracia, ed. 1996. *Puerto Rican Women and Work: Bridges in Transnational Labor*. Philadelphia: Temple University Press.

Pacyga, Dominic A. 1995. "New City." In *Local Community Fact Book Chicago Metropolitan Area 1990*, eds. The Chicago Fact Book Consortium. Chicago: Academy.

Padilla, Elena. 1947. "Puerto Rican Immigrants in New York and Chicago: A Study in Comparative Assimilation." M.A. thesis, University of Chicago.

Padilla, Felix M. 1987. *Puerto Rican Chicago*. Notre Dame, IN: University of Notre Dame Press.

————. 1985. *Latino Ethnic Consciousness: The Case of Mexican Americans and Puerto Ricans in Chicago*. Notre Dame, IN: University of Notre Dame Press.

Paz, Frank X. January 1948. *Mexican Americans in Chicago, a General Survey*. Chicago: Welfare Council of Metropolitan Chicago.

Peltz, Jennifer. 2000. "Landlord Gets Prison in Slaying of Activist." *Chicago Tribune*, March 8.

Pérez, Gina M. 2004. *The Near Northwest Side Story: Migration, Displacement, and Puerto Rican Families*. Berkeley: University of California Press.

Peréz y Gonzáles, María Elizabeth. 1997. "Latina Women in a Traditionally Male-Dominated Institution-the Church." *Latino Studies Journal* 8: 19-35.

Portes, Alejandro, and Rubén G. Rumbaut. 1996. *Immigrant America, a Portrait*. Berkeley: University of California Press.

Prieto, Jorge. 1989. *Harvest of Hope: The Pilgrimage of a Mexican American Physician*. Notre Dame, IN: University of Notre Dame Press.

————. 1994. *The Quarterback Who Almost Wasn't*. Houston, TX: Arte PublicoPress.

Puente, Teresa. 1998. "Latino Radio Pioneer is one of the Family." *Chicago Tribune*, December 13.

————. 2000. "Church Loses its Home, But Not it's Spirit." *Chicago Tribune*, January 7.

————. 1998. "Guatemalan's Visit Protested, Some Suspicious of Country's Chief Despite Peace Accord." *Chicago Tribune*, June 12.

————. 2001. "Columbia Strife Inflicts Far-Reaching Pain." *Chicago Tribune*,

January 2.

Puente, Teresa, and Ray Quintanilla. 1997. "Bringing it Together." *Chicago Tribune*, April 13.

Puente, Teresa, and Stephen Franklin. 2000. "Janitors' 1-Day Strike Move to Suburbs." *Chicago Tribune*, April 18.

Queralt, Magaly. 1984. "Understanding Cuban Immigrants: a Cultural Perspective," *Social Work* 29: 115-121.

Quintanilla, Ray. 2001. "Hispanic Area May Get 2 High School City Plans Include a Third School, But Not Enough Cash." *Chicago Tribune*, August 21.

Ramos-Zayas, Ana Y. 2003. *National Performances: The Politics of Class, Race, and Space in Puerto Rican Chicago*. University Press of Chicago.

Reisler, Mark. 1977. *By the Sweat of Their Brow: Mexican Immigrant Labor in the United States, 1900-1940*. Westport, CT: Greenwood Press.

———. 1976. "Always the Laborer, Never the Citizen: Anglo Perceptions of the Mexican Immigrant During the 1920s." *Pacific Historical Review* 37: 231-54.

———. 1973. "The Mexican Immigrant in the Chicago Area During the 1920s." *Illinois State Historical Association Journal* 6: 144-158.

Rey, Roberto. 1995. "Humboldt Park." In *Local Community Fact Book Chicago Metropolitan Area 1990*, eds. The Chicago Fact Book Consortium. Chicago: Academy.

Romero, Mary, Pierrette Hondagneu-Sotelo, and Vilma Ortiz, eds. 1997. *Challenging Fronteras: Structured Latino and Latina Lives in the U.S.* New York: Routledge.

Rosales, Francisco Arturo. 1976. "The Regional Origins of Mexicano Immigrants to Chicago During the 1920s." *Aztlán* 7: 187-201.

Rosales, Francisco Arturo, and Daniel T. Simon. 1975. "Chicano Steel Workers and Unionism in the Midwest, 1919-1945." *Aztlán* 6: 267-275.

———. 1981. "Mexican Immigrant Experience in the Urban Midwest: East Chicago, Indiana, 1919-1945." *Indiana Magazine of History* 72: 333-357.

Rodríguez, Clara E. 1991. *Puerto Ricans Born in the U.S.A.* Boulder, Colorado: Westview Press.

Rodríguez, Clara E., and Virginia E. Sánchez Korrol, eds. 1996. *Historical Perspectives on Puerto Rican Survival in the United States*. Princeton: Markus Wiener.

Rodríguez, Luis J. 1993. *Always Running La Vida Loca: Gang Days in L.A.* New York: Simon & Schuster.

Ropka, Gerald W. 1980. *The Evolving Residential Pattern of the Mexican, Puerto Rican and Cuban Population in the City of Chicago*. New York: Arno Press.

Rosales, Francisco Arturo. 1978. "Mexican Immigration to the Urban Midwest During the 1920s." Ph.D. diss., Indiana University.

Rotzoll, Brenda Warner. 1998. "School is a Lesson in Activism." *Chicago Sun-Times*, October 29.

Rumbler, Bill. 1999. "Helping Hands Throughout Chicago's Neglected Neighborhoods, Church Groups Lead a Housing Revival." *Chicago Sun-Times*, June 8.

Safa, Helen I. 1988. "Migration and Identity: A Comparison of Puerto Rican and Cuban Migrants in the United States." In *The Hispanic Experience in the United States, Contemporary Issues and Perspectives*, eds. Edna Acosta-Belen and Barbara R. Sjostrom. Westport, CT: Praeger.

Samora, Julian, and Richard A Lamanna. 1967. *Mexican-Americans in a Midwest*

Metropolis: A Study of East Chicago. Los Angeles: University of California Press.

Sánchez, George J. 1993. *Becoming Mexican American, Ethnicity, Culture and Identity in Chicano Los Angeles, 1900-1945.* New York: Oxford University Press.

Sánchez Korrol, Virginia E. 1983. *From Colonia to Community, the History of Puerto Ricans in New York City.* Berkeley: University of California Press.

Schmid, Jon. 1996. "Near W. Side Church Celebrates 2 Rebirths." *Chicago Sun-Times,* April 8.

Schultz, Susy. 1998. "Legislators Threaten UIC's Budget, Hearing Set on Minority Hiring, Enrollment." *Chicago Sun-Times,* January 23.

Sepúlveda, Ciro. 1976. "La Colonia del Harbor: a History of Mexicanos in East Chicago, Indiana, 1919-1932." Ph.D. diss., University of Notre Dame.

Sister Schwendinger, M. Paula. May 22, 1989. *Our Lady of Guadalupe Parish 1928-1989, Reality of Mexican Americans.* Unpublished paper. Chicago: Our Lady of Guadalupe Parish.

Skerrett, Ellen, Edward R. Kantowicz, and Steven M. Avella. 1993. *Catholicism, Chicago Style.* Chicago: Loyola University of Chicago.

Skerry, Peter. 1993. *Mexican Americans, the Ambivalent Minority.* Cambridge, MA: Harvard University Press.

Skertic, Mark. 2002. "White Ethnic Groups Fade." *Chicago Sun-Times,* August 21.

Slayton, Robert A. 1986. *Back of the Yards: the Making of a Local Democracy.* Chicago: University of Chicago Press.

Smith, Bryan. 2000. "Shepherd of the Streets, a Tough Road: Saving Gang Members With Faith." *Chicago Sun-Times,* May 7.

Sorrell, Victor A., and Mark Rogovin. 1987. The Barrio Murals/Murales del Barrio. Chicago: *Mexican Fine Arts Center Museum.*

Steelworkers Research Project. 1985. *Chicago Steelworkers: the Cost of Unemployment.* Chicago: Steelworkers Research Project.

Spielman, Fran. 2000. "Food Vendors Face Regulation." *Chicago Sun-Times,* September 19.

Suro, Roberto. 1999. *Strangers Among us, Latinos Lives in a Changing America.* New York: Vintage Books.

Swanson, Stevenson, ed. 1997. *Chicago Days, 150 Defining Moments in the Life of a Great City.* Wheaton, IL: Contemporary Books.

Sweet, Lynn. 2001. "Daley, Gutierrez Patch it up Mayor Pledges Support for Congressman's Re- election After June Talks Irons out Differences." *Chicago Tribune,* July 26.

Taller de Estudios Comunitarios. *1984. Rudy Lozano, His Life, His People.* Chicago: Taller de Estudios Comunitarios.

Taylor, Paul. 1932. *Mexican Labor in the United States: Chicago and the Calumet Region.* Berkeley: University of California Press.

The Neighborhood Capital Budget Group. 1999. *Rebuilding Our Schools, Brick by Brick.* Chicago: The Neighborhood Capital Budget Group.

"The Puerto Rican Chicago." 1967. *Chicago Tribune,* June 11.

The Woodstock Institute. November 1998. *A Rising Tide...But Some Leaky Boats.* Chicago: The Woodstock Institute.

"30 Seized in Tuley Melee; 6 Cops Hurt." 1973. *Chicago Sun-Times,* February 1.

Toro-Morn, Maura. 2001. "Yo Era Muy Arriesgada: a Historical Overview of the Work Experiences of Puerto Rican Women in Chicago." *Centro: Journal of the*

Center for Puerto Rican Studies 13 (2): 24-44.

Torres, Andrés, and José E. Velázquez, eds. 1998. *The Puerto Rican Movement: Voices from the Diaspora*. Philadelphia: Temple University Press.

Torres, Andres and Frank Bonilla. 1993. "Decline Within Decline: the New York Perspective." In *Latinos in a Changing U.S. Economy: Comparative Perspectives on Growing Inequality*, eds. Rebecca Morales and Frank Bonilla. Newbury Park, CA: Sage Publications.

Torres, Carlos Antonio, Hugo Rodriguez Vecchini and William Burgos, eds. 1994. *The Commuter Nation: Perspectives on Puerto Rican Migration*. Puerto Rico. Universidad de Puerto Rico.

Torres, María de los Angeles. 1999. "Cuba Comes To Chicago." *Chicago Sun-Times*, November 22.

————. 1991. "The Commission on Latino Affairs: a Case of Community Empowerment." In *Harold Washington and the Neighborhoods Progressive City Government in Chicago, 1983-1987*, eds. Pierre Clavel and Wim Wiewel. New Brunswick, NJ: Rutgers University Press.

Torres, María de los Angeles, and Arcy Obejas. 1989. "Freedom Means a Cuban Orchestra Should Perform." *Chicago Tribune*, April.

Torres, Maximino DeJesus. 1983. "An Attempt to Provide Higher Educational Opportunity to Hispanics: The Evolution of Proyecto Pa'lante at Northeastern Illinois University—1971-1976." Ed.D. diss., Loyola University.

Tucker, Ernest. 1998. "For Cubans, It's a Matter of Faith." *Chicago Sun-Times*, January 21.

Tuttle, William M. Jr. 1970. *Race Riot: Chicago in the Red Summer of 1919*. New York: Antheneum.

U. S. Census Bureau. 2000. *Hispanic Population by Type for Regions, States, and Puerto Rico: 1990 and 2000*. Washington D.C.: Government Printing Office.

Valdes, Dionicio Nodin. 2000. *Barrios Nortenos, St. Paul and Midwestern Mexican Communities in the Twentieth Century*. Austin, TX: University of Texas Press.

Valdez, Virginia. April 2000. *Progress Report: an Evaluation of the Chicago Public School's Efforts to Relieve Overcrowding at Elementary Schools*. Chicago: Mexican American Legal Defense and Educational Fund.

Vargas, Zaragosa. 1993. *Proletarians of the North: a History of Mexican Industrial Workers in Detroit and the Midwest, 1917-1933*. Berkeley: University of California Press.

Vélez, William, ed. 1998. *Race and Ethnicity in the United States, an Institutional Approach*. Dix Hills, New York: General Hall.

Vidal, Jaime R. 1994. "Beyond New York." In *Puerto Rican and Cuban Catholics in the U. S., 1900-1965*, eds. Jay P. Dolan and Jaime R.Vidal. Notre Dame, IN: University of Notre Dame Press.

————. 1994 "The Rejection of the Ethnic Parish Model." In *Puerto Rican and Cuban Catholics in the U. S., 1900-1965*, eds. Jay P. Dolan and Jaime R.Vidal. Norte Dame, IN: University of Norte Dame Press.

Walton, John, Luis Salces, and Joanne Belechia. 1977. *The Political Organization of Chicago's Latino Communities*. Evanston, IL: Northwestern University.

Washburn, Gary. 2000. "Study Criticizes Chicago TIFs." *Chicago Tribune*, March 12.

————. 2000. "Daley Backs School Board Chief Sees no Conflict in Chico's Lobbying and his Position." *Chicago Tribune*, March 15.

————. 2001. "City Ward Remap Okd by 48-1 Vote." *Chicago Tribune*, December

20.

Washington, Laura, and Wilfredo Cruz. 1983. "Two-Thirds of Adult Latinos Have no High School Diplomas." *The Chicago Reporter*, January 1983.

Whalen, Carmen Teresa. 2001. *From Puerto Rico to Philadelphia: Puerto Rican Workers and Postwar Economies*. Philadelphia: Temple University Press.

Wille, Lois. 1966. "The Puerto Rican 'Doodlers'." *Chicago Daily News*, June 23.

Zambrana, Ruth E. ed. 1995. *Understanding Latino Families: Scholarship, Policy, and Practice*. London: Sage Publications.

Index

About the Author

Wilfredo Cruz was born and raised in Chicago. He earned his Ph.D. in Social Service Administration from the University of Chicago. Cruz was formerly an assistant press secretary for the late Mayor Harold Washington, and director of the Office of Public Information for the Chicago Public Library. He was also an investigative reporter for The Chicago Reporter. Cruz is currently a faculty member in the Liberal Education Department at Columbia College Chicago. He teaches various courses in sociology, and his research interests include Latinos, immigration, race-relations, politics, and community organizing. Cruz is the author of *Puerto Rican Chicago*.

woman and children
on horses. All small children

- Young woman

CPSIA information can be obtained at www.ICGtesting.com
233020LV00002B/16/P